Plus
Workbook and Disk

Learning dBASE III Plus by Creating a Sales Analysis Model

Michael J. Clifford

revised by
James J. Bauman

Que™ Corporation
Carmel, Indiana

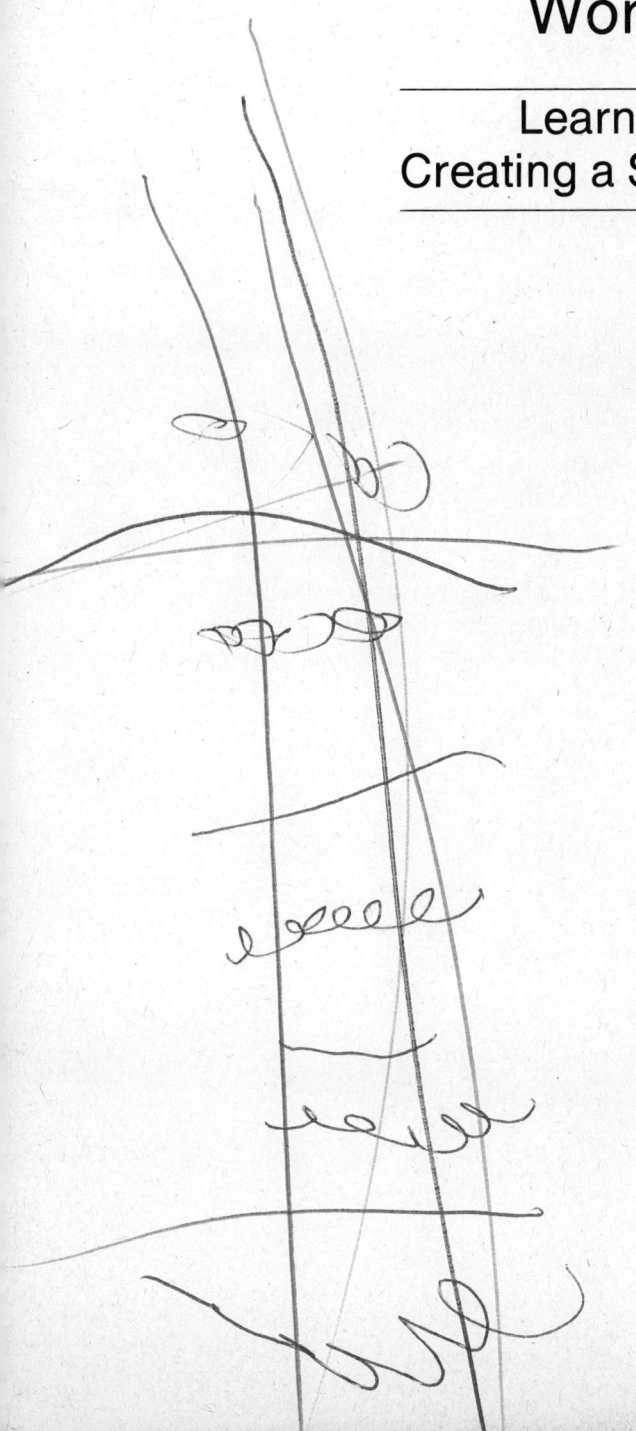

Table of Contents

How To Use Your Workbook Data Disk

Introduction

Who Should Use This Workbook? 1
What Does This Workbook Contain? 1
What Is dBASE III Plus? 2
   A Few Definitions 3
   The Keys To Using dBASE III Plus 4
   Rules of the Road: Operating dBASE III Plus 5
   When You Need an Assist 6
   A Little Help from Your Friend 8

Lesson 1

Designing an Application, Creating a Structure, and Building a Database

Sales Analysis: Saltwater Sally's Sales
   Management System 14
   Building an Application: Design, Identify,
     and Create the Structure 15
     In the Beginning There Was a Plan 15
     Putting the Plan into Action: Creating the Database..... 19
   Making a Few Changes 31
     Modifying the Structure 31
     Choosing a Database 35
     Adding Information to the Database 37
     Exiting APPEND Mode 47
     Building the Data File 49
   Summary of Concepts Presented in Lesson 1 56
   Lesson 1 Exercise 59

Lesson 2

Moving About, Cleaning Up, and Browsing

Navigating between Records: Getting
   to the Top and Bottom 67
Revising and Refining Data 71
   The EDIT Command 71
   Command Qualifications 73
   The CHANGE Command 75
   The BROWSE Command 79
Summary of Concepts Presented in Lesson 2 83
Lesson 2 Exercise 85

Lesson 3

Extracting and Ordering Data

The LIST Command 87
Search Strategies.. 89
Search Conditions... 97
The DISPLAY Command 101
Summary of Concepts Presented in Lesson 3 104
Lesson 3 Exercise 105

Lesson 4

Global Alterations and Deletions, and Date Arithmetic

Changing the Plan... 107
   Global Alterations 115
   Mass Replacements.. 119

Deleting Records from a Database 123
Performing Date Arithmetic 127
Summary of Concepts Presented in Lesson 4 133
Lesson 4 Exercise 135

Lesson 5

Statistics Commands and Memory Variables

The Statistics Commands 137
    The COUNT Command 139
    The SUM Command 141
    The AVERAGE Command 147
Memory Manipulation 149
Summary of Concepts Presented in Lesson 5 150
Lesson 5 Exercise 151

Lesson 6

Labels and Reports

Designing the Label Form File 155
Issuing and Modifying the Label Form File 163
Designing the Report Form File 167
Issuing and Modifying the Report Form File 181
Summary of Concepts Presented in Lesson 6 187
Lesson 6 Exercise 189

Lesson 7

Indexing and Searching

Indexing a Database 193
Searching a Database 203
Using FIND for an Instant Search 207
Summary of Concepts Presented in Lesson 7 210
Lesson 7 Exercise 211

Lesson 8

Producing Polished Products

Conditional Reports 213
Other Reports 219
    The Detailed Financial Report 219
    The Customer Notes Report 229
Summary of Concepts Presented in Lesson 8 231
Lesson 8 Exercise 232

Lesson 9

Automation (or Let dBASE Do the Typing)

Automating Commands 239
Setting a Field List 239
Setting a Database Filter 243
Making Filters and Field Lists Permanent..................... 245
Creating a View File 253
Writing Programs 261
    Interacting with the Program............................... 267
    Looping the Program 271
    Running a Loop Indefinitely 275

Cleaning Up the Program 277
Summary of Concepts Presented in Lesson 9 281
Lesson 9 Exercise 283

Lesson **10**

The Ties That Bind: Writing Menus

Jogging Your Memory with a Menu 287
Building the Main Menu 299
Trapping User Errors 307
Summary of Concepts Presented in Lesson 10 312
Lesson 10 Exercise 313

Lesson **11**

Screen Formatting: The Add, Edit, and Search Programs

Creating Screens and Format Files 321
Using Pictures and Ranges To Prevent Errors 335
    Pictures 335
    Ranges 339
Writing the Screen-Oriented Programs 343
Summary of Concepts Presented in Lesson 11 354
Lesson 11 Exercise 355

Lesson 12

The Professional Touch: Relating Databases

Splitting the MX_SALES Database 363
Setting a Relation 367
Using a Relation To Write a Report............................. 373
Building a Data Entry Program for Two
    Related Databases 379
    The Format Files... 379
    The Data Entry Program 383
Going through the New Menu 393
The End of the Beginning 393
Summary of Concepts Presented in Lesson 12................ 396
Lesson 12 Exercise.. 396

Trademark Acknowledgments

Product Director
Bill Nolan

Editorial Director
David F. Noble, Ph.D.

Acquisitions Editor
Pegg Kennedy

Editor
Steven L. Wiggins

Book Design and Production
Dan Armstrong
Jennifer Matthews
Cindy L. Phipps
Joe Ramon
Dennis Sheehan
Peter Tocco
Carrie L. Torres
Sharon Hilgenberg
Laura Koehler

Composed in Megaron by
Que Corporation

Screen shots produced with Inset software from
Inset Systems, Inc.

How To Use Your Workbook Data Disk

The data disk accompanying *dBASE III Plus Workbook and Disk* contains files corresponding to the lessons for creating a Sales Analysis model in the workbook. This software is designed for use with Que Corporation's *dBASE III Plus Workbook and Disk*. The workbook serves as primary documentation for this software.

This user's guide will help you begin using dBASE III Plus more quickly but is not a substitute for the workbook, which explains the commands and principles of data management with dBASE III Plus. Please read this guide carefully before you start to use your disk.

What You Need To Get Started

You will need the following computer equipment and materials to complete all the workbook lessons:

1. An IBM® or IBM-compatible microcomputer with at least 256K of RAM memory and two disk drives

2. The dBASE III Plus program disks

3. Que's book *dBASE III Plus Handbook*, 2nd Edition

4. A printer that can print at least 80 characters of text across a page (optional)

Preparing Your Equipment and Disks

If your computer system is new to you, you first should read the instructions provided with your system. Some basic operations you will need to know are

*   How to turn on your computer

*   How to load (boot) the disk operating system (DOS)

*   How to format a new disk

*   How to copy files from one disk to another

For instructions about each operation, refer to the manuals provided with your computer system. Beware: certain steps, such as preparing (formatting) a disk or copying a disk, can destroy information previously recorded on the receiving disk.

Making a Backup Copy

As soon as you open this package, you should make a backup copy of your new workbook data disk. Your computer's operating manual should include instructions about copying a disk.

If you are going to complete the workbook lessons on a computer with two floppy disk drives, copy the contents of the data disk to another disk. If you have a computer with a hard disk drive, copy the contents to the correct drive and directory on which the dBASE III Plus program has been installed.

The disk files on the workbook data disk are Que's original exercise files. Although you can create and alter copies of the files, one problem exists: when you complete and save each exercise, the program will "write over" and destroy a file with the same name if it is on the disk. To preserve the original file, the name of each file that you complete during the workbook lessons is prefaced by MX (for **M**y e**X**ercise)—for example,

QUE's Original	Your Exercise
QX1SALES.DBF	MX_SALES.DBF
QX_FRM1.FRM	MX_SALES.FRM

Copying Restrictions

Under the terms of the license agreement, you can make backup copies of your workbook data disk, as long as the copies are for your use only on a single computer.

Configuring dBASE III Plus

dBASE III Plus has a provision that allows you to predetermine a number of features. These features, such as size of memory or shape of the cursor, will be active when dBASE III Plus is first started. Most features are not used during the workbook lessons; however, some must be set correctly before you begin.

The following factors also may determine configuration:

- Whether you have a two-floppy system or a computer with one floppy and one hard disk

- The copy protection used by each version of dBASE III Plus

To ensure the correct settings, a preparation program (called QPREP) is included in this software guide. From dBASE III Plus, the preparation program permits easy resumption of one lesson after quitting another. In addition, most of the dBASE III Plus options are set to those most favorable to each lesson. Directions for using QPREP follow.

Starting dBASE III Plus and the Workbook Data Disk

This section of the user's guide shows you how to load dBASE III Plus and the workbook data disk into your computer. If you have installed dBASE III Plus properly and have a computer with two floppy disk drives, insert System Disk #1 into drive A. Place the workbook data disk (or, preferably, a copy of the disk) into drive B. At the A> prompt, type *dBASE* and press the Return (or Enter) key. After about a minute, the following prompt appears:

    Insert System Disk #2 and press ENTER
        or type CTRL-C to abort

Remove System Disk #1 from drive A. Insert System Disk #2 and press Return.

If you have a computer with a hard disk drive and if dBASE III Plus is properly installed, copy the contents of the workbook data disk to the hard disk. At the C> prompt, type *dBASE* and press Return.

If you have a computer with two floppy disk drives, type

    SET DEFAULT TO B:

and press Return.

For a hard disk system, type

    SET DEFAULT TO C:

and press Return.

The drive used by hard disk systems is usually designated as drive C. dBASE III Plus now searches the default drive for all files and saves the results to the default drive.

Now, to be sure that all of dBASE III Plus's many features have been set properly for the workbook lessons, run QPREP. QPREP is a program on the workbook data disk that is written in the dBASE language for this purpose. Type

    DO QPREP

and press Return.

The screen clears, and you are asked to enter the number of the lesson that you will be starting (see fig. 1). After you enter the number, the program calls up the work files and announces that the program is prepared. The program prompts you to press any key; then the dot prompt appears. You now can start the exercises.

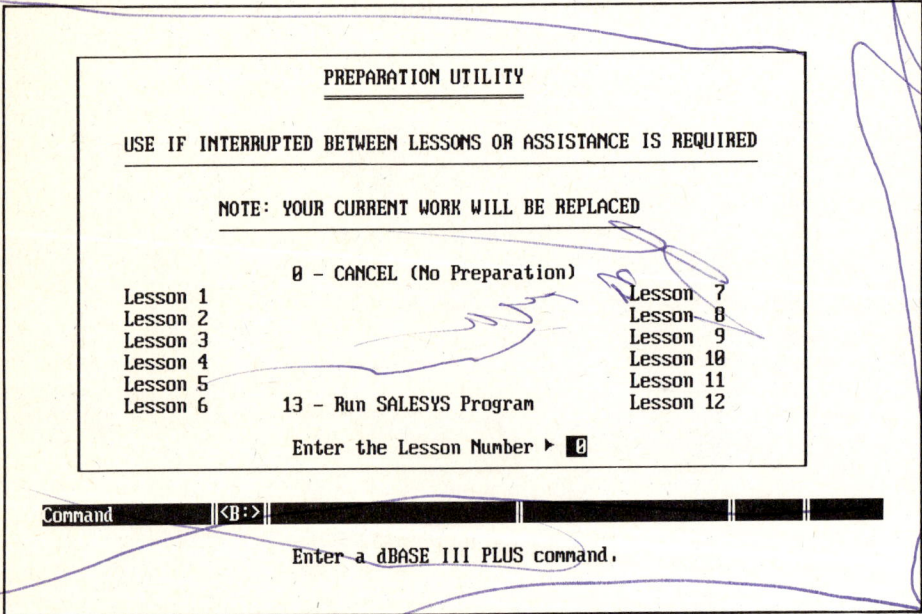

```
                    PREPARATION UTILITY
                    ═══════════════════

      USE IF INTERRUPTED BETWEEN LESSONS OR ASSISTANCE IS REQUIRED
      ──────────────────────────────────────────────────────────

            NOTE: YOUR CURRENT WORK WILL BE REPLACED


                 0 - CANCEL (No Preparation)
   Lesson 1                                        Lesson  7
   Lesson 2                                        Lesson  8
   Lesson 3                                        Lesson  9
   Lesson 4                                        Lesson 10
   Lesson 5                                        Lesson 11
   Lesson 6        13 - Run SALESYS Program        Lesson 12

              Enter the Lesson Number ▶ 0


 Command         <B:>

              Enter a dBASE III PLUS command.
```

Fig. 1. *The QPREP screen.*

You need to run QPREP only at the start of a work session. If you work through all the lessons in the workbook without interruption, then preparing the files again is not necessary. If you exit dBASE III Plus between lessons (using the QUIT command), you need to run QPREP before you resume the exercises.

QPREP allows you to stop at the end of any lesson and begin later with the next lesson. However, be aware that if you quit and start later, dBASE III Plus automatically warns you if an existing file is to be replaced by another with the same name. QPREP, if issued again, restores from an archive the files necessary to begin a lesson; many of these files have the same name as those used in a previous lesson. The file restored most often from the archive is MX_SALES, the exercise data that contains names and numbers. If you or a friend has worked through the exercises or previously run QPREP, the following safety message may be issued:

    MX_SALES already exists, overwrite it? (Y/N)

Do not be concerned. Answer Y (for Yes) if you want QPREP to function; answer N (for No) if you want to keep the exercises you have created from being overwritten.

Troubleshooting Guide

You will avoid many problems by making backup copies of your disks. If your master disk is damaged or your files are lost accidentally, backup disks will protect both your investment and your work. If you have trouble using the workbook data disk, refer to this troubleshooting chart.

Sympton	Probable Cause	Solution
dBase III Plus will not load.	dBASE III Plus is not configured properly to your computer. Your computer does not have enough memory.	See your user's manual.
The workbook data disk will not load.	The wrong disk is in the drive you are loading from.	Use the correct disk.
	Drive door is not shut.	Shut the door.
	Disk is in backward.	Invert the disk.
	Your computer has less than 256K available memory.	Increase your RAM. Remove other software in memory (for example, Sidekick).
Booting the disk Que sent you does not work; the disk just spins.	The disk Que sent you does not have your DOS on it.	Follow your instructions on making a backup copy of your disk.
Typing DO QPREP results in the File not found message.	The default is not set to the drive on which the QPREP program resides.	Set the default to the proper drive.

File Contents

The following list describes files that are stored on your workbook data disk. These files support the primary exercises in Lessons 1 through 12 of the workbook.

File Name	Description
ADD_INV.PRG	Invoice data entry program
INVOICE.VUE	Data entry view file
QX_PURCH.DBF	Purchase data file
QX_PURCH.FMT	Purchase format file
QX_OWED.FRM	Customer report form
QPREP.PRG	Main preparation menu
QX1SALES.DBF	Sales data file—first version
QX1SALES.DBT	Sales memo file—first version
QX4SALES.DBF	Sales data file—third version
QX4SALES.DBT	Sales memo file—third version
QX_ADD.PRG	Add record program
QX_CN.FRM	Customer notes form
QX_CUSTL.LBL	Customer label form
QX_EDIT.PRG	Edit record program
QX_MENU.PRG	Main sales menu
QX_REPT.PRG	Report program
QX_SEAR.PRG	Search program
QX_SF.FRM	Financial report form
QX_SFORM.FMT	Screen format file
QX2SALES.DBF	Sales data file—second version
QX2SALES.DBT	Sales memo file—second version
QX_SALES.FRM	Sales Report
QX_PERF.PRG	Sales statistics program
QX_GA.QRY	Sales query file
QX_SALES.VUE	Sales view file
QX_CUST.DBF	Customer data file
QX_CUST.DBT	Customer memo file
QX_CUST.FMT	Customer format
SALESYS.PROG	Sales system program

In addition to these files, the workbook data disk contains an additional file called EXERCISE, which actually is a directory. By setting your directory to EXERCISE, you can access the following files, which support the supplemental exercises (the exercises at the end of each lesson) in Lessons 1 through 12.

BILLS.PRG	Billing program
GENBILLS.FRM	Vendor report form
SSACCTS.DBF	Vendor information file
SSBILLS.DBF	Vendor data file
SSBILLS1.DBF	Billing information file
SSSFORM.FMT	Screen form file
SS_ADD.PRG	Add record program
SS_EDIT.PRG	Change record program
SS_MENU.PRG	Main menu program
SS_REPT.PRG	Report program
SS_SEAR.PRG	Search program
SS_TOTAL.PRG	Billing program

These last 12 files on the workbook data disk are provided for the convenience of instructors teaching dBASE III Plus courses. If necessary, an instructor can copy these files to a student's disk. For example, Exercise 7 in the *dBASE III Plus Instructor's Guide* requires that all the workbook's supplemental exercises be completed before doing the exercise. If a student has not completed all the exercises, the instructor can provide that student with these files so that the exercise can be completed.

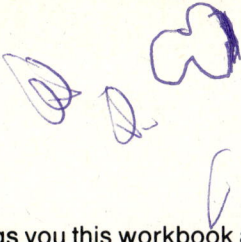

Introduction

Que brings you this workbook as a companion to the book *dBASE III® Plus Handbook*, 2nd Edition. Rather than repeat topics in the handbook, the workbook supplements those topics with a series of practical, hands-on exercises. These exercises help you use dBASE III Plus to store, edit, and retrieve information.

The lessons in the *dBASE III Plus Workbook and Disk* provide step-by-step instructions for developing a dBASE III Plus application. With the help of files on the workbook data disk, you will develop Saltwater Sally's Sales System. Saltwater Sally's is a successful one-store retailer of hot tubs and pools. The sales system application analyzes and reports the store's sales of hot tubs, swimming pools, and accessories.

Who Should Use This Workbook?

This workbook is written for a variety of users:

- Owners of dBASE III Plus who want to apply the program to personal data management applications

- Instructors of dBASE III Plus workshops, seminars, and courses who desire a complete course package: workbook, disk, text, and instructor's manual

- Trainers who lead classes and labs in business and industry. The materials can be used for both group instruction and for self-paced learning.

What Does This Workbook Contain?

The workbook is organized into the following sections:

1. Lessons. The workbook contains 12 lessons developed around one model, Sales Analysis. The model was chosen because everybody sells something: time, ideas, services, materials, or finished goods. Creating the information system in this workbook helps you learn all the major dBASE III Plus commands and operating concepts. The lessons contain detailed descriptions of the model and a list of the steps and commands.

   To complete the lessons, you will use the steps given throughout the workbook as well as the files on the workbook data disk. These files add supplemental features to the model. You also can use these files to restore selected files if your work should get lost or damaged.

2. Figures and charts. In each lesson, numerous figures and screens help you learn the dBASE III Plus commands and steps.

3. Review sections. At the end of each lesson are summaries to help you review the concepts and procedures covered. You also can use these summaries for quick reference when you need help with successive lessons.

4. Additional exercises. Each lesson contains an additional exercise that you can use to continue practicing the important elements of dBASE III Plus as you create the information system.

5. References to the *dBASE III Plus Handbook*, 2nd Edition. Each lesson contains references to specific sections in the handbook. Consult the handbook for more detailed explanations of the commands and concepts as you complete the exercises in the workbook.

What Is dBASE III Plus?

Before you begin the exercises, read the following brief introduction to dBASE III Plus, its capabilities, and the general rules of operation. Then read the more detailed introduction to data management software and to dBASE III Plus in Chapters 1 and 2 of the *dBASE III Plus Handbook*, 2nd Edition.

dBASE III Plus is a database management system (DBMS), a system that automates the entry, validation, ordering, and reporting of information. The equivalent of an electronic file cabinet, DBMS software electronically shuffles information stored on magnetic disks rather than on paper. The results can help you make important decisions and solve problems.

With dBASE III Plus, you can process information into meaningful reports. The software helps you understand and structure data, enter and validate it, and extract it in almost any form. Only a few years ago, these feats would have required extensive programming on a large mainframe computer. Today you can do it all on a microcomputer.

dBASE® accepts commands in one of two ways: individually typed from the keyboard or in programmed sets. Individual commands are typed, entered, and processed one at a time; programmed commands are written and saved into a program file, and the program file is submitted as a unit. dBASE processes the commands in a program file one after the other, without any further human intervention. Knowledgeable users often write large or complex applications as a series of program files to reduce the possibility of human error.

dBASE III Plus creates and uses several types of files, each of which is stored on disk under its own file name. Each file name consists of two parts: a root name (QO_SALES, for example) and a file extension or identifier (DBF, for example). A period separates the two parts (for example, QO_SALES.DBF).

File extensions designate different types of dBASE III Plus files. Table I.1 lists the types of file extensions.

Table I.1
File Extensions

Type of File	Ends In
Database	.DBF
Database Memo	.DBT
Index	.NDX
Command (or Program)	.PRG
Label Form	.LBL
Memory	.MEM
Report Form	.FRM
Text Output	.TXT
Format	.FMT
Screen	.SCR
Query	.QRY
View	.VUE
Catalog	.CAT

A Few Definitions

To use dBASE III Plus, you should understand a few basic terms used in database-management: data item, field, record, database structure, database, and database file.

A *data item* is a single bit of information concerning some object, person, place, thing, event, or so on.

A *field* is a complete set of data items related to a particular category of information. In a personnel database, employee IDs, names, and salaries are examples of different information categories, and each would be stored in a different field.

A *record* is a complete set of data items on a single entry in the database. An entry could be an employee in a personnel file, a part description in an inventory system, or the details of a purchase in a sales management database.

The *database structure* consists of descriptions of each field category. Each description includes the name of the field and the size and type of data to be stored in the field.

A *database* is a collection of data items comprising all fields and all records for a single database structure. A database is organized to provide information in the form of reports or answers to individual questions.

A *database file* refers to the database in the form it is stored on a computer disk.

dBASE III Plus has a few constraints:

- 1 billion records per data file
- 128 fields per data file
- 10 data files in use at the same time
- 4,000 characters per record
- 254 characters stored per character field

Your applications are unlikely to exceed these limitations. But even if they do, you can meet your goals by using dBASE III Plus's relational features to link two or more databases.

The Keys To Using dBASE III Plus

In operating dBASE, you eventually will have to use most of the keys on the keyboard. Study the layout of keys on your keyboard to familiarize yourself with the location of the major key groups: the function keys, the alphanumeric keys, the cursor and editing keys, and the control keys. Figure I.1 illustrates the IBM® PC keyboard.

Fig. I.1. *The IBM PC keyboard.*

The *function keys* generally are labeled F1 to F10. Some computer keyboards have more than ten function keys, but dBASE does not make use of the extra ones. In dBASE, any function key except F1 can be programmed to store and execute one or more commands. The F1 key is reserved for calling up help screens.

The *alphanumeric keys* are labeled with the names of letters, numbers, and punctuation marks. Use them to enter text and numbers into a database and to write dBASE commands.

The *cursor* and *editing keys* generally are labeled with arrows pointing in different directions or with names such as PgUp, PgDn, End, Home, Ins, and Del. These keys move the cursor in any operation that requires entering or editing data and commands. The Ins and Del keys control inserting and deleting characters at the cursor. The Backspace key moves the cursor to the left, deleting characters as it goes.

The *control keys* include the Esc, Alt, Ctrl, Num Lock, and Shift keys.

- The *Ctrl key* is used together with certain cursor keys to carry out special cursor movements.

- The *Shift key* is used as it would be on a typewriter, to change from lowercase to uppercase or to enter the special symbols above the number row on the keyboard.

- The *Esc key* is used to backtrack to a previous step or to cancel an operation already underway.

- The *Num Lock key* switches the function of the numeric keypad at the right of the keyboard from carrying out cursor movements to entering numbers.

- The *Alt key* is not used in dBASE.

Rules of the Road: Operating dBASE III Plus

The dBASE language consists of over 150 commands and functions, each of which controls a particular database management operation. You make your request for a command or function either by typing its name and options from the keyboard or by selecting it from a menu of possibilities. The workbook refers to the first method as operating from the *dot prompt* and to the second method as operating from the *Assistant*.

When you start dBASE III Plus, you are located in the Assistant. If you want to type your commands, you switch to the dot prompt by pressing the Esc key. To switch back to the Assistant, you type the command *ASSIST* after the dot prompt. The next section gives an overview of the rules needed to operate the Assistant.

Although the Assistant has definite advantages for persons with little computer background or with weak typing skills, the emphasis in this workbook is on operating dBASE from the dot prompt. This method of entering commands tends to better reinforce learning and leads eventually to a surer footing in the command language. The payoff for the extra work particularly comes in better preparation for learning the programming language. Also, the dot prompt is the only method of entering commands that cannot be entered with the Assistant. The basic command set does not include many of these commands, but when you need one you have no alternative to the dot prompt.

The screens for the Assistant menu and the dot prompt share two informative elements, the message line and the status bar (see fig. I.2 for the Assistant menu). The *message line* is at the bottom of the screen and tells you specifically what will happen if you execute the highlighted option. The message line also provides error messages in certain operating modes.

The highlighted line on the screen is the *status bar*. The status bar acts as a kind of scoreboard to keep track of how the working environment is currently defined. The status bar is divided into six panels, the first of which identifies the current operating mode. When you are working in the Assistant, the first panel of the status bar reads ASSIST.

The second panel of the status bar identifies the *current* or *default disk drive*. This is the drive on which dBASE will search for files or onto which it will store files created during your work session. You can override the default drive by specifying another drive when you name the file you want to retrieve or create.

The fourth panel of the status bar initially displays the number of the option currently highlighted within the pull-down menu. For example, if you are at the fourth option of six in the menu, the fourth panel reads, Opt: 4/6. After you have selected a database to work with, this panel provides more helpful information.

The status bar is a common feature of all the dBASE III Plus operating modes, including the dot prompt. Because you will see the status bar later, other functions of the status bar panels will be described as you acquire a better understanding of how dBASE works.

In the exercises, the workbook summarizes the sequence of steps you would take if you were entering a dot prompt command. The steps in the sequence are in the order they must be carried out. If a step requires you to select a menu option, the option is written in **boldface** type. If a step requires you to type something, what you type is written in *italics*. Anything in italics should be typed exactly as it appears. Pay particular attention to typing uppercase and lowercase letters correctly.

When You Need an Assist

The dBASE III Plus Assistant is a menu-based method of entering commands to dBASE. The menu *options* (the choices on the menu) are organized in a row across the top of the Assistant menu (see fig. I.2). You use the left-arrow and right-arrow keys to move to the option you want to select. An alternative to the arrow keys is to type the first letter of the option name—for example, *T* for **Tools**.

Menu options

Set Up Create Update Position Retrieve Organize Modify Tools   11:55:44 am

| Database file |
| Format for Screen Query |
| Catalog View |
| Quit dBASE III PLUS |

Submenu of Set Up

Current number
of option
in use

Current disk drive

ASSIST   <C:>   Opt: 1/6
Move selection bar – ↑↓, Select – ◄┘, Leave menu – ↔, Help – F1, Exit – Esc,
Select a database file,

Status bar

Navigation line   Message line

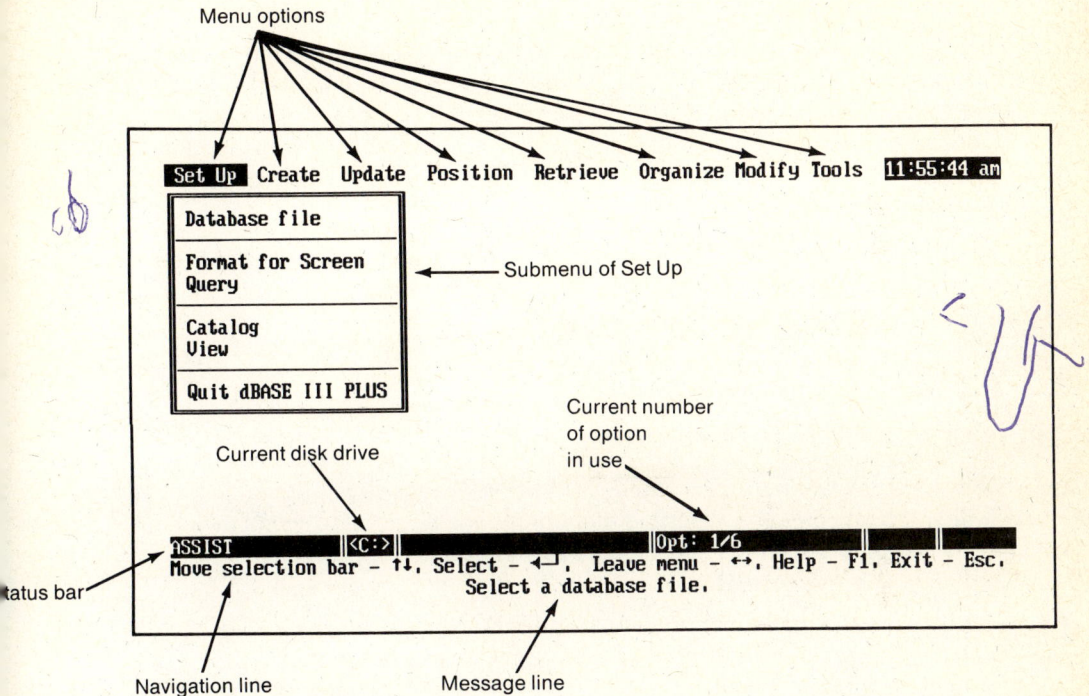

Fig. I.2. *The Assistant menu.*

Immediately above the message line on the Assistant menu is the *navigation line*, which identifies the actions you can take at any point in the menu system. At startup, the navigation line lists all the actions necessary to highlighting and selecting the command you want (the arrow keys), calling for help (the F1 key), and exiting back to the dot prompt (the Esc key).

As you move from one option to another, a "pull-down" submenu associated with that option appears on the screen. Each pull-down submenu offers a number of second-level options within the main option. Each of these second-level options corresponds directly to a dBASE command. To call up one of these commands, use the up-arrow and down-arrow keys to move to the option you want within the pull-down submenu.

When you have located the command you want, press the Return key to execute the command. Depending on the command you are using, one of two things will happen: the command will be executed immediately, or you will be asked to specify some further point of detail. If the command you have selected requires more detail, the Assistant will prompt you for that information either by pulling down another submenu or by placing a window on the screen, into which you type the information.

Most of the time, the action you have to take will be obvious from the choices available. If you have trouble understanding what is required, you can check the message line, which tells you what will happen if you execute the highlighted option. You also can call up a *help screen* by pressing the F1 key, which gives you a more detailed explanation of the command. Be careful when using help screens, however. They are written in terms of how the command would be typed from the dot prompt. The explanation of what the command does is accurate, but the method explained is not appropriate to the way the Assistant carries out the command.

If you make a mistake entering a step, back out of your mistake by pressing the Esc key. In most cases the Assistant will take you back to the previous menu, and you can reenter your option. If you need to go back all the way to the Assistant menu, press the Esc key repeatedly.

A Little Help from Your Friend

Any software as comprehensive as dBASE III Plus offers an array of options that may at first bewilder the novice user. Learning the commands and their options eventually eliminates the bewilderment, but until that time comes you will need occasional help to get commands to operate correctly.

dBASE III Plus provides some of this help in the form of a series of *help screens*. These help screens are arranged in two complementary series. The first series consists of screens of general definitions for terms and procedures used in working with dBASE. The second series consists of informational screens on each of the commands and functions in the dBASE command language. The second series makes full use of the terms defined in the first series, so you are advised to learn those definitions before calling up a screen for a particular command.

The help screens are accessible from the dot prompt by typing the command *HELP* or by pressing the F1 key. Either of these actions brings up the Help Main Menu illustrated in figure I.3. In the Assistant, pressing F1 will only call up a screen specific to the highlighted command. You cannot access the help screens for definitions from the Assistant. The help screens for a command differ between the Assistant and the dot prompt, with the dot prompt help screen generally providing more information.

When you call up the Help Main Menu from the dot prompt, use the cursor arrow keys to move the cursor to the desired subject; then press the Return (or Enter) key, ↵. The related help message appears. A screen label in the upper right of the screen identifies the help topic, and the message at the bottom of the screen outlines the available options for exiting or requesting more help. Pressing Esc always exits the help system. If several help screens exist for a topic, you can press the PgDn and PgUp keys to move forward and backward through the series of related topics. You press the F10 key to return to the previous help system menu.

You also can take a shortcut through the menu system by calling for help on a particular topic. In this case, do not use the F1 key. Instead, if you are at the dot prompt, type *HELP* plus the screen label for the screen you want to see. The screen label for a command

```
                                                              MAIN MENU

                    Help Main Menu
                    ──────────────


                    ┌─────────────────────┐
                    │ 1 - Getting Started │
                    └─────────────────────┘
                      2 - What Is a ...
                      3 - How Do I ...
                      4 - Creating a Database File
                      5 - Using an Existing Database File
                      6 - Commands and Functions




 HELP          ‖<C:>‖
      Position selection bar - ↑↓, Select - ⏎, Exit with Esc or enter a command,
                    ENTER >
```

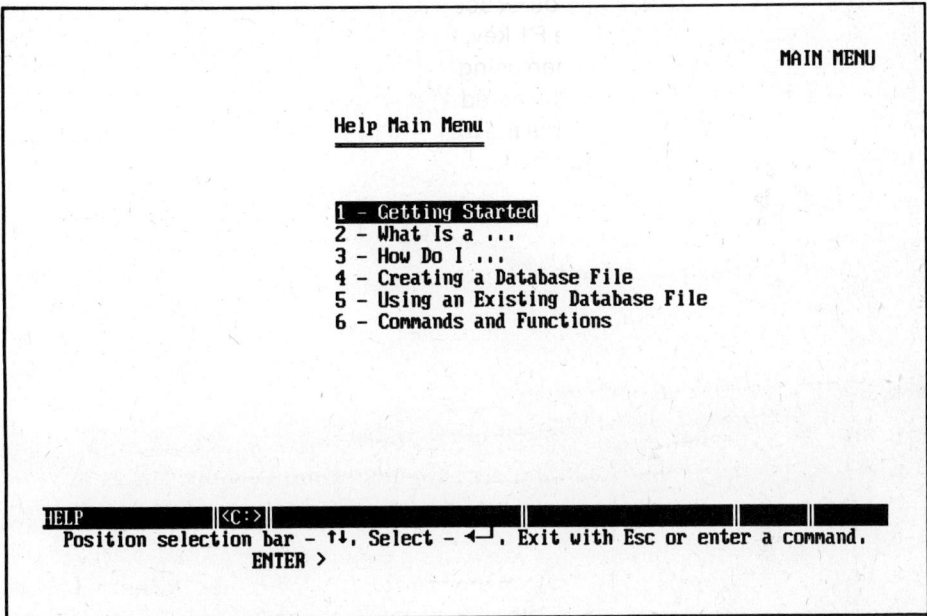

Fig. I.3. *The Help Main Menu.*

or function is normally the same as the command or function name. If you are already in the help screens and the ENTER > prompt at the bottom of the screen is displayed, you can simply type the screen label and press the Return key. You will immediately see the screen you want.

To make things easier for you, the name of each of the commands and functions in the command language can be used as a screen label to call up that help screen. For instance, to call up the help screen for the DISPLAY command, type *HELP DISPLAY* at the dot prompt or simply *DISPLAY* after the ENTER > prompt.

The screen labels for the definition screens are not as easy to recall as the screen labels for command and function help screens. For your convenience, the most important screen labels are listed in table I.2. As with the command and function help screens, you type the name of the screen you want after the HELP command. For instance, at the dot prompt type *HELP FIELD NAME* to bring up the screen describing the rules for naming database fields.

Table I.2
Screen Labels for Definition Help Screens

Screen Label	Definition Help Screen
SYNTAX	Symbols used in explaining how to write command line options
WHAT	Menu of definitions for all types of command qualifications. Each qualification has a separate screen.
NARRATIVE	Terms used in defining a database structure
DATABASE NAME	Rules for naming database files
FIELD NAME	Rules for naming database fields
FIELD TYPE	Limitations of different types of database fields
FIELD SIZE	Definitions of field size options
STARTER	List of commands in the basic or starter set
ADVANCED	List of commands in the advanced set

1

Designing an Application, Creating a Structure, and Building a Database

Related sections in *dBASE III Plus Handbook*, 2nd Edition: Chapters 4 and 9.

As mentioned in the introduction to this workbook, the lessons are developed around one application: a sales analysis information system. The entire application already is on the workbook data disk, and all files are prefaced by QX, which stands for **Q**ue e**X**ercise. A number of the files also include an underscore (_); the underscore is part of the file name and must be entered when you enter the file name. Throughout the rest of this workbook, you will be given step-by-step instructions on how to re-create each file. To distinguish your files from the QX files, you will use the prefix MX, which stands for **M**y e**X**ercise.

This lesson introduces the major dBASE III Plus commands, along with several important principles for identifying a data management problem, designing a remedy, and implementing the solution.

In this lesson, you will learn the following:

- How to plan a database
- How to create a database
- How to select a database
- How to add to a database

First, set the stage.

NOTES

Sales Analysis: Saltwater Sally's Sales Management System

Saltwater Sally's Hot Tubs and Pools is a one-store retailer of hot tubs and pools. The owner is Harold (Admiral) Hornblower. Three salespeople work for him: Doug Kornfeld, Frank McGuire, and Lucy Murray.

Saltwater Sally's is a small but growing business. Harold purchased a PC and dBASE III Plus a couple weeks ago and asked Doug to bring the paperwork under control.

"We are awash in paper," said Harold. "We constantly are writing invoices, calculating commissions, and addressing promotional fliers. Not even Captain Blye had to endure this tedium. Take the computer and the software and see what you can do, Doug. I need some way to figure out which salesperson sold what, the amount of the commissions, the items sold, and the amount of purchase."

Fortunately, Doug was able to find a model sales management system that was already developed in dBASE. The model served as a guide for addressing Harold's concerns for managing the paper burden at Saltwater Sally's. With the help of the model, Doug cut down considerably the amount of time usually needed to learn dBASE, and he built a complete application. Within three weeks, he was able to show Harold a working system.

"Let's see what you've got, Doug," said Harold.

Doug booted up dBASE III Plus, set the default to the data drive, and typed DO MX_MENU. A menu appeared.

Said Doug, "By making a selection from the Main Menu, we can add, edit, or check on sales. By pressing another button, we can print a series of management reports, including sales commissions calculations. No more paper, calculators, and scribbled reports!

"Moreover, we can print customer addresses, and, with not too much more work, we also can send a form letter to each customer. Each letter will appear to be individually typed by the salesperson who sold the item."

"Well done!" said Harold. "Excellent. Your work, dBASE III Plus, and the PC will go a long way to getting this outfit shipshape. By the way, how did you do it, Doug?"

"Well, therein lies a tale," replied Doug. "And it's not a fish story."

NOTES

Building an Application: Design, Identify, and Create the Structure

Doug had been given a task: design a sales management system. He was familiar with the use of word-processing and spreadsheet software, but not with data management and dBASE III Plus.

He called Henry Hacker, a friendly computer hobbyist, and described the problem. "What should I do?" asked Doug.

"Do nothing," replied Henry. "Turn off the computer. Think. What are you trying to accomplish? What data do you need in order to manage your sales? Remember, an electronic file system must do the same things that a paper-based file system does. Keep calm and design it on paper as though the information system were based on paper rather than software."

Doug did not know it, but Henry's advice saved him many hours of chasing down "electronic blind alleys." Henry's parting words to Doug were, "Remember, especially with computers, in the beginning there was a plan—with a capital P."

In the Beginning There Was a Plan

Consider the information contained in Saltwater Sally's Sales Management System. This information includes the following:

- Customers—who and where they are
- Sales—the items sold, when the items were sold, and for how much
- Salespeople—who sold what

Doug borrowed information from the standard invoice form used at Saltwater Sally's (see fig. 1.1) and devised a plan for storing information. Each sales entry would store the following categories of data:

Customer Data

Customer name
Telephone number
Additional customer notes

Sales Data

Product code
Purchase amount
Number of items purchased
Date of purchase
Paid-in-full marker

NOTES

Employee Data

Person selling product

After the data categories are identified, the next step is to define each category. You define a data category by examining three concerns:

- How will you refer to the data category?

- How do you intend to use the data category to report information?

- How much space is required to store individual data items within the category?

The invoice (see fig. 1.1) gives some indication of how these concerns were addressed in setting up the paper form. For instance, the customer is identified by name, the address is given more space than the city, the amount of the sale is used to calculate a total, some space is reserved for recording miscellaneous comments about the sale, and so on. The invoice in effect represents a definition of each data category.

```
                    Saltwater Sally's Hot Tubs and Pools
                            We Soak You Good!
     Date: _____

     Customer Name: _____     Phone: _____

     Address: _____ City: _____   State: __  Zip: _____
     Salesperson: _____

     Item    Quantity   Description                         Amount
     ____    ____       _____            ____

     ____    ____       _____            ____

                                                 Total      ____

     Comments: _____
               _____
```

Fig. 1.1. *Saltwater Sally's current invoice.*

When you work with an electronic filing system such as dBASE III Plus, the results of your planning are used to define the structure of a *database* rather than a paper-based form. The same concerns apply, but all you do is lay out the specifications for your database. The "electronic form" used to store the data is automatically generated.

NOTES

In the workbook, the term *field* is now used to refer to what previously was called a data category. Setting up the structure of the database, then, is a matter of defining each field to be included in the database. Three specifications are needed for each field:

- *Name*—how you will refer to the field. Names must be 10 characters or fewer; the first character must be a letter, and other characters can be letters, digits, or the underscore (_).

- *Type*—what kind of data the field will store. The different types of data are listed in table 1.1.

- *Size*—the length of the longest item of data the field is expected to store. If the field is typed as numeric and includes decimals, add one extra position for the decimal point.

Table 1.1
Types of Fields and Symbols for Each

C	Character	Text information
N	Numeric	Numbers to be processed
D	Date	Date or calendar information
M	Memo	Notepad of up to five pages
L	Logical	Yes/No data

Putting the Plan into Action: Creating the Database

The process of developing and storing a structure for a dBASE III Plus database is the function of the CREATE command. In this part of the lesson, you will create a structure for a database to be called MX_SALES. When you finish setting up this database, it should correspond exactly to the **Q**ue e**X**ercise database named QX1SALES.

First, start the lesson. If you are not already in dBASE III Plus, follow the instructions at the front of this workbook to boot up dBASE III Plus, enter the program, and press the Esc key to leave the Assistant. You are now in dot prompt mode, and the first panel of the status bar reads Command Line (see fig. 1.2). The second panel identifies the default drive. If you loaded dBASE III Plus from a hard disk, the second panel reads ⟨C:⟩; if you loaded it from a floppy disk, the panel reads ⟨A:⟩.

To change the default drive, use the SET DEFAULT TO command followed by the letter of the new default—for example, *SET DEFAULT TO B.*

Step 1: Prepare the lesson. Type *DO QPREP.* You will see a menu of lessons (see fig. 1.3). Select 1 after the prompt.

```
┌─────────────────────────────────────────────────────────────────┐
│                                                                   │
│                                                                   │
│                                                                   │
│                                                                   │
│                                                                   │
│ Command Line    ║<C:>║                                            │
│                    Enter a dBASE III PLUS command.                │
│                                                                   │
└─────────────────────────────────────────────────────────────────┘
```

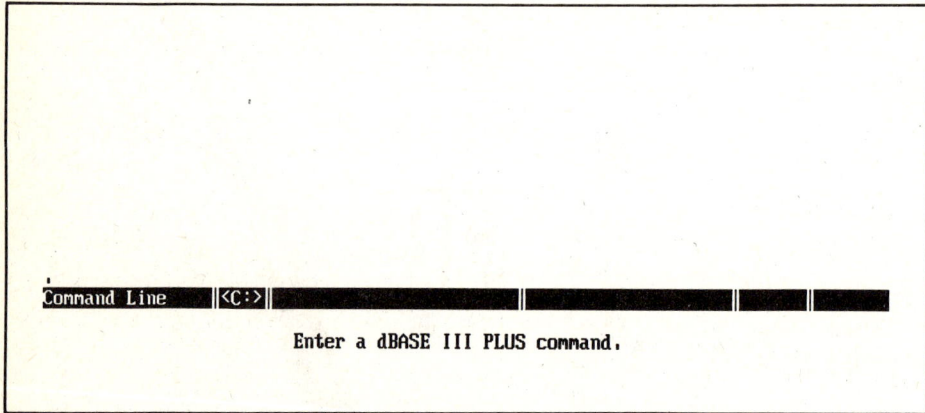

Fig. 1.2. *The dot prompt operating mode.*

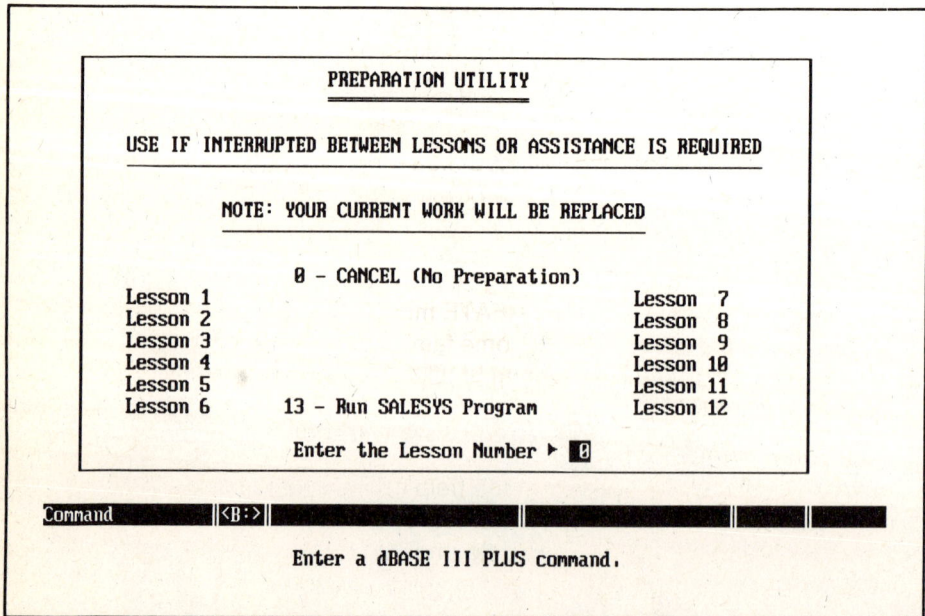

```
┌─────────────────────────────────────────────────────────────────┐
│      ┌──────────────────────────────────────────────────┐        │
│      │                PREPARATION UTILITY                │        │
│      │                ══════════════════                 │        │
│      │                                                   │        │
│      │  USE IF INTERRUPTED BETWEEN LESSONS OR ASSISTANCE IS REQUIRED │
│      │                                                   │        │
│      │        NOTE: YOUR CURRENT WORK WILL BE REPLACED   │        │
│      │                                                   │        │
│      │            0 - CANCEL (No Preparation)            │        │
│      │  Lesson 1                             Lesson  7   │        │
│      │  Lesson 2                             Lesson  8   │        │
│      │  Lesson 3                             Lesson  9   │        │
│      │  Lesson 4                             Lesson 10   │        │
│      │  Lesson 5                             Lesson 11   │        │
│      │  Lesson 6     13 - Run SALESYS Program   Lesson 12 │       │
│      │        Enter the Lesson Number ► 0                │        │
│      └──────────────────────────────────────────────────┘        │
│ Command         ║<B:>║                                            │
│                    Enter a dBASE III PLUS command.                │
└─────────────────────────────────────────────────────────────────┘
```

Fig. 1.3. *The QPREP screen.*

Step 2: Create the structure. Type *CREATE MX_SALES* and press Return. Figure
1.4 shows what appears on the screen.

```
                                                  Bytes remaining:   4000

 ┌─────────────────┐ ┌─────────────┐ ┌─────────────┐ ┌──────────────────┐
 │ CURSOR  <-- -->  │ │  INSERT     │ │  DELETE     │ │ Up a field:    ↑  │
 │ Char:    ← →     │ │ Char:  Ins  │ │ Char:   Del │ │ Down a field:  ↓  │
 │ Word: Home End   │ │ Field: ^N   │ │ Word:   ^Y  │ │ Exit/Save:   ^End │
 │ Pan:    ^← ^→    │ │ Help:  F1   │ │ Field:  ^U  │ │ Abort:       Esc  │
 └─────────────────┘ └─────────────┘ └─────────────┘ └──────────────────┘

    Field Name  Type    Width Dec        Field Name  Type    Width  Dec
                                        ────────────────────────────────
 1  ████████   Character  ██    ██


 ┌──────────────────────────────────────────────────────────────────────┐
 │CREATE         ║<C:>║MX_SALES              ║Field: 1/1 ║        ║       ║
 └──────────────────────────────────────────────────────────────────────┘
                        Enter the field name.
   Field names begin with a letter and may contain letters, digits and underscores
```

Fig. 1.4. *Creating MX_SALES.DBF.*

dBASE III Plus is now in the CREATE mode of operation (see fig. 1.4). Note that the first
panel of the status bar identifies the CREATE mode. The third panel identifies the name
of the database you are creating, and the fourth panel identifies which field you are
currently defining—field 1 of 1.

At the top of the screen is a help block that gives key mappings for all the cursor control
and editing functions available in the CREATE mode. As you will see, each operating
mode has its own help block. As you become familiar with moving the cursor and with
editing, you might want to turn off the help block to free more screen space. Pressing
the F1 key turns off the help block. Pressing F1 a second time turns the help block
back on.

Each cursor and editing function within the help block is identified by the key or key
combination that executes the control. Most of these you are already familiar with from
the introduction. Those you might be a little uncertain about are the ones beginning
with the caret (^) symbol.

The caret indicates that the Ctrl key must be held down while the second key is pressed.
For example, the function in the fourth panel that saves your screen and exits back to

NOTES

the dot prompt (Exit/Save: ^End) is called by holding down the Ctrl key and pressing the End key.

While in CREATE mode, dBASE III Plus prompts for the name, type, and size specifications for each field. The size is specified with a width and, if the type is numeric, the number of decimal places. Make sure that the size you give is large enough to hold the longest data value in your set. On the other hand, do not make the size so long that you end up storing a lot of empty space for each record. Remember, for numeric fields, you must count one extra position for the decimal point if numbers have decimal places.

Step 3: Enter the field name. The first item of information is the name of the customer. Type the field name *CNAME*, which stands for the customer's name, and press Return.

Step 4: Enter the type. You do not need to worry about the field type for the first field; dBASE III Plus offers the character option as a default. Press Return to register CNAME as a character field.

Step 5: Enter the width. Add a width of *20*, and press Return.

When you have completed the specifications for the first field, dBASE III Plus puts you in position to define the second field (see fig. 1.5). Notice that the Bytes remaining: indicator at the top right corner of the screen has decreased from 4000 to 3980. The width of the CNAME field has been subtracted from the total available.

Step 6: Define the telephone number field. Add the field name by typing *CPHONE* (see fig. 1.6).

Designate the telephone number as a character field by pressing C or by pressing Return. Give the phone number eight digits (seven for the digits and one for the hyphen).

When is a number not a number? You might think that the phone number should be typed numerically because it consists of digits. However, to test whether a field should be numeric, answer this question: "Can I use this so-called number in calculations?"

In this case, if you plan to add, subtract, multiply, or divide phone numbers, go ahead and make them numeric. If you do so, then you must also leave off the hyphens, because the numeric field contains only digits and decimal points. If arithmetic with your field makes no sense (and it does not with a phone number), then make the field a character field.

Step 7: Define a field to store comments. Enter a memo field by typing *CNOTE* (see fig. 1.7). Plan for the unexpected by allowing several pages of notes to be entered for one client. Next, press M (for memo), and dBASE III Plus automatically reserves a width of 10.

```
                                        Bytes remaining:    3980

 ┌─────────────┬─────────────┬─────────────┬──────────────────┐
 │ CURSOR <-- -->│   INSERT    │   DELETE    │ Up a field:    ↑ │
 │ Char:   ← →  │ Char:  Ins  │ Char:   Del │ Down a field:  ↓ │
 │ Word: Home End│ Field:  ^N  │ Word:   ^Y  │ Exit/Save:   ^End│
 │ Pan:   ^← ^→ │ Help:   F1  │ Field:  ^U  │ Abort:       Esc │
 └─────────────┴─────────────┴─────────────┴──────────────────┘

     Field Name  Type    Width  Dec        Field Name  Type    Width  Dec
     ─────────────────────────────         ─────────────────────────────
   1 CNAME       Character  20
   2 ▮▮▮▮▮▮▮     Character  ▮▮     ▮▮


 CREATE          |<C:>|MX_SALES          |Field: 2/2  |        | Caps
                        Enter the field name.
       Field names begin with a letter and may contain letters, digits and underscores
```

Fig. 1.5. *Entering the customer name field.*

```
                                        Bytes remaining:    3972

 ┌─────────────┬─────────────┬─────────────┬──────────────────┐
 │ CURSOR <-- -->│   INSERT    │   DELETE    │ Up a field:    ↑ │
 │ Char:   ← →  │ Char:  Ins  │ Char:   Del │ Down a field:  ↓ │
 │ Word: Home End│ Field:  ^N  │ Word:   ^Y  │ Exit/Save:   ^End│
 │ Pan:   ^← ^→ │ Help:   F1  │ Field:  ^U  │ Abort:       Esc │
 └─────────────┴─────────────┴─────────────┴──────────────────┘

     Field Name  Type    Width  Dec        Field Name  Type    Width  Dec
     ─────────────────────────────         ─────────────────────────────
   1 CNAME       Character  20
   2 CPHONE      Character   8
   3 ▮▮▮▮▮▮▮     Character  ▮▮     ▮▮


 CREATE          |<C:>|MX_SALES          |Field: 3/3  |        | Caps
                        Enter the field name.
       Field names begin with a letter and may contain letters, digits and underscores
```

Fig. 1.6. *Entering the telephone number field.*

```
                                          Bytes remaining:   3962

 ┌─────────────────┐┌──────────────┐┌──────────────┐┌─────────────────────┐
 │ CURSOR  <-- -->  ││   INSERT     ││   DELETE     ││ Up a field:     ↑   │
 │ Char:    ← →     ││ Char:   Ins  ││ Char:   Del  ││ Down a field:   ↓   │
 │ Word: Home End   ││ Field: ^N    ││ Word:   ^Y   ││ Exit/Save:    ^End  │
 │ Pan:    ^← ^→    ││ Help:   F1   ││ Field:  ^U   ││ Abort:        Esc   │
 └─────────────────┘└──────────────┘└──────────────┘└─────────────────────┘

     Field Name  Type     Width  Dec        Field Name  Type    Width  Dec

  1  CNAME       Character   20
  2  CPHONE      Character    8
  3  CNOTE       Memo        10
  4  ▓▓▓▓▓▓▓     Character  ▓▓▓   ▓▓

 CREATE        │<C:>│MX_SALES           │Field: 4/4       │      │     Caps
                       Enter the field name.
  Field names begin with a letter and may contain letters, digits and underscores
```

Fig. 1.7. *Entering a comments or memo field.*

Any comments you add to a record are not stored in the database itself; they are stored in a database text (DBT) file. dBASE III Plus automatically creates the DBT file when you specify that you want a memo field.

Step 8: Enter the date of purchase field by typing *PDATE* (see fig. 1.8). Press D (for date), and dBASE III Plus automatically reserves a width of eight characters for the date.

Step 9: Enter the stock code of the item purchased by typing *PCODE* (see fig. 1.9). Codes can be P-47, HT-2, or other similar combinations of letters and digits. After you type the name, enter the character field type and a width of *4*.

Step 10: Enter the number of items purchased by typing *PNO*. Saltwater Sally's sells accessories, such as bottles of chemical treatments, which customers often buy in quantity. The PNO field stores the number of duplicate items purchased.

Unlike other fields defined up to this point, the data that PNO stores is to be calculated into totals and averages. In this case, the condition is satisfied by setting up the field numerically; to do this, press the N key to change to numeric type.

```
                                              Bytes remaining:    3954

┌─────────────────┬─────────────────┬─────────────────┬──────────────────────┐
│ CURSOR  <── ──>  │     INSERT      │     DELETE      │ Up a field:       ↑  │
│ Char:     ← →    │ Char:  Ins      │ Char:    Del    │ Down a field:     ↓  │
│ Word: Home End   │ Field: ^N       │ Word:    ^Y     │ Exit/Save:      ^End │
│ Pan:     ^← ^→   │ Help:  F1       │ Field:   ^U     │ Abort:          Esc  │
└─────────────────┴─────────────────┴─────────────────┴──────────────────────┘
       Field Name   Type      Width  Dec        Field Name   Type    Width  Dec

   1   CNAME        Character    20
   2   CPHONE       Character     8
   3   CNOTE        Memo         10
   4   PDATE        Date          8
   5   ▓▓▓▓▓▓▓▓     Character  ▓▓▓▓  ▓▓▓▓

┌CREATE          ║<C:>║MX_SALES             ║Field: 5/5    ║        ║ Caps ┐
                     Enter the field name.
  Field names begin with a letter and may contain letters, digits and underscores
```

Fig. 1.8. *Entering the purchase date field.*

```
                                              Bytes remaining:    3950

┌─────────────────┬─────────────────┬─────────────────┬──────────────────────┐
│ CURSOR  <── ──>  │     INSERT      │     DELETE      │ Up a field:       ↑  │
│ Char:     ← →    │ Char:  Ins      │ Char:    Del    │ Down a field:     ↓  │
│ Word: Home End   │ Field: ^N       │ Word:    ^Y     │ Exit/Save:      ^End │
│ Pan:     ^← ^→   │ Help:  F1       │ Field:   ^U     │ Abort:          Esc  │
└─────────────────┴─────────────────┴─────────────────┴──────────────────────┘
       Field Name   Type      Width  Dec        Field Name   Type    Width  Dec

   1   CNAME        Character    20
   2   CPHONE       Character     8
   3   CNOTE        Memo         10
   4   PDATE        Date          8
   5   PCODE        Character     4
   6   ▓▓▓▓▓▓▓▓     Character  ▓▓▓▓  ▓▓▓▓

┌CREATE          ║<C:>║MX_SALES             ║Field: 6/6    ║        ║ Caps ┐
                     Enter the field name.
  Field names begin with a letter and may contain letters, digits and underscores
```

Fig. 1.9. *Entering the stock code field.*

Only one digit is required for the width, because the assumption is made that selling more than nine items is not possible. For the first time, the cursor moves to a fourth column, the Dec or decimals option. Press 0 or Return, because fractional units are not possible (see fig. 1.10).

```
                                              Bytes remaining:   3949


  ┌───────────────────┬───────────────────┬───────────────────┬────────────────────┐
  │ CURSOR  <-- -->   │     INSERT        │    DELETE         │ Up a field:    ↑   │
  │  Char:    ← →     │  Char:  Ins       │  Char:   Del      │ Down a field:  ↓   │
  │  Word: Home End   │  Field: ^N        │  Word:   ^Y       │ Exit/Save:    ^End │
  │  Pan:    ^← ^→    │  Help:  F1        │  Field:  ^U       │ Abort:         Esc │
  └───────────────────┴───────────────────┴───────────────────┴────────────────────┘

       Field Name  Type    Width  Dec      Field Name   Type    Width  Dec

   1  CNAME       Character  20
   2  CPHONE      Character   8
   3  CNOTE       Memo       10
   4  PDATE       Date        8
   5  PCODE       Character   4
   6  PNO         Numeric     1     0
   7  ▉▉▉▉▉▉▉▉    Character ▉▉▉   ▉▉▉


  CREATE           ▐C:▌MX_SALES              ▐Field: 7/7         ▌            Caps
                         Enter the field name.
  Field names begin with a letter and may contain letters, digits and underscores
```

Fig. 1.10. *Entering the number of items purchased.*

Step 11: Enter the field name for amount of purchase, *PAMT* (see fig. 1.11). This is also numeric information. Decimals are required for the fraction of a dollar. Sally's has never had a sale of more than $9,999. The width can be determined by the largest expected number of digits plus one for the decimal point. Enter a width of 7, and enter 2 for the number of decimal places.

Step 12: Enter the cash/charge field, *PPIF* (see fig. 1.12). This field indicates whether the customer has paid in full or has opted for layaway. PPIF (purchase paid in full) is either yes or no. A logical field type (L) permits only true or false data values. If dBASE III Plus displays an .T. (for true), then the hot tub or pool is paid in full; if it displays an .F., the hot tub or pool is not paid in full. No in-between exists for a logical field.

After you enter PPIF for the name of the field, press L for the type. dBASE III Plus fills in a width of 1.

```
                                                      Bytes remaining:    3942

┌─────────────────┬─────────────────┬─────────────────┬──────────────────────┐
│ CURSOR  <-- -->│     INSERT      │     DELETE      │ Up a field:      ↑   │
│ Char:     ← →  │ Char:   Ins    │ Char:    Del   │ Down a field:    ↓   │
│ Word: Home End │ Field:  ^N     │ Word:    ^Y    │ Exit/Save:      ^End │
│ Pan:    ^← ^→  │ Help:   F1     │ Field:   ^U    │ Abort:           Esc │
└─────────────────┴─────────────────┴─────────────────┴──────────────────────┘

    Field Name   Type      Width Dec        Field Name   Type      Width  Dec

 1  CNAME        Character   20
 2  CPHONE       Character    8
 3  CNOTE        Memo        10
 4  PDATE        Date         8
 5  PCODE        Character    4
 6  PNO          Numeric      1    0
 7  PAMT         Numeric      7    2
 8  ▆▆▆▆▆▆▆      Character         ▆▆▆▆

┌──────────┬────────┬──────────────────┬────────────┬────────┬────────┐
│CREATE    ║<C:>║MX_SALES             ║Field: 8/8   ║       ║       │
                        Enter the field name.
Field names begin with a letter and may contain letters, digits and underscores
```

Fig. 1.11. *Entering the amount of purchase.*

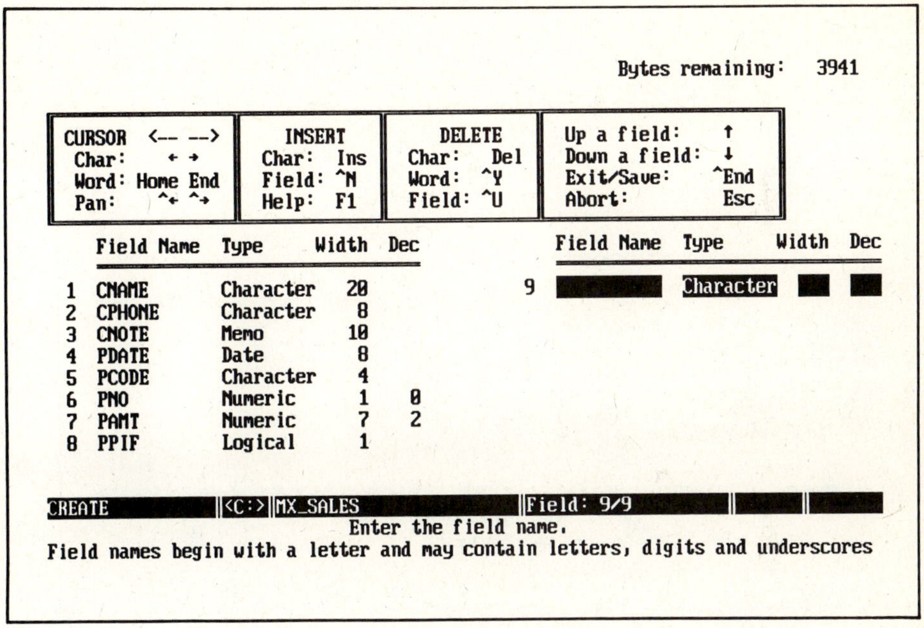
Bytes remaining: 3941
CURSOR <-- -->
Char: ← →
Word: Home End
Pan: ^← ^→
INSERT
Char: Ins
Field: ^N
Help: F1
DELETE
Char: Del
Word: ^Y
Field: ^U
Up a field: ↑
Down a field: ↓
Exit/Save: ^End
Abort: Esc
Field Name Type Width Dec
1 CNAME Character 20
2 CPHONE Character 8
3 CNOTE Memo 10
4 PDATE Date 8
5 PCODE Character 4
6 PNO Numeric 1 0
7 PAMT Numeric 7 2
8 PPIF Logical 1
Field Name Type Width Dec
9 Character
CREATE <C:> MX_SALES Field: 9/9
Enter the field name.
Field names begin with a letter and may contain letters, digits and underscores

Fig. 1.12. *Entering the purchase paid in full field.*

Step 13: Enter the salesperson field, *ESP*, to store the initials of the salesperson (see fig. 1.13). ESP (employee sales person) can hold a maximum of three characters. Note that if your menu is on the screen, ESP is placed in the second column of fields on the right.

Step 14: Save your work by using the all-purpose dBASE III Plus save command, Ctrl-End. That is, press the Ctrl key and hold it down while you press the End key. When the message `Press ENTER to confirm` appears, press Return.

The screen clears. dBASE III Plus asks, `Input data records now? (Y/ N)`. Press N for no. The dot prompt appears. Note that the fourth panel of the status bar now indicates the number of records currently stored in the MX_SALES database, namely `None`.

Step 15: Document your work. If you have a printer, prepare it for printing and type *LIST STRUCTURE TO PRINT*. If you do not have a printer, type *LIST STRUCTURE*.

A recap of the current structure should appear on the screen and on paper. The outline should look similar to figure 1.14.

```
                                          Bytes remaining:    3938

  ┌─────────────────┬─────────────┬─────────────┬────────────────────┐
  │ CURSOR  <── ──> │   INSERT    │   DELETE    │ Up a field:    ↑   │
  │ Char:    ← →    │ Char:  Ins  │ Char:  Del  │ Down a field:  ↓   │
  │ Word: Home End  │ Field: ^N   │ Word: ^Y    │ Exit/Save:    ^End │
  │ Pan:    ^← ^→   │ Help:  F1   │ Field: ^U   │ Abort:        Esc  │
  └─────────────────┴─────────────┴─────────────┴────────────────────┘

       Field Name   Type     Width  Dec        Field Name   Type     Width  Dec

    1  CNAME        Character   20        9     ESP          Character    3
    2  CPHONE       Character    8       10     ▮▮▮▮▮▮       Character  ▮▮   ▮▮
    3  CNOTE        Memo        10
    4  PDATE        Date         8
    5  PCODE        Character    4
    6  PNO          Numeric      1    0
    7  PAMT         Numeric      7    2
    8  PPIF         Logical      1

 ┌CREATE          ┐┌<C:>┐┌MX_SALES        ┐┌Field: 10/10    ┐┌      ┐┌    ┐
                         Enter the field name.
   Field names begin with a letter and may contain letters, digits and underscores
```

Fig. 1.13. *Entering the salesperson field.*

```
Structure for database: A:mx_sales.dbf
Number of data records:        0
Date of last update   : 07/01/85
Field   Field Name  Type       Width   Dec
    1   CNAME       Character     20
    2   CPHONE      Character      8
    3   CNOTE       Memo          10
    4   PDATE       Date           8
    5   PCODE       Character      4
    6   PNO         Numeric        1
    7   PAMT        Numeric        7      2
    8   PPIF        Logical        1
    9   ESP         Character      3
** Total **                      63
```

Fig. 1.14. *Listing of structure of MX_SALES.*

Que Tip: Document the structure. Whenever you create a structure (data file), print the structure on paper. First, prepare the printer. Then, type the dBASE III Plus command *LIST STRUCTURE TO PRINT*.

Making a Few Changes

Doug thought he had everything solved. "This is easy, but, just to make sure, I'll let Henry Hacker have a look. I'll take the printed structure over to him."

Henry had only a couple of suggestions. "Remember, Doug, you may want to sort on the customer's name. The first few characters determine the sort order of each name. If the whole name is stored to CNAME by the first name, you would get this order:

Alan Smith
James Calhoun
Sam Abbot

"Is this what you want?" Henry asked. "Alan Smith sorts before the others because his first name, Alan, comes before all the other first names."

"Well," replied Doug, "I was thinking that sorting by the last name would be better, especially as we add more customers."

"Then keep the first and last names in separate fields," explained Henry. "Sort by last name later. Most last names have more characters than first names, so allocate eight characters for the first name and call it CFNAME. Call the last name CLNAME and give it a width of 10 spaces."

Modifying the Structure

As needs change, the structure can be altered without losing information. Fields can be added or deleted; field names, widths, and types also can be changed.

Step 1: Modify the structure by typing *MODIFY STRUCTURE*. Figure 1.15 shows the screen readied for modifications.

Make sure that MX_SALES appears in the third panel of the status bar. If it does not appear, type *USE MX_SALES* beforehand.

Step 2: Modify the first field. Move the cursor to the first field name, CNAME. Change the name to *CFNAME*, the customer's first name. Move the cursor over to the width field and change the number to *8*.

```
                                              Bytes remaining:    3938

 ┌──────────────────┬──────────────┬──────────────┬──────────────────────┐
 │ CURSOR  <-- -->  │   INSERT     │   DELETE     │ Up a field:     ↑    │
 │ Char:    ← →     │ Char:   Ins  │ Char:   Del  │ Down a field:   ↓    │
 │ Word: Home End   │ Field:  ^N   │ Word:   ^Y   │ Exit/Save:     ^End  │
 │ Pan:    ^← ^→    │ Help:   F1   │ Field:  ^U   │ Abort:          Esc  │
 └──────────────────┴──────────────┴──────────────┴──────────────────────┘

        Field Name  Type    Width Dec        Field Name  Type    Width Dec
     ───────────────────────────────      ───────────────────────────────
     1  CNAME       Character   20    ▮   9  ESP         Character    3
     2  CPHONE      Character    8
     3  CNOTE       Memo        10
     4  PDATE       Date         8
     5  PCODE       Character    4
     6  PNO         Numeric      1   0
     7  PAMT        Numeric      7   2
     8  PPIF        Logical      1
```

MODIFY STRUCTURE|<C:>|MX_SALES |Field: 1/9 || ||
                     Enter the field name.
   Field names begin with a letter and may contain letters, digits and underscores

Fig. 1.15. *Modifying MX_SALES.*

Make use of the editing keys to avoid having to retype everything. For instance, to insert the letter F in CNAME, move the cursor under the letter N, press the Ins key once, and type *F*. Notice that when you press Ins, the fifth panel of the status bar shows an Ins indicator. Pressing Ins again turns off the insert editing control. Panel six of the status bar has separate indicators for the Num Lock and the Caps Lock keys.

Step 3: Add a field on the second line. Move the cursor down to the second field. Press the Ctrl key and hold it down while you press N. (Ctrl-N moves the existing fields down one from the cursor.) Now you have room for another field between CFNAME and CPHONE (see fig. 1.16).

```
                                          Bytes remaining:   3950

  ┌─────────────────┬────────────────┬───────────────┬──────────────────────┐
  │ CURSOR  <── ──> │  INSERT        │  DELETE       │ Up a field:     ↑     │
  │ Char:    ← →    │  Char:   Ins   │  Char:   Del  │ Down a field:   ↓     │
  │ Word: Home End  │  Field:  ^N    │  Word:   ^Y   │ Exit/Save:    ^End    │
  │ Pan:    ^← ^→   │  Help:   F1    │  Field:  ^U   │ Abort:         Esc    │
  └─────────────────┴────────────────┴───────────────┴──────────────────────┘

      Field Name  Type      Width Dec        Field Name  Type       Width Dec

   1  CFNAME      Character    8           9  PPIF        Logical      1
   2  ▮▮▮▮▮▮▮     Character  ▮▮▮  ▮▮      10  ESP         Character    3
   3  CPHONE      Character    8
   4  CNOTE       Memo        10
   5  PDATE       Date         8
   6  PCODE       Character    4
   7  PNO         Numeric      1   0
   8  PAMT        Numeric      7   2

 ▌MODIFY STRUCTURE▐▌<C:>▐▌MX_SALES▐         ▌Field: 2/10▐        ▌Ins▐   ▌Caps▐
                      Enter the field name.
 Field names begin with a letter and may contain letters, digits and underscores
```

Fig. 1.16. *Inserting a new field.*

Step 4: Enter *CLNAME*, the character field type, and a width of *10* (see fig. 1.17).

Step 5: Save your work by pressing Ctrl-End and then Return. The structure is now revised and saved.

Step 6: Document your work. Prepare your printer and run the *LIST STRUCTURE TO PRINT* procedure. Your printout should look similar to figure 1.18.

```
                                        Bytes remaining:   3948

 ┌─────────────────┬─────────────────┬─────────────────┬────────────────────┐
 │ CURSOR  <-- -->  │   INSERT        │    DELETE       │ Up a field:     ↑   │
 │ Char:    ← →     │ Char:   Ins     │ Char:    Del    │ Down a field:   ↓   │
 │ Word: Home End   │ Field: ^N       │ Word:    ^Y     │ Exit/Save:    ^End  │
 │ Pan:     ^← ^→   │ Help:   F1      │ Field:   ^U     │ Abort:        Esc   │
 └─────────────────┴─────────────────┴─────────────────┴────────────────────┘

     Field Name   Type    Width Dec         Field Name   Type    Width Dec

   1 CFNAME      Character   8            9 PPIF        Logical     1
   2 CLNAME      Character  10           10 ESP         Character   3
   3 CPHONE      Character   8
   4 CNOTE       Memo       10
   5 PDATE       Date        8
   6 PCODE       Character   4
   7 PNO         Numeric     1    0
   8 PAMT        Numeric     7    2

 ┌─────────────────────────────────────────────────────────────────────────┐
 │ MODIFY STRUCTURE ||<C:>||MX_SALES        |Field: 2/10    ||Ins  ||  Caps  │
 └─────────────────────────────────────────────────────────────────────────┘
                  Enter the field name.
   Field names begin with a letter and may contain letters, digits and underscores
```

Fig. 1.17. *New field inserted in structure.*

```
   Structure for database: A:mx_sales.dbf
   Number of data records:        0
   Date of last update    : 07/01/85
   Field   Field Name   Type      Width     Dec
       1   CFNAME       Character      8
       2   CLNAME       Character     10
       3   CPHONE       Character      8
       4   CNOTE        Memo          10
       5   PDATE        Date           8
       6   PCODE        Character      4
       7   PNO          Numeric        1
       8   PAMT         Numeric        7       2
       9   PPIF         Logical        1
      10   ESP          Character      3
   ** Total **                        61
```

Fig. 1.18. *Modified structure of MX_SALES.*

Now update your plan to reflect the change from one name field to two. This is now the current plan:

Customer Data	*Field Name*
Customer first name	CFNAME
Customer last name	CLNAME
Telephone number	CPHONE
Additional customer notes	CNOTE

Sales Data	
Product code	PCODE
Purchase amount	PAMT
Number of items purchased	PNO
Date of purchase	PDATE
Paid-in-full marker	PPIF

Employee Data	
Initials of person selling product	ESP

Choosing a Database

You have created the structure for MX_SALES, but the sales database can be one of many stored on the disk. dBASE III Plus needs to know which database is active. The USE command, followed by the name of a database, opens the data file.

The USE command also performs one other vital service. Recently added records can be in memory and not yet saved permanently to disk. USE by itself closes the current database and saves all records to disk. USE followed by a second file name closes one database and opens another.

A way to save your work periodically, particularly if power failures are a possibility, is to type USE and the current file name. If you already are working with MX_SALES, the command USE MX_SALES saves the contents, closes the sales file, and then opens it again. Every record is saved.

Open databases can be closed in two other ways. One is to use the CLOSE DATA-BASES command; the other is to use the CLEAR ALL command. These commands close not only the current database but also any other open databases, as well as certain other types of files.

For example, to save your database to disk and then reopen it, close and reopen MX_SALES by typing *USE MX_SALES*.

NOTES

Que Tip: Save your work periodically. At the dot prompt, type *USE* and the file name.

Adding Information to the Database

Records are entered most easily by putting dBASE III Plus in APPEND mode. This command enables you to enter records into the database in use.

Step 1: Put dBASE III Plus in APPEND mode. Type *APPEND.* Figure 1.19 shows the data entry screen that results.

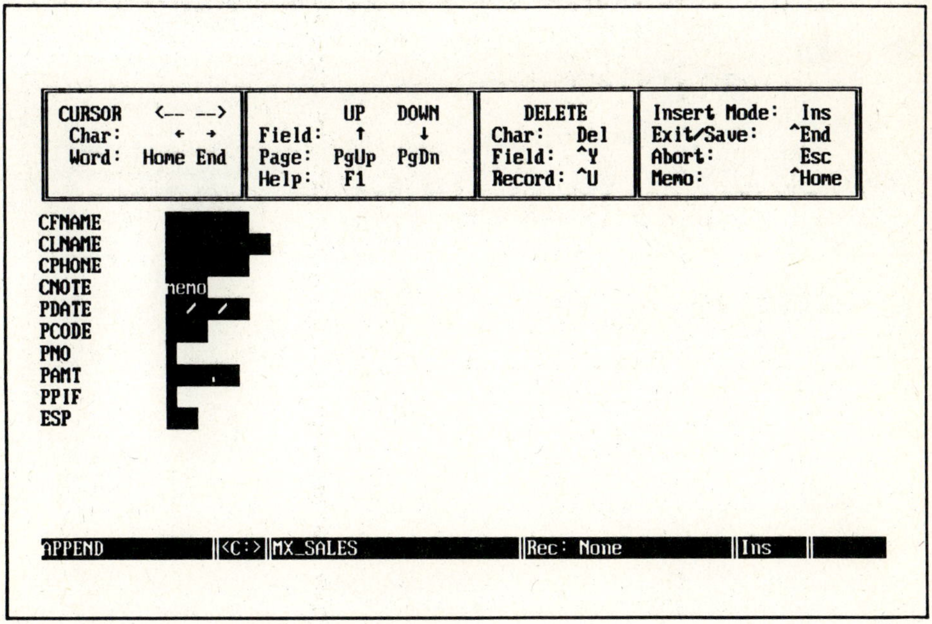

Fig. 1.19. *The APPEND data entry screen.*

The names of the fields are on the left, down the screen. The width of each is highlighted to the right.

Step 2: Enter the first field for the first record (see fig. 1.20). Suppose that you want to add the customer's first name, CFNAME. For the first customer, type *James* and press Return. Remember to capitalize the first letter and type the other letters in lowercase. Do not use the Caps Lock key.

As you enter the data for each field, do not worry about mistakes for now. You will have a chance to correct errors in Lesson 2.

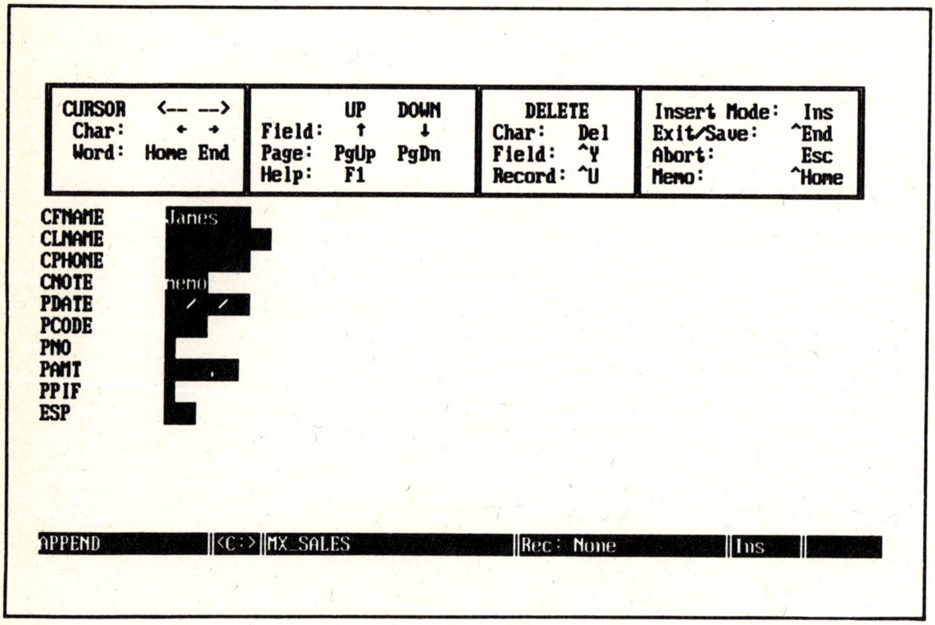

```
 CURSOR    <--  -->          UP   DOWN     DELETE          Insert Mode:   Ins
 Char:       ←   →     Field:  ↑     ↓     Char:   Del     Exit/Save:    ^End
 Word:   Home End      Page: PgUp  PgDn    Field:  ^Y      Abort:        Esc
                       Help:  F1            Record: ^U      Memo:        ^Home

CFNAME       James
CLNAME
CPHONE
CNOTE       memo
PDATE        /  /
PCODE
PNO
PAMT          .
PPIF
ESP


 APPEND          |<C:>|MX_SALES           |Rec: None        | Ins  |
```

Fig. 1.20. *Entering a value for first name.*

Step 3: Enter the last name for the first record. The cursor moves to CLNAME. Type *Blair* and press Return. The cursor moves down to the third field, CPHONE.

Step 4: Now press the up-arrow key (at the upper right of the keyboard). The cursor moves up to the second field. Arrow keys move the cursor up, down, right, and left. Return the cursor to the CPHONE field.

Step 5: Enter the telephone number for the first record (see fig. 1.21). At the CPHONE field, type *351-8923*. Note that a beep sounds when the telephone number fills the field width. dBASE III Plus beeps when the information has either the same number of characters as the field or more characters than the field can accept. The beep is a reminder that the cursor has moved to the next field.

```
┌─────────────────────────────────────────────────────────────────────────────┐
│                                                                               │
│  ┌─────────────────────────┬──────────────────┬──────────────┬─────────────┐ │
│  │ CURSOR    <── ──>        │        UP   DOWN │ DELETE       │ Insert Mode: Ins│
│  │ Char:      ←   →    Field:│       ↑     ↓    │ Char:   Del  │ Exit/Save:  ^End│
│  │ Word:   Home End   Page: │  PgUp  PgDn      │ Field:  ^Y   │ Abort:      Esc │
│  │                    Help: │   F1             │ Record: ^U   │ Memo:      ^Home│
│  └─────────────────────────┴──────────────────┴──────────────┴─────────────┘ │
│   CFNAME     James                                                            │
│   CLNAME     Blair ▐                                                           │
│   CPHONE     351-8923                                                          │
│   CNOTE      memo                                                             │
│   PDATE      ▌ /  /                                                            │
│   PCODE      ▐                                                                │
│   PNO        ▌                                                                │
│   PAMT         .  ▌                                                            │
│   PPIF       ▐                                                                │
│   ESP        ▌                                                                │
│                                                                               │
│  ▐APPEND        ║<C:>║MX_SALES          ║Rec: None     ║Ins ║                  │
└─────────────────────────────────────────────────────────────────────────────┘
```

Fig. 1.21. *First three fields completed.*

Step 6: Enter the comments for the first record. Notes about the customer's satisfaction can be entered in the memo field, CNOTE. Memo fields enable you to store several lines of notes about the record. Only four highlighted spaces with the word memo are visible. To enter comments, you must "zoom" into the dBASE III Plus word processor.

NOTES

Before you zoom, make sure that the cursor is on the CNOTE field. Then press Ctrl and hold it down while you press Home. The APPEND screen clears, the message `Edit: CNOTE` appears in the upper left corner, and a new help block appears (see fig. 1.22).

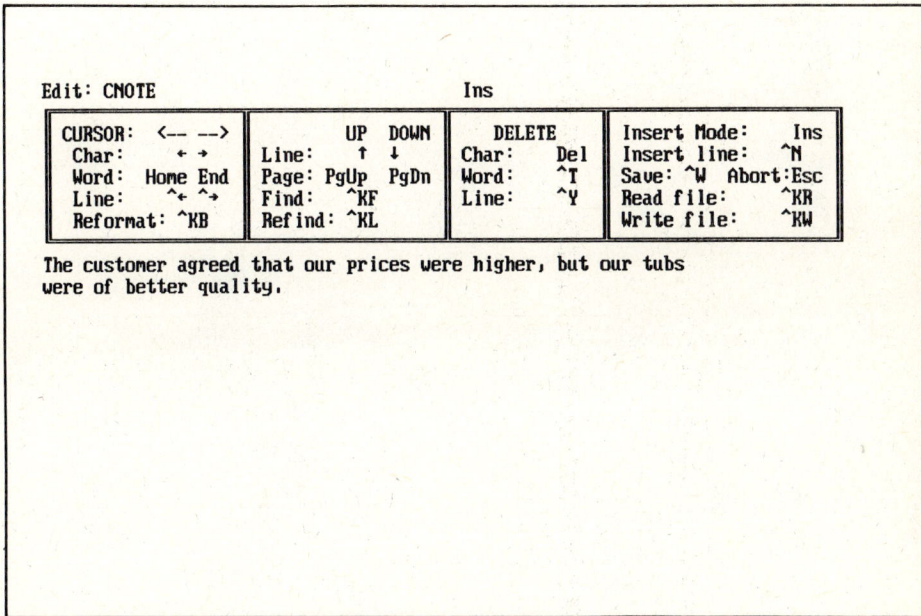

```
Edit: CNOTE                              Ins
┌──────────────────┬──────────────────┬──────────────┬──────────────────────┐
│ CURSOR: <-- -->  │          UP  DOWN │   DELETE     │ Insert Mode:     Ins │
│ Char:     ← →    │ Line:    ↑   ↓    │ Char:    Del │ Insert line:  ^N     │
│ Word:  Home End  │ Page: PgUp  PgDn │ Word:    ^T  │ Save: ^W  Abort:Esc  │
│ Line:     ^← ^→  │ Find:    ^KF     │ Line:    ^Y  │ Read file:    ^KR    │
│ Reformat: ^KB    │ Refind:  ^KL     │              │ Write file:   ^KW    │
└──────────────────┴──────────────────┴──────────────┴──────────────────────┘

The customer agreed that our prices were higher, but our tubs
were of better quality.
```

Fig. 1.22. *Entering a memo in the word processor.*

Next you will type the comments observed by the salesperson. Type until you reach about the 50th column. dBASE III Plus's word-wrap feature will automatically move the rest of the paragraph down to the next line. Now enter the comment:

The customer agreed that our prices were higher, but our tubs were of better quality.

Note that you can move the cursor to any word. Use the Ins (Insert) and Del (Delete) keys to add to or delete from the notes.

When you finish typing, save your work by pressing Ctrl and holding it down while you press End. This sequence always saves work in dBASE III Plus. Ctrl-W also works in this instance. After saving, you are zoomed from the notepad back to the memo field shown in figure 1.21.

Step 7: Enter the date for the first record. This field and the ones that follow save purchase information. PDATE retains the date of purchase. With your cursor on the PDATE field, enter the date *02/30/85* (see fig. 1.23).

```
┌──────────────────────────────────────────────────────────────────────────────┐
│  ┌─────────────────┬──────────────────┬──────────────────┬──────────────────┐ │
│  │ CURSOR  <-- -->  │      UP   DOWN   │     DELETE       │ Insert Mode:  Ins │ │
│  │ Char:    ←  →    │ Field:   ↑    ↓  │ Char:    Del     │ Exit/Save:   ^End │ │
│  │ Word:  Home End  │ Page:  PgUp PgDn │ Field:   ^Y      │ Abort:        Esc │ │
│  │                  │ Help:    F1      │ Record:  ^U      │ Memo:       ^Home │ │
│  └─────────────────┴──────────────────┴──────────────────┴──────────────────┘ │
│  CFNAME     James                                                              │
│  CLNAME     Blair                                                              │
│  CPHONE     351-8923                                                           │
│  CNOTE      memo                                                               │
│  PDATE      02/30/85                                                           │
│  PCODE                                                                         │
│  PNO                                                                           │
│  PAMT                                                                          │
│  PPIF                                                                          │
│  ESP                                                                           │
│                                                                                │
│  APPEND          │<C:>│MX_SALES            │Rec: None        │Ins │            │
│                      Invalid date. (press SPACE)                               │
└──────────────────────────────────────────────────────────────────────────────┘
```

Fig. 1.23. *Entering the date field (incorrectly).*

What happens? The message Invalid date. (press SPACE) appears on the screen. dBASE III Plus prohibits entry of invalid dates (February does not have 30 days). You can enter a wrong date but not an invalid date. Press the space bar and type *06/15/85*.

Step 8: Enter the item code for the first record. At the PCODE field, enter *H-27*.

Step 9: Enter the number of items purchased for the first record. PNO records this data. Assume that PCODE H-27 represents a hot tub and that this customer bought one unit. Enter *1*.

Figure 1.24 shows the data entry screen completed through field number seven. Check to make sure your screen reads the same.

```
 ┌──────────────────────────────────────────────────────────────────────────┐
 │                                                                            │
 │  ┌─────────────────┬───────────────────┬──────────────┬─────────────────┐ │
 │  │ CURSOR  <── ──>  │            UP  DOWN │   DELETE      │ Insert Mode: Ins │ │
 │  │ Char:    ← →     │ Field:    ↑    ↓   │ Char:   Del  │ Exit/Save:  ^End │ │
 │  │ Word:  Home End  │ Page:  PgUp  PgDn  │ Field:  ^Y   │ Abort:      Esc  │ │
 │  │                  │ Help:   F1        │ Record: ^U   │ Memo:       ^Home│ │
 │  └─────────────────┴───────────────────┴──────────────┴─────────────────┘ │
 │  CFNAME     Janes                                                          │
 │  CLNAME     Blair                                                          │
 │  CPHONE     351-8923                                                       │
 │  CNOTE      memo                                                           │
 │  PDATE      06/15/85                                                       │
 │  PCODE      H-27                                                           │
 │  PNO        1                                                              │
 │  PAMT       .                                                              │
 │  PPIF                                                                      │
 │  ESP                                                                       │
 │                                                                            │
 │  ─APPEND──────────────<C:>──MX_SALES─────────────Rec: None──────Ins──────  │
 └──────────────────────────────────────────────────────────────────────────┘
```

Fig. 1.24. *First record for fields 1 through 7.*

Step 10: Enter the amount of purchase for the first record. At PAMT, type *4000* and pause. Note the movement of the cursor and the decimal point. Press Return. The decimal point as well as zeros to the right of the decimal point are provided if none are entered.

NOTES

Step 11: Enter the ninth field for the first record: the fully paid indicator, PPIF. PPIF is a logical field type that indicates whether the invoice has been paid in full. A logical field allows entry of only four data values: T (true) or Y (yes) if logically true, and F (false) or N (no) if not true. A question mark appears if a logical field has never been used before, and the omission of an entry is assumed to be false.

Press any key except for T, F, Y, or N. What happens? A beep sounds, and the cursor remains in the PPIF field. No other entries are allowed. The locking-out is a verification feature. dBASE III Plus ensures that only logical information can be entered into a logical field. Now enter *T* to indicate full payment.

Step 12: Enter the sales person's initials for the first record into the ESP field. Type *DWK,* for Douglas William Kornfeld. All information has now been entered for the first record (see fig. 1.25). The cursor jumps immediately to the second record.

```
┌─────────────────────────────────────────────────────────────────────┐
│                                                                       │
│  ┌────────────────┐┌──────────────────┐┌──────────────┐┌───────────────────┐
│  │ CURSOR  <── ──>││          UP  DOWN││   DELETE     ││Insert Mode:  Ins  │
│  │ Char:    ←  →  ││ Field:   ↑    ↓  ││ Char:   Del  ││Exit/Save:   ^End  │
│  │ Word:  Home End││ Page:  PgUp PgDn ││ Field:  ^Y   ││Abort:        Esc  │
│  │                ││ Help:   F1       ││ Record: ^U   ││Memo:       ^Home  │
│  └────────────────┘└──────────────────┘└──────────────┘└───────────────────┘
│   CFNAME     James                                                    │
│   CLNAME     Blair                                                     │
│   CPHONE     351-8923                                                  │
│   CNOTE      memo                                                      │
│   PDATE      06/15/85                                                  │
│   PCODE      H-27                                                      │
│   PNO        1                                                         │
│   PAMT       4000.00                                                   │
│   PPIF       T                                                         │
│   ESP        DWK                                                       │
│                                                                       │
│  APPEND          ||<C:>||MX_SALES              ||Rec: 1/1  ||    ||    │
└─────────────────────────────────────────────────────────────────────┘
```

Fig. 1.25. *First record for fields 1 through 10.*

NOTES

Step 13: Once the ESP information is entered, the cursor moves to the second record. Record 1 is automatically saved when you move to record 2. To scroll back to record 1, press PgUp. Make changes if necessary; then press PgDn to return to record 2 (see fig. 1.26).

Record 2 is indicated indirectly. After you add the first record, the fourth panel of the status bar reads, Rec: EOF/1. This message is dBASE shorthand indicating that you will be appending the next record to the end of the file (EOF) of a database that currently contains one record (/1).

```
┌─────────────────────────────────────────────────────────────────────────┐
│                                                                           │
│  ┌──────────────────┬────────────────────┬──────────────┬──────────────┐ │
│  │ CURSOR   <-- -->  │         UP   DOWN  │   DELETE     │Insert Mode: Ins│
│  │ Char:      ← →    │ Field:   ↑    ↓    │ Char:   Del  │Exit/Save: ^End │
│  │ Word:   Home End  │ Page:  PgUp  PgDn  │ Field:  ^Y   │Abort:     Esc  │
│  │                   │ Help:   F1         │ Record: ^U   │Memo:     ^Home │
│  └──────────────────┴────────────────────┴──────────────┴──────────────┘ │
│   CFNAME                                                                   │
│   CLNAME                                                                   │
│   CPHONE                                                                   │
│   CNOTE    memo                                                            │
│   PDATE     /  /                                                           │
│   PCODE                                                                    │
│   PNO                                                                      │
│   PAMT        .                                                            │
│   PPIF                                                                     │
│   ESP                                                                      │
│                                                                           │
│  APPEND         ║<C:>║MX_SALES            ║Rec: EOF/1    ║      ║          │
└─────────────────────────────────────────────────────────────────────────┘
```

Fig. 1.26. *Data entry screen for second record.*

Exiting APPEND Mode

To stop adding records, exit in one of these ways:

1. Press Esc to exit *without saving* the current record.

2. Press Ctrl-End to exit *saving* the current record.

NOTES

Building the Data File

Add nine more records of purchases to the database. If you exited from APPEND, type *APPEND* at the dot prompt. A blank record appears. Add one record at a time from the list that follows.

If you want to interrupt the exercise and exit dBASE III Plus, type *QUIT* at the dot prompt.

To start again (for a two floppy drive system), type the following:

    DBASE
    SET DEFAULT TO B:
    DO QPREP

Then select the lesson you want to review.

The complete list of records in the data file follows. You already have entered the first record, so start with record 2 and enter the data in the right-hand column of each record.

Record No.	1	
CFNAME	James	
CLNAME	Blair	
CPHONE	351-8923	
CNOTE	========>	The customer agreed that our prices were higher, but our tubs were of better quality.
PDATE	06/15/85	
PCODE	H-27	
PNO	1	
PAMT	4000.00	
PPIF	T	
ESP	DWK	

Record No.	2
CFNAME	Francis
CLNAME	Connors
CPHONE	
CNOTE	
PDATE	06/16/85
PCODE	H-22
PNO	1
PAMT	6600.35
PPIF	T
ESP	LEM

NOTES

Record No.	3
CFNAME	Thomas
CLNAME	Jones
CPHONE	971-9412
CNOTE	=========> Customer is purchasing a vacation home in six months. Give him a call about sale at that time.
PDATE	06/17/85
PCODE	H-19
PNO	1
PAMT	3523.17
PPIF	T
ESP	DWK
Record No.	4
CFNAME	Sam
CLNAME	Aster
CPHONE	371-2341
CNOTE	
PDATE	06/18/85
PCODE	P-11
PNO	1
PAMT	9042.00
PPIF	F
ESP	FSM
Record No.	5
CFNAME	Harold
CLNAME	Stephens
CPHONE	621-1517
CNOTE	
	06/19/85
	H-19
PNO	1
PAMT	3523.17
PPIF	F
ESP	FSM

NOTES

Record No.   6
CFNAME   Molly
CLNAME   Brown
CPHONE   876-1252
CNOTE
PDATE   06/22/85
PCODE   H-22
PNO   1
PAMT   6600.35
PPIF   F
ESP   LEM

Record No.   7
CFNAME   John
CLNAME   Clark
CPHONE   351-1118
CNOTE   =========>   Customer wishes to install deck. Give
                              contractor a call.

PDATE   06/25/85
PCODE   P-14
PNO   1
PAMT   8097.00
PPIF   F
ESP   DWK

Record No.   8
CFNAME   Susan
CLNAME   Jones
CPHONE   370-4726
CNOTE
PDATE   06/27/85
PCODE   H-27
PNO   1
PAMT   4000.00
PPIF   T
ESP   LEM

NOTES

Record No.   9
CFNAME   William
CLNAME   Abbott
CPHONE   875-2212
CNOTE
PDATE   07/01/85
PCODE   P-11
PNO   1
PAMT   9042.00
PPIF   T
ESP   FSM

Record No.   10
CFNAME   Barbara
CLNAME   Hoffsmith
CPHONE   542-1199
CNOTE   =========>   Customer remarked that the price for
                                         the 55-gallon drums of pool cleaner
                                         was the lowest price in town.

PDATE   07/02/85
PCODE   P-10
PNO   2
PAMT   152.52
PPIF   T
ESP   DWK

When you finish entering the records, you need to exit APPEND. If you are at a blank record, you can press Esc to exit. If you are at a record you want to save, press Ctrl-End to exit. After exiting APPEND, if you want to end your work session now and continue at a later time, type *QUIT* to close the file and leave dBASE III Plus.

☐ SUMMARY OF CONCEPTS
PRESENTED IN LESSON 1

---

1. Before building an application, plan for it. Use business forms (such as invoices and customer lists) as inspiration.

2. The dBASE III Plus CREATE command builds the general layout of the database—the structure.

3. The structure contains field characteristics: the name, type, width, and number of decimals, if applicable.

4. The field name can be up to 10 letters long. Use a name that is descriptive of the information in the field.

5. Five types of fields exist. Select one according to the type of information to be stored.

Character information	C
Numeric information	N
Date or calendar data	D
Extended notes—Memo	M
Yes/No data—Logical	L

6. Select N, for numeric, only if the information is to be operated on mathematically. Do not confuse a math field with Social Security, ZIP code, or telephone "numbers."

7. Save the created structure by pressing Ctrl-End. This key combination always saves work in dBASE III Plus.

8. Always document your structure. If a printer is available, print the structure by typing DISPLAY STRUCTURE TO PRINT.

9. Select a current data file with the USE command. USE also closes the previous data file.

10. To enter data into records, type APPEND. To stop entering data, exit APPEND by pressing Ctrl-End (saving the current screen contents) or by pressing the Esc key (not saving the current screen contents).

11. APPEND mode verifies entries according to the type of field. Digits and decimal points can be entered into numeric fields. A logical field accepts only Yes or No entries or True or False entries. Only valid dates can go into date fields.

12. To zoom into the notepad, place the cursor in the memo field, press Ctrl-Home, enter notes, and save by pressing Ctrl-End.

13. You can revise records while in APPEND mode by pressing PgUp to move the cursor up to previous records. Pressing PgDn moves the cursor to the following record.

NOTES

**LESSON 1
EXERCISE**

The Saltwater Sally Sales Management system tracks sales. The system includes information about credit sales (accounts receivable) and keeps track of how much the customers owe you, the seller.

An accounts payable system does the opposite, tracking the funds you owe others, notably vendors. *Vendors* are people or companies who provide you with the goods that you resell to your customers.

The fields used in an accounts payable system often resemble those in an accounts receivable application. Examine the following series of fields. Do they contain the data necessary to pay your bills?

Field 1	VNAME	Company name of vendor
Field 2	VATTN	Name of contact person at vendor's company
Field 3	VPHONE	Vendor's phone number
Field 4	VNOTE	Memo field—supplementary vendor information
Field 5	DATEIN	Date of bill receipt
Field 6	VBILLNO	The bill number
Field 7	VAMT	Amount of bill
Field 8	VPIF	Now paid in full? (Yes or No)

Follow the steps to create a data file to store accounts payable information. Complete the steps carefully, because later exercises build on the accounts payable data file.

Step 1: Create the SSBILLS data file. At the dBASE III Plus dot prompt, type *CREATE SSBILLS.*

NOTES

Step 2: Enter the field names, types, widths, and decimals as outlined. Save your work by pressing Ctrl-End.

Field 1	VNAME	C	20
Field 2	VATTN	C	15
Field 3	VPHONE	C	8
Field 4	VNOTE	M	
Field 5	DATEIN	D	
Field 6	VBILLNO	C	5
Field 7	VAMT	N	7 2
Field 8	VPIF	L	

Step 3: Now add a few bills. If you must interrupt your work session after creating the structure for SSBILLS, type *USE SSBILLS* to open the file again before adding the bills.

Step 4: Enter the current accounts payable data that follows. Type *APPEND*. When you finish, press Ctrl-End to save your work.

Record No.	1
VNAME	Aquarius Pool Supp.
VATTN	Mr. James Smith
VPHONE	283-2123
DATEIN	06/19/85
VBILLNO	323
VAMT	1923.20
VPIF	F
Record No.	2
VNAME	Tidewater Tillie's
VATTN	Ms. C. Maid
VPHONE	593-9200
DATEIN	06/29/85
VBILLNO	3453
VAMT	1284.32
VPIF	F

NOTES

Record No.	3
VNAME	Acme Chlorine
VATTN	Mr. Sam Lyons
VPHONE	932-1253
DATEIN	07/02/85
VBILLNO	121
VAMT	842.23
VPIF	F

Record No.	4
VNAME	Southern Bell
VATTN	Business Office
VPHONE	953-4243
DATEIN	07/03/85
VBILLNO	2131
VAMT	112.00
VPIF	F

Record No.	5
VNAME	Trust Realty Co.
VATTN	Mr. Roger Bix
VPHONE	312-3292
DATEIN	07/05/85
VBILLNO	3
VAMT	634.00
VPIF	F

NOTES

2

Moving About, Cleaning Up, and Browsing

Related sections in *dBASE III Plus Handbook*, 2nd Edition: Chapters 4 and 5.

In the previous lesson, you added new information to the database. In this lesson, you will practice working with existing records in the database.

Information changes rapidly, and revisions must be made to records in order to reflect the changes. In addition, people often make mistakes when entering records: names are misspelled, addresses are entered incorrectly, and amounts are omitted.

dBASE III Plus has a number of techniques that can ensure the validity of data. For example, records can be inspected easily and revised. To do so, however, requires the capability to focus on one record at a time.

In this lesson, you will move about the existing database and learn two powerful techniques for inspecting records and altering them. Specifically, you will learn about the following commands:

- The GO command

- The EDIT command

- The CHANGE command

- The BROWSE command

NOTES

Navigating between Records: Getting to the Top and Bottom

The MX_SALES data file you constructed in the previous lesson now contains 10 records. In this lesson, you will be changing data in some of these records. To make changes, you locate the record you want to change, make your changes, advance to the next record that needs correction, make changes there, and so forth.

dBASE III Plus can operate on only a single record at any one time. This record, called the *current record*, is identified in the fourth panel of the status bar by the number before the slash. For instance, if you have just opened MX_SALES with its 10 records, the current record is record 1 and the status bar reads Rec: 1/10, indicating that the current record is record 1 of 10.

The status bar indicates the current position of the database *record pointer*, an internal electronic arrow always positioned at one record. Processing or making changes to a record, then, involves moving the record pointer to the correct record beforehand.

dBASE III Plus has several ways to move the record pointer, including the command GO (which also can be written GOTO) and the command SKIP. The GO command moves the pointer to a particular record based on its *record number*, a sequential number that dBASE assigns to each record as it is appended to the database. The next record you append to MX_SALES, for instance, would be assigned record number 11. The SKIP command moves the pointer to the record immediately following the current record. You also can skip longer distances and even move backwards by putting a number after SKIP. For example, SKIP 5 moves the record pointer 5 records forward; SKIP -1 moves the pointer 1 record back.

To move the record pointer using GO, simply type GO followed by a record number. If the record number you named does not exist, dBASE returns the message Record is out of range. You also can go to two named locations in the database:

TOP	The first record
BOTTOM	The last record

In addition to the records themselves, any database also includes two special positions:

BOF	Beginning of file	Position before the first record
EOF	End of file	Position after the last record

Your 10-record file therefore has 12 positions (see fig. 2.1).

NOTES

BOF	1	2	3	4	5	6	7	8	9	10	EOF

Fig. 2.1. *Possible locations for record pointer.*

You might recall when you were appending records that panel four in the status bar indicated you were at EOF. The EOF indicator also appears any other time the record pointer is positioned at the end of the file. The BOF position has no indicator in the status bar, but you rarely have to be concerned about it.

With the following four expressions, you can test the movement commands:

GO TOP
GO BOTTOM
GO 5 (GO and a record number)
SKIP

Follow these steps to test the movement commands. As you carry out each step, look at panel four of the status bar to keep track of the position of the pointer.

Step 1: Type *DO QPREP*. Select Lesson 2.

Step 2: Open the sales file. Type *USE MX_SALES*.

The status bar reads, Rec: 1/10.

Step 3: Move to the fifth record. Type *GO 5.*

The status bar reads, Rec: 5/10.

Step 4: Go to the bottom of the file. Type *GO BOTTOM.*

The status bar reads, Rec: 10/10.

The tenth record is the bottom of the data file and is now the current record. However, the bottom record is not the end of the file. Use the SKIP command to advance the record pointer one record to the end of the file.

Step 5: Move past the last record to EOF. Type *SKIP.*

The status bar reads, Rec: EOF/10.

The end of file is the "Twilight Zone." dBASE III Plus functions differently after the end of a file is reached. If you type a command and nothing happens, check whether the record pointer is at the end of file. Go to the top of the file if necessary and issue the command again.

NOTES

Step 6: Move back to the top of the file. Type *GO TOP.*

Que Tip: If a command produces no response, check for end of file by typing *? EOF( ).* dBASE responds either .T., meaning you are at EOF, or .F., meaning you are not at EOF. Type *GO TOP*, if necessary. Then issue the original command again.

Revising and Refining Data

Data is seldom entered without errors the first time. Typographical errors occur and must be corrected. Information also must be revised as data changes. You often need to update records when people change names or if stock numbers were entered incorrectly.

dBASE III Plus offers a number of commands to revise the database. Among them are EDIT, CHANGE, and BROWSE. You will use these three commands to revise your database in this lesson.

The EDIT Command

The all-purpose command to change data already stored in the database is EDIT. If you have a database in use, just type *EDIT* at the dot prompt, and the current record is brought to the screen. If you want to edit a specific record, type EDIT followed by its record number. You cannot use TOP or BOTTOM after EDIT; type *GO TOP* or *GO BOTTOM* first and then *EDIT.*

Step 1: Use the EDIT command. Make sure you are using MX_SALES and are at the first record, and type *EDIT.* Figure 2.2 shows what appears. Move the cursor to any field. Move to any other record by pressing the PgUp and PgDn keys.

Step 2: Make necessary revisions. Refer to the list of records you entered in Lesson 1. If you have entered any fields incorrectly, you should make the needed corrections. To make a correction, first check the fifth panel of the status bar on your computer screen to make sure that the indicator Ins appears. If Ins does not appear, press the Ins key at the lower right of your keyboard. You may now position your cursor at any field and revise it.

Step 3: Save your work and exit the EDIT mode as you exited APPEND mode. Move the cursor past the last record, or press Ctrl-End. (If you do not want to save your current edit, press Esc to exit.)

```
┌─────────────────────────────────────────────────────────────────────┐
│                                                                       │
│  ┌──────────────────┬───────────────────┬───────────────┬──────────┐ │
│  │ CURSOR  <── ──>  │      UP   DOWN     │   DELETE      │Insert Mode: Ins │
│  │ Char:    ←   →   │ Field:   ↑    ↓    │ Char:   Del   │Exit/Save:  ^End │
│  │ Word:  Home End  │ Page:  PgUp  PgDn  │ Field:  ^Y    │Abort:       Esc │
│  │                  │ Help:   F1         │ Record: ^U    │Memo:      ^Home │
│  └──────────────────┴───────────────────┴───────────────┴──────────┘ │
│    CFNAME      James                                                  │
│    CLNAME      Blair                                                  │
│    CPHONE      351-8923                                               │
│    CNOTE       memo                                                   │
│    PDATE       06/15/85                                               │
│    PCODE       H-27                                                   │
│    PNO         1                                                      │
│    PAMT        4000.00                                                │
│    PPIF        T                                                      │
│    ESP         DWK                                                    │
│                                                                       │
│                                                                       │
│                                                                       │
│   EDIT             |<C:>|MX_SALES              |Rec: 1/10    |Ins|     │
│                                                                       │
└─────────────────────────────────────────────────────────────────────┘
```

Fig. 2.2. *Editing records.*

Step 4: Edit record 5. Type *EDIT 5.* Mr. Stephens actually spells his name *Stevens*, and his old telephone number was entered. His new number is *543-9850*. Make the necessary changes to the invoice. Your screen should look like figure 2.3 when you finish.

```
┌──────────────────────────────────────────────────────────────────────────┐
│                                                                            │
│   ┌─────────────────┬──────────────────┬──────────────────┬─────────────┐ │
│   │ CURSOR  <-- -->  │      UP   DOWN   │    DELETE        │Insert Mode:  Ins │
│   │ Char:    ←  →    │Field:   ↑    ↓   │ Char:   Del      │Exit/Save:  ^End │
│   │ Word:  Home End  │Page:  PgUp PgDn  │ Field:  ^Y       │Abort:       Esc │
│   │                  │Help:   F1        │ Record: ^U       │Memo:      ^Home │
│   └─────────────────┴──────────────────┴──────────────────┴─────────────┘ │
│                                                                            │
│    CFNAME    Harold                                                        │
│    CLNAME    Stevens                                                       │
│    CPHONE    543-9850                                                      │
│    CNOTE     memo                                                          │
│    PDATE     06/19/85                                                      │
│    PCODE     H-19                                                          │
│    PNO       1                                                             │
│    PAMT      3523.17                                                       │
│    PPIF      F                                                             │
│    ESP       FSM                                                           │
│                                                                            │
│                                                                            │
│   EDIT          <C:> MX_SALES          Rec: 5/10           Ins             │
│                                                                            │
└──────────────────────────────────────────────────────────────────────────┘
```

Fig. 2.3. *Editing record 5.*

The EDIT command allows you to change all the fields in all the records in the database, one record at a time. You select the starting point for the edit session by specifying a particular record number.

Command Qualifications

In certain situations you may want to restrict the view of the database so that only the records or fields you need to change are presented on the screen. For example, if you need to make changes only in the name fields, then you do not need to be bothered with any of the other fields. To restrict the view, you can apply one or a combination of three qualifications to the command:

NOTES

- A *field list*—a listing of the names of the fields you want to display or change

- A *scope*—a range of records you want to restrict the command to

- A *search condition*—a selection of records sharing one or more data elements that you want the command to operate on

You type the name of the command and follow it on the same command line with the particular qualification you want. As with anything else in dBASE III Plus, you must follow certain rules for writing each of these qualifications into a statement.

Construct a *field list* by typing the keyword FIELDS followed by the name of the fields you want to view. Use a comma (,) to separate each field from the next one in the list. Certain commands specify a field list by leaving off the keyword FIELDS. You will have to learn which commands require FIELDS and which do not as you learn dBASE.

Specify a *scope* by using one of four keywords:

- RECORD, followed by a particular record number. For example, RECORD 8 restricts the scope to only record 8.

- NEXT, followed by the number of records you want to scope including the current record. For example, NEXT 5 scopes out the current record and the next four.

- ALL. This keyword includes all the database records in the scope.

- REST. This keyword includes in the scope all records from the current one to the end of the database.

The *search condition* requires a detailed discussion and is explained in Lesson 3.

The CHANGE Command

Whereas the EDIT command allows you to revise all the fields for one record at a time, the CHANGE command enables you to select a subset of the existing record for review and alteration.

Step 1: Invoke the CHANGE command on a field list. Type *CHANGE ALL FIELDS CFNAME,ESP*. Figure 2.4 shows a clear screen, with only the two fields for the first record appearing for alteration. Do not change the fields now.

Step 2: Press PgDn until you reach the bottom of the file. The dot prompt appears after CHANGE displays the last record. You also can use Ctrl-End to exit CHANGE at any time.

The CHANGE command is especially helpful if records have many fields and you want to alter just a couple of fields, or if you need to change only a few records in a certain range of records.

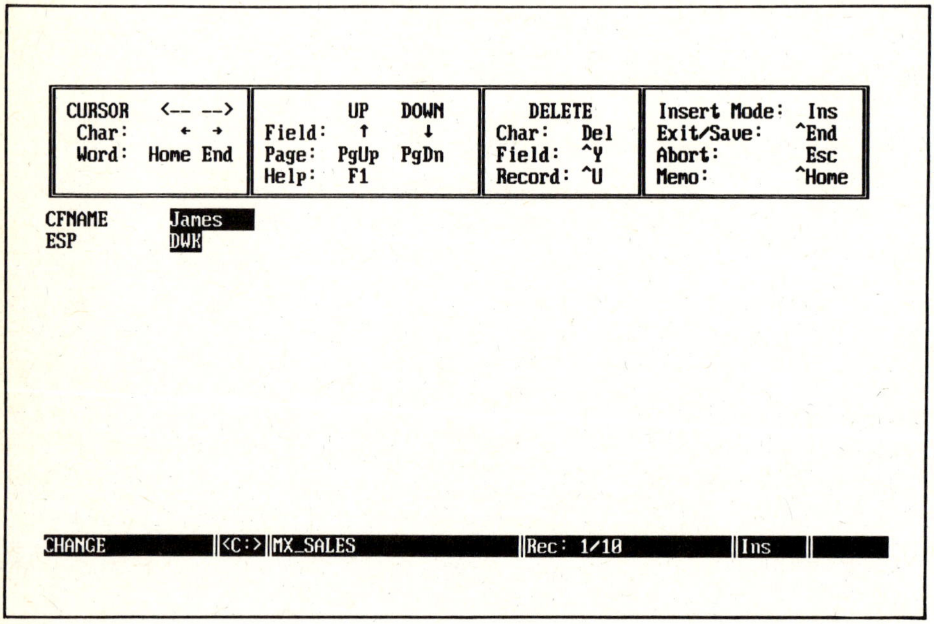

```
┌──────────────────────────────────────────────────────────────────────┐
│                                                                        │
│  ┌──────────────────┬──────────────────┬──────────────┬────────────┐  │
│  │ CURSOR   <-- -->  │        UP   DOWN │    DELETE    │ Insert Mode: Ins│
│  │ Char:     ←   →   │ Field:   ↑    ↓  │ Char:   Del  │ Exit/Save:  ^End│
│  │ Word:  Home End   │ Page:  PgUp PgDn │ Field:  ^Y   │ Abort:      Esc │
│  │                   │ Help:   F1       │ Record: ^U   │ Memo:     ^Home │
│  └──────────────────┴──────────────────┴──────────────┴────────────┘  │
│  CFNAME    │James  │                                                    │
│  ESP       │DWK│                                                        │
│                                                                        │
│                                                                        │
│  CHANGE        │<C:>│MX_SALES         │Rec: 1/10      │Ins │            │
└──────────────────────────────────────────────────────────────────────┘
```

Fig. 2.4. *Changing selected fields (record 1).*

Step 3: CHANGE with a scope qualification. With CHANGE, you also can designate only one or a few records to change. The most restrictive scope is a single record. Type the following:

CHANGE FIELDS CFNAME,ESP RECORD 5

Figure 2.5 shows what appears on the screen.

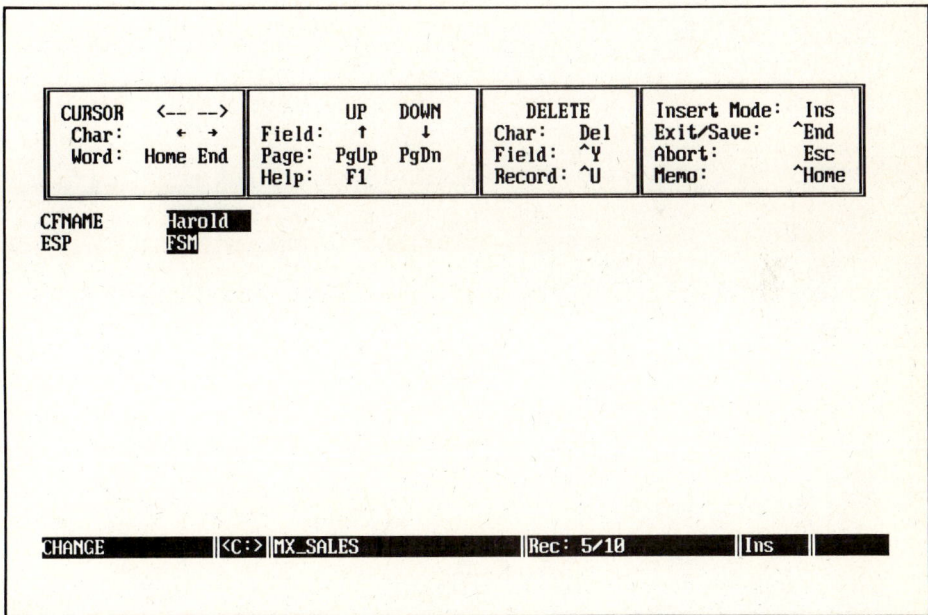

```
┌─────────────────────────────────────────────────────────────────────────┐
│                                                                           │
│                                                                           │
│  ┌──────────────────────┬──────────────────┬──────────────┬────────────┐ │
│  │ CURSOR    <-- -->     │        UP   DOWN │   DELETE     │Insert Mode: Ins│
│  │  Char:    ←  →        │ Field:  ↑    ↓   │ Char:   Del  │Exit/Save:  ^End│
│  │  Word:  Home End      │ Page:  PgUp  PgDn│ Field:  ^Y   │Abort:      Esc │
│  │                       │ Help:  F1        │ Record: ^U   │Memo:      ^Home│
│  └──────────────────────┴──────────────────┴──────────────┴────────────┘ │
│  CFNAME      Harold                                                        │
│  ESP         FSM                                                           │
│                                                                           │
│                                                                           │
│                                                                           │
│ CHANGE          <C:> MX_SALES            Rec: 5/10          Ins           │
└─────────────────────────────────────────────────────────────────────────┘
```

Fig. 2.5. *Changing fields for a single record scope.*

Like EDIT, CHANGE accesses the fifth record. Unlike EDIT, CHANGE displays only the two designated fields and quits operating after record 5 is revised. Both EDIT and CHANGE move the record pointer to record 6 after the revision.

Step 4: CHANGE over a range of more than one record. Type the following:

CHANGE FIELDS CFNAME,ESP NEXT 3

Then press PgDn three times. dBASE displays three records and exits to the dot prompt, leaving the record pointer at record 9.

Starting at the current record (record 6), the CHANGE command you issued operated on the next three records: 6, 7, and 8.

NOTES

EDIT does not work with a scope or a field list; CHANGE does. With the notable exceptions of CREATE, USE, and APPEND, most commands in dBASE III Plus do operate using a scope or a field list or both.

The BROWSE Command

BROWSE is a powerful command with which you can display and alter several fields for several records at once. The format that BROWSE uses to display records looks like a spreadsheet.

Step 1: Enter BROWSE mode. Type *BROWSE*. Figure 2.6 shows what appears on the screen.

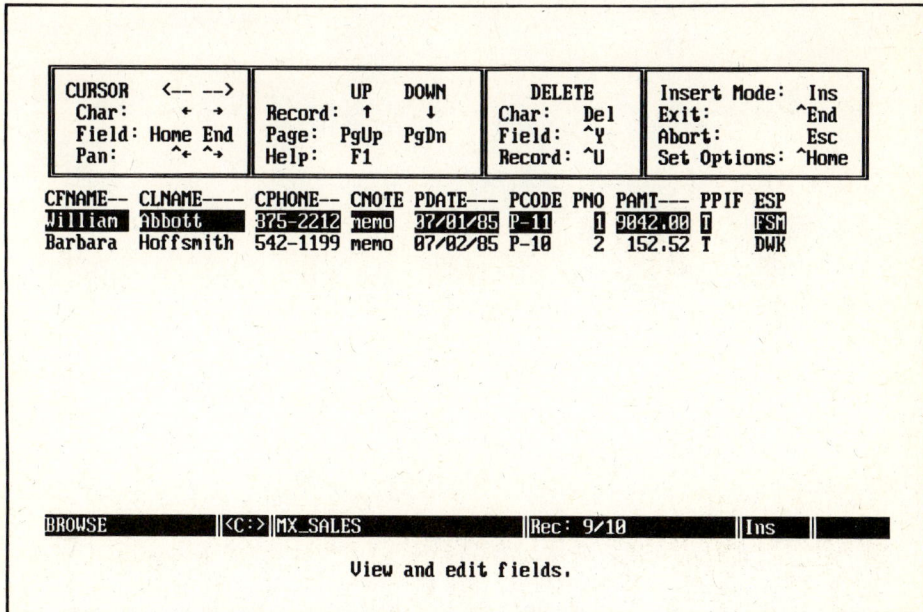

```
┌──────────────────────────────────────────────────────────────────────────┐
│                                                                            │
│  ┌─────────────────────┬──────────────────┬──────────────┬──────────────┐ │
│  │ CURSOR    <-- -->    │        UP   DOWN  │   DELETE     │ Insert Mode: Ins│
│  │ Char:      ← →        │ Record:  ↑    ↓   │ Char:   Del  │ Exit:     ^End │
│  │ Field: Home End       │ Page: PgUp PgDn   │ Field:  ^Y   │ Abort:     Esc │
│  │ Pan:      ^← ^→        │ Help:   F1        │ Record: ^U   │ Set Options: ^Home│
│  └─────────────────────┴──────────────────┴──────────────┴──────────────┘ │
│  CFNAME-- CLNAME----- CPHONE-- CNOTE PDATE--- PCODE PNO PAMT--- PPIF ESP    │
│  William  Abbott       375-2212 memo  07/01/85 P-11   1  9042.00 T   FSM    │
│  Barbara  Hoffsmith    542-1199 memo  07/02/85 P-10   2   152.52 T   DWK    │
│                                                                            │
│                                                                            │
│                                                                            │
│  BROWSE        │<C:>│MX_SALES            │Rec: 9/10        │Ins │          │
│                   View and edit fields.                                    │
└──────────────────────────────────────────────────────────────────────────┘
```

Fig. 2.6. *Browsing from the record pointer.*

BROWSE is particularly useful in working with databases with a large number of fields. With a FIELDS list statement, you can select just those fields you want to view. But beyond this capability, BROWSE also gives you some maneuvering room within the command itself. In a sense, BROWSE incorporates the GO command and a form of the FIELDS list qualification. These capabilities are accessed from the BROWSE Assistant menu, which is accessed by pressing Ctrl-Home (see fig. 2.7).

```
┌──────────────────────────────────────────────────────────────────────────┐
│  Bottom          Top          Lock          Record No.        Freeze  10:33:24 am │
│  ┌────────────────────────┐┌────────────────────┐┌───────────────┐┌─────────────────────────┐ │
│  │ CURSOR    <-- -->      ││         UP   DOWN   ││   DELETE      ││ Insert Mode:  Ins       │ │
│  │ Char:      ←  →        ││ Record:  ↑    ↓     ││ Char:    Del  ││ Exit:         ^End      │ │
│  │ Field: Home End        ││ Page:  PgUp  PgDn   ││ Field:    ^Y  ││ Abort:        Esc       │ │
│  │ Pan:       ^←  ^→      ││ Help:  F1           ││ Record:   ^U  ││ Set Options:  ^Home     │ │
│  └────────────────────────┘└────────────────────┘└───────────────┘└─────────────────────────┘ │
│                                                                            │
│ CFNAME-- CLNAME----  CPHONE-- CNOTE PDATE--- PCODE PNO PAMT--- PPIF ESP    │
│ Jillian  Abbott      375-2212 memo  07/01/85 P-11   1  9042.00 T   FSM     │
│ Barbara  Hoffsmith   542-1199 memo  07/02/85 P-10   2   152.52 T   DWK     │
│                                                                            │
│                                                                            │
│                                                                            │
│                                                                            │
│                                                                            │
│                                                                            │
│                                                                            │
│ BROWSE           |<C:>|MX_SALES            |Rec: 9/10       |          ||  │
│          Position selection bar with ↔.  Select with ←┘.                  │
│                     Go to end of the file.                                 │
└──────────────────────────────────────────────────────────────────────────┘
```

Fig. 2.7. *The BROWSE Assistant menu.*

The menu includes five options, which are executed by highlighting the option and pressing the Return key:

Bottom	Moves the pointer to the last record in the database
Top	Moves the pointer to the first record in the database
Lock	Locks onto the screen one or more of the leftmost fields on the screen. This capability is important if the database contains more fields than will fit on the screen at once.
Record No.	Moves the pointer to a particular record number
Freeze	Specifies one field to which changes can be made. **Freeze** will not permit changes to any other fields.

Step 2: Move to the top of the data file. Press Ctrl-Home, move the selection bar to highlight **Top**, and press the Return key. Your screen should now look similar to figure 2.8.

BROWSE is a multipurpose command. As with EDIT and CHANGE, you can use BROWSE to review and revise data. You even can append records within BROWSE.

Step 3: Append records within BROWSE. First, move to the end of the data file by pressing the PgDn key and then the down-arrow key. A prompt appears in the message area (see fig. 2.9):

  ===> Add new records? (Y/N)

Responding Yes brings up a blank record; responding No returns the record pointer to the last record. Type N at this time.

To exit from BROWSE, press Ctrl-End to save your most current changes or Esc to abort the last change made.

```
 ┌─────────────────────────────────────────────────────────────────────────┐
 │ ┌──────────────────┬──────────────────┬──────────────┬─────────────────┐ │
 │ │ CURSOR  <-- -->  │      UP   DOWN   │   DELETE     │ Insert Mode: Ins│ │
 │ │ Char:    ←  →    │ Record:  ↑    ↓  │ Char:   Del  │ Exit:      ^End │ │
 │ │ Field: Home End  │ Page:  PgUp PgDn │ Field:  ^Y   │ Abort:      Esc │ │
 │ │ Pan:    ^← ^→    │ Help:    F1      │ Record: ^U   │ Set Options:^Home│ │
 │ └──────────────────┴──────────────────┴──────────────┴─────────────────┘ │
 │                                                                           │
 │ CFNAME-- CLNAME----- CPHONE-- CNOTE PDATE--- PCODE PNO PAMT--- PPIF ESP    │
 │ James    Blair       351-8923 memo  06/15/85 H-27   1 4000.00 T  DWK       │
 │ Francis  Connors     975-0807 memo  06/16/85 H-22   1 6600.35 T  LEM       │
 │ Thomas   Jones       971-9412 memo  06/17/85 H-19   1 3523.17 T  DWK       │
 │ Sam      Aster       371-2341 memo  06/18/85 P-11   1 9042.00 F  FSM       │
 │ Harold   Stevens     543-9850 memo  06/19/85 H-19   1 3523.17 F  FSM       │
 │ Molly    Brown       876-1252 memo  06/22/85 H-22   1 6600.35 F  LEM       │
 │ John     Clark       351-1118 memo  06/25/85 P-14   1 8097.00 F  DWK       │
 │ Susan    Jones       370-4726 memo  06/27/85 H-27   1 4000.00 T  LEM       │
 │ William  Abbott      875-2212 memo  07/01/85 P-11   1 9042.00 T  FSM       │
 │ Barbara  Hoffsmith   542-1199 memo  07/02/85 P-10   2  152.52 T  DWK       │
 │                                                                           │
 │ BROWSE        <C:> MX_SALES        │Rec: 1/10                             │
 │                   View and edit fields.                                   │
 └───────────────────────────────────────────────────────────────────────────┘
```

Fig. 2.8. *Browsing from top of file.*

```
 ┌─────────────────────────────────────────────────────────────────────────┐
 │ ┌──────────────────┬──────────────────┬──────────────┬─────────────────┐ │
 │ │ CURSOR  <-- -->  │      UP   DOWN   │   DELETE     │ Insert Mode: Ins│ │
 │ │ Char:    ←  →    │ Record:  ↑    ↓  │ Char:   Del  │ Exit:      ^End │ │
 │ │ Field: Home End  │ Page:  PgUp PgDn │ Field:  ^Y   │ Abort:      Esc │ │
 │ │ Pan:    ^← ^→    │ Help:    F1      │ Record: ^U   │ Set Options:^Home│ │
 │ └──────────────────┴──────────────────┴──────────────┴─────────────────┘ │
 │                                                                           │
 │ CFNAME-- CLNAME----- CPHONE-- CNOTE PDATE--- PCODE PNO PAMT--- PPIF ESP    │
 │ Barbara  Hoffsmith   542-1199 memo  07/02/85 P-10   2  152.52 T  DWK       │
 │                                                                           │
 │ BROWSE        <C:> MX_SALES        │Rec: 10/10                            │
 │              ===> Add new records? (Y/N)                                  │
 │                   View and edit fields.                                   │
 └───────────────────────────────────────────────────────────────────────────┘
```

Fig. 2.9. *Appending within BROWSE.*

■ SUMMARY OF CONCEPTS
PRESENTED IN LESSON 2

1. A data file is composed of a beginning of file (BOF), an end of file (EOF), and in-dividual records. A record pointer in dBASE III Plus can reference at one time the top of the file, the bottom of the file, or only one of the records.

2. You can move the record pointer to any position in the file by using the GO command:

    GO TOP   Position pointer at the top of the file
    GO BOTTOM   Position pointer at the bottom of the file
    GO 5   Position pointer at the fifth record

3. Commands such as CHANGE and BROWSE can be qualified with the addition of a field list, scope, or search condition. A field list generally is introduced by the keyword FIELDS. A scope is introduced by one of four keywords:

    RECORD #
    NEXT #
    ALL
    REST

    The pound sign (#) indicates that a number is typed after the keyword.

4. Move from one record to the next with SKIP. Skip forward and backward in larger moves by typing a positive or negative number after SKIP.

5. EDIT enables you to revise existing records in the file.

6. With CHANGE, you can revise existing records. Unlike the EDIT command, CHANGE also enables you to designate fields to be revised for each record. CHANGE also can revise one record and automatically return to the dot prompt.

7. With BROWSE, you can display and revise several fields and records on the screen at the same time. You also can jump the record pointer within BROWSE and append records.

NOTES

LESSON 2
EXERCISE

Follow these steps to verify that the accounts payable file is correct:

Step 1: Alter the other data file, SSBILLS, by typing *USE SSBILLS*.

Step 2: Move the record pointer to the third record. Type *GO 3*.

Step 3: Check your work. Type *EDIT*. dBASE displays the third record in the database, in EDIT mode.

Step 4: Verify your work by comparing your records to the list in Lesson 1. Move to a record and revise if necessary. Press PgUp to move to records 1 and 2; press PgDn to move to records 4 and 5.

Step 5: Browse and view the final result. Type *GO TOP* and *BROWSE*.

NOTES

3

Extracting and Ordering Data

Related sections in *dBASE III Plus Handbook*, 2nd Edition: Chapters 4 and 7.

The main objective of data management is to generate output products: reports, labels, totals, and summaries. In this lesson, you will learn the following:

- The basic dBASE III Plus search strategies
- How to use the LIST and DISPLAY commands
- How to derive new information from existing information

The LIST Command

The LIST command lists to the screen or printer the data for all fields for all records of the file in use.

Step 1: Type *DO QPREP*. Select Lesson 3.

Step 2: Use the LIST command. Type *USE MX_SALES*. Then type *LIST*. Figure 3.1 shows what appears on the screen.

On the first line are descriptive headings of the record number and field names. The actual record number and each field for the record follow on successive lines. Because memo fields would not fit neatly into a column, they are excluded from this simple list in order to preserve the concise tabular appearance.

```
, USE MX_SALES
, LIST
Record#  CFNAME    CLNAME      CPHONE    CNOTE PDATE    PCODE PNO    PAMT PPIF ESP
      1  James     Blair       351-8923  Memo  06/15/85 H-27    1 4000.00 ,T. DWK
      2  Francis   Connors     975-0007  Memo  06/16/85 H-22    1 6600.35 ,T. LEM
      3  Thomas    Jones       971-9412  Memo  06/17/85 H-19    1 3523.17 ,T. DWK
      4  Sam       Aster       371-2341  Memo  06/18/85 P-11    1 9042.00 ,F. FSM
      5  Harold    Stevens     543-9050  Memo  06/19/85 H-19    1 3523.17 ,F. FSM
      6  Molly     Brown       876-1252  Memo  06/22/85 H-22    1 6600.35 ,F. LEM
      7  John      Clark       351-1118  Memo  06/25/85 P-14    1 8097.00 ,F. DWK
      8  Susan     Jones       370-4726  Memo  06/27/85 H-27    1 4000.00 ,T. LEM
      9  William   Abbott      875-2212  Memo  07/01/85 P-11    1 9042.00 ,T. FSM
     10  Barbara   Hoffsmith   542-1199  Memo  07/02/85 P-10    2  152.52 ,T. DWK
,
```

Command Line   <C:> MX_SALES   Rec: EOF/10   Caps

Enter a dBASE III PLUS command,

Fig. 3.1. *Result of LIST command.*

Step 3: Suppress the record number with OFF. Type *LIST OFF*. Figure 3.2 shows
what dBASE displays.

```
. LIST OFF
  CFNAME    CLNAME      CPHONE    CNOTE PDATE    PCODE PNO    PAMT PPIF ESP
  James     Blair       351-8923  Memo  06/15/85 H-27    1 4000.00 .T. DWK
  Francis   Connors     975-0807  Memo  06/16/85 H-22    1 6600.35 .T. LEM
  Thomas    Jones       971-9412  Memo  06/17/85 H-19    1 3523.17 .T. DWK
  Sam       Aster       371-2341  Memo  06/18/85 P-11    1 9042.00 .F. FSM
  Harold    Stevens     543-9850  Memo  06/19/85 H-19    1 3523.17 .F. FSM
  Molly     Brown       876-1252  Memo  06/22/85 H-22    1 6600.35 .F. LEM
  John      Clark       351-1118  Memo  06/25/85 P-14    1 8097.00 .F. DWK
  Susan     Jones       370-4726  Memo  06/27/85 H-27    1 4000.00 .T. LEM
  William   Abbott      875-2212  Memo  07/01/85 P-11    1 9042.00 .T. FSM
  Barbara   Hoffsmith   542-1199  Memo  07/02/85 P-10    2  152.52 .T. DWK

Command Line    ||<C:>||MX_SALES              ||Rec: EOF/10       ||        || Caps

            Enter a dBASE III PLUS command.
```

Fig. 3.2. *Result of LIST OFF command.*

Step 4: Redirect output to a printer. If you have a printer, send the output to it by
typing *TO PRINT* after LIST OFF.

Search Strategies

Lesson 2 described two types of qualifications for dBASE III Plus commands: field lists
and scopes. This lesson describes the third member of the trio, search conditions. Together these three qualifications make up the basic components of a dBASE search
strategy. Many of the commands in dBASE III Plus can take one or more of these qualifications to build a search strategy that can extract from a database as little or as much
information as you want.

NOTES

Constructing a search strategy follows roughly the same rules for all commands. Table 3.1 shows several search strategies involving the LIST command.

Table 3.1
Basic Command Line Search Strategies

Verb	Field List	Scope	Search Condition
LIST	CFNAME,PAMT	NEXT 10	FOR PAMT > 2500
LIST	CFNAME,CPHONE	ALL	FOR ESP = 'DWK'
LIST	PCODE,PNO,PDATE	RECORD 6	
LIST		REST	FOR PPIF
LIST	CFNAME,CNOTE		FOR PCODE = 'P-10'

Notice from table 3.1 that each search strategy must contain a command verb as its first component. Following the command verb is a combination of one or more optional qualifications: a field list, a scope, and a search condition.

Notice that with certain commands, such as LIST, the field list does not begin with the keyword FIELDS. dBASE III Plus is inconsistent in the use of FIELDS; you will have to learn for each command whether the keyword is required or not. If FIELDS is required, it cannot be left out; if FIELDS is not required, it cannot be included.

Each command has a default value for its scope—either ALL or the current record. The default for the LIST command is the ALL scope. In other words, if you do not specify otherwise, LIST will display all records.

The search condition always begins with the keyword FOR. Search conditions are discussed in more detail in the following section.

Practice building some simple search strategies with LIST.

Step 1: Use LIST to list the first three records. Type the following:

```
GO TOP
LIST NEXT 3 OFF
```

Figure 3.3 shows what appears on the screen.

Step 2: List a single record. The LIST command with the keyword RECORD and a record number moves the record pointer to the record and lists the results. Type *LIST RECORD 5*. dBASE III Plus moves to the fifth record, lists it, and the record pointer moves up one, to the sixth record. Figure 3.4 shows what the screen displays.

```
. GO TOP
. LIST NEXT 3 OFF
CFNAME    CLNAME     CPHONE    CNOTE PDATE     PCODE PNO     PAMT PPIF ESP
James     Blair      351-8923  Memo  06/15/85  H-27    1  4000.00 .T.  DWK
Francis   Connors    975-8807  Memo  06/16/85  H-22    1  6600.35 .T.  LEM
Thomas    Jones      971-9412  Memo  06/17/85  H-19    1  3523.17 .T.  DWK
```
```
Command Line    |<C:>|MX_SALES              |Rec: 3/10    |      |    | Caps
```
```
         Enter a dBASE III PLUS command.
```

Fig. 3.3. *Listing three records.*

```
. LIST RECORD 5
Record#  CFNAME    CLNAME       CPHONE    CNOTE PDATE     PCODE PNO     PAMT PPIF ESP
      5  Harold    Stevens      543-9850  Memo  06/19/85  H-19    1  3523.17 .F.  FSM
```
```
Command Line    |<C:>|MX_SALES              |Rec: 5/10    |      |    | Caps
```
```
         Enter a dBASE III PLUS command.
```

Fig. 3.4. *Listing a single record.*

Step 3: List designated fields. List only the purchase amounts, the number of items purchased, and names of the customers. Type *LIST CFNAME,CLNAME,PNO,PAMT OFF*. Figure 3.5 shows what dBASE III Plus displays. The number of items purchased and the amount paid for the item(s) purchased follow the first and last names of each purchaser.

```
. LIST CFNAME,CLNAME,PNO,PAMT OFF
CFNAME    CLNAME      PNO    PAMT
James     Blair         1 4000.00
Francis   Connors       1 6600.35
Thomas    Jones         1 3523.17
Sam       Aster         1 9042.00
Harold    Stevens       1 3523.17
Molly     Brown         1 6600.35
John      Clark         1 8097.00
Susan     Jones         1 4000.00
William   Abbott        1 9042.00
Barbara   Hoffsmith     2  152.52
.
Command Line    ||<C:>||MX_SALES               ||Rec: EOF/10     ||      ||    Caps
        Enter a dBASE III PLUS command.
```

Fig. 3.5. *Listing designated fields.*

Note the last record: two items were purchased for a total of $152.52. You can derive new information from old information.

Step 4: List other fields. The order of fields extracted for each record can be altered easily: just change the field list. Type *LIST CLNAME,CFNAME,PAMT,PNO OFF*. Figure 3.6 shows what appears.

Step 5: List the memo field. The memo field also can be extracted by specifying CNOTE in the field list. To combine the memo field with the last name, type *LIST CLNAME,CNOTE*. You should see the material shown in figure 3.7.

```
. LIST CLNAME,CFNAME,PAMT,PNO OFF
CLNAME      CFNAME      PAMT  PNO
Blair       James    4000.00    1
Connors     Francis  6600.35    1
Jones       Thomas   3523.17    1
Aster       Sam      9042.00    1
Stevens     Harold   3523.17    1
Brown       Molly    6600.35    1
Clark       John     8097.00    1
Jones       Susan    4000.00    1
Abbott      William  9042.00    1
Hoffsmith   Barbara   152.52    2
.
```

| Command Line | <C:> MX_SALES | Rec: EOF/10 | Caps |

Enter a dBASE III PLUS command.

Fig. 3.6. *Reordering a field list.*

```
. LIST CLNAME,CNOTE
Record#  CLNAME      CNOTE
      1  Blair       The customer agreed that our prices were higher,
                     but our tubs were of better quality.
      2  Connors
      3  Jones       Customer is purchasing a vacation home in six
                     months. Give him a call about sale at that time.

      4  Aster
      5  Stevens
      6  Brown
      7  Clark       Customer wishes to install deck. Give contractor a
                     call.

      8  Jones
      9  Abbott
     10  Hoffsmith   Customer remarked that the price for the 55-gallon
                     drums of pool cleaner was the lowest price in
                     town.
```

| Command Line | <C:> MX_SALES | Rec: EOF/10 | Caps |

Enter a dBASE III PLUS command.

Fig. 3.7. *Listing a memo field.*

Step 6: Type *LIST CLNAME,PAMT,PNO,PAMT/PNO*, to calculate the cost per item while listing. Figure 3.8 shows the result. The cost per item sold, PAMT divided by PNO, is calculated and then displayed for each record. The slash (/) indicates a division of the first term, PAMT, by the second term, PNO.

```
. LIST CLNAME,PAMT,PNO,PAMT/PNO
Record#  CLNAME      PAMT PNO PAMT/PNO
      1  Blair     4000.00   1  4000.00
      2  Connors   6600.35   1  6600.35
      3  Jones     3523.17   1  3523.17
      4  Aster     9042.00   1  9042.00
      5  Stevens   3523.17   1  3523.17
      6  Brown     6600.35   1  6600.35
      7  Clark     8097.00   1  8097.00
      8  Jones     4000.00   1  4000.00
      9  Abbott    9042.00   1  9042.00
     10  Hoffsmith  152.52   2    76.26
```

```
Command Line    ‖<C:>‖MX_SALES            ‖Rec: EOF/10      ‖           ‖ Caps
              Enter a dBASE III PLUS command.
```

Fig. 3.8. *Listing a calculated field.*

Step 7: Enclose identifiers or labels while listing. dBASE III Plus inserts these so-called "strings" of characters if they are enclosed in quotation marks. Type the following (all on one line):

> LIST CLNAME,PAMT,PNO,"SELLING PRICE PER ITEM",PAMT/PNO

Your screen should look similar to figure 3.9.

Remember two other useful command qualifications. Suppress record numbers by adding OFF to the command. Send the data to the printer by adding TO PRINT.

```
. LIST CLNAME,PAMT,PNO,"SELLING PRICE PER ITEM",PAMT/PNO
Record#  CLNAME        PAMT PNO "SELLING PRICE PER ITEM" PAMT/PNO
       1 Blair       4000.00  1 SELLING PRICE PER ITEM    4000.00
       2 Connors     6600.35  1 SELLING PRICE PER ITEM    6600.35
       3 Jones       3523.17  1 SELLING PRICE PER ITEM    3523.17
       4 Aster       9042.00  1 SELLING PRICE PER ITEM    9042.00
       5 Stevens     3523.17  1 SELLING PRICE PER ITEM    3523.17
       6 Brown       6600.35  1 SELLING PRICE PER ITEM    6600.35
       7 Clark       8097.00  1 SELLING PRICE PER ITEM    8097.00
       8 Jones       4000.00  1 SELLING PRICE PER ITEM    4000.00
       9 Abbott      9042.00  1 SELLING PRICE PER ITEM    9042.00
      10 Hoffsmith    152.52  2 SELLING PRICE PER ITEM      76.26
.
Command Line    <C:> MX_SALES              Rec: EOF/10       Ins    Caps

            Enter a dBASE III PLUS command.
```

Fig. 3.9. *Listing a character string.*

Search Conditions

Who still owes the store money? Which customers did Doug Kornfeld sell to? How much did we sell in August? How many H-22 units did we sell last year? All these questions share one similarity: they can be answered by examining only a portion of the records in the database. The problem is to pull out just the records with the useful information. The solution to the problem is to build a search condition that requests just those records.

In English, you would express a search condition by giving the name of a field and then specifying which data values you want from that field. For instance, to learn who owes the store money, you might ask, "Which records have a value of false for the PPIF field?" Or, to learn which customers Doug Kornfeld sold to, you might ask, "What are the customer last names (CLNAME) for records in which the ESP field has the value DWK?"

Translating the English questions into dBASE III Plus command language requires carefully laying out the search condition. In the first request, where the question is being asked of a logical field, the search condition is expressed as follows:

    FOR .NOT. PPIF

For the LIST command, the full command line is

    LIST FOR .NOT. PPIF

In this case the word .NOT. is called a *logical operator*, and it must have a period before and after. To search for the opposite condition—those customers who have paid in full—simply leave off the .NOT.:

    FOR PPIF

    Step 1: Use a conditional expression with a logical field. Find out the last names of all who have paid in full. Type *LIST ALL CLNAME FOR PPIF*. Figure 3.10 shows what appears on the screen.

dBASE III Plus interprets the command to mean, "Give me the last names for all records that have recorded a T for true in the PPIF field."

    Step 2: List the outstanding balances (they are probably of more interest), and extract a phone list of the people who owe money. Type *LIST ALL CLNAME,CPHONE FOR .NOT. PPIF OFF*. Your screen should show the list in figure 3.11.

```
. LIST ALL CLNAME FOR PPIF
Record#  CLNAME
      1  Blair
      2  Connors
      3  Jones
      8  Jones
      9  Abbott
     10  Hoffsmith
.
Command Line     |<C:>|MX_SALES                 |Rec: EOF/10      |Ins  |  Caps
              Enter a dBASE III PLUS command.
```

Fig. 3.10. *Customers who have paid in full.*

```
. LIST ALL CLNAME,CPHONE FOR .NOT. PPIF OFF
CLNAME      CPHONE
Aster       371-2341
Stevens     543-9850
Brown       876-1252
Clark       351-1118
.
Command Line     |<C:>|MX_SALES                 |Rec: EOF/10      |     |  Caps
              Enter a dBASE III PLUS command.
```

Fig. 3.11. *Customers with outstanding balances.*

The second question asked earlier results in a more typical kind of search condition, one that uses a *relational operator* (see table 3.2). Relational operators specify an acceptable range of values for the search field. The record values may have to match exactly the search condition, they may have to be greater than or less than the search condition, or they may be required not to match in some way.

Table 3.2
Common Relational Operators

=	Equal
<> or #	Not Equal
<	Less Than
>	Greater Than
<=	Less Than or Equal
>=	Greater Than or Equal

Building a search condition with a numeric, character, or date field as the reference is done by linking the name of the field and the search value with the appropriate relational operator. For example, to answer the question regarding DWK's customers, type the following command:

LIST CLNAME FOR ESP = 'DWK'

Notice that if the search is on a character field, the search value—here, DWK—must be enclosed in quotation marks. They may be either single (') or double quotation marks ("), but they both should be the same. Numeric field values are not enclosed in quotation marks. Date fields require some special consideration and are discussed further in Lesson 4. Memo fields cannot be searched at all. Multiple search conditions, which consist of more than one search condition, are explained in Lesson 9.

Step 3: Use a conditional expression with a numeric field to extract purchases under $5000. Type *LIST CLNAME,PCODE,PAMT FOR PAMT < 5000*. Figure 3.12 shows the listing.

Step 4: Use the following expression to first calculate an expression, then extract records based on the results. Type the following:

LIST CLNAME,PAMT FOR PAMT/PNO = (152.52 / 2)

The screen shown in figure 3.13 should appear. Only records with a per unit sale price of $76.26 are extracted—in this case, the tenth record.

Step 5: Use a conditional expression with a character field. Extract a list of all salespersons who have sold items in the P-11 product code. Type *LIST ESP,PCODE FOR PCODE = 'P-11'*. Your result should look like figure 3.14.

```
. LIST CLNAME,PCODE,PAMT FOR PAMT < 5000
Record#  CLNAME      PCODE    PAMT
      1  Blair       H-27    4000.00
      3  Jones       H-19    3523.17
      5  Stevens     H-19    3523.17
      8  Jones       H-27    4000.00
     10  Hoffsmith   P-10     152.52
```

```
Command Line    ||<C:>||MX_SALES              ||Rec: EOF/10       ||     || Caps
```

Enter a dBASE III PLUS command.

Fig. 3.12. *Purchases under $5000.*

```
. LIST CLNAME,PAMT FOR PAMT/PNO = (152.52 / 2)
Record#  CLNAME       PAMT
     10  Hoffsmith   152.52
```

```
Command Line    ||<C:>||MX_SALES              ||Rec: EOF/10       ||     || Caps
```

Enter a dBASE III PLUS command.

Fig. 3.13. *Using a calculated search condition.*

```
. LIST ESP,PCODE FOR PCODE = 'P-11'
Record#  ESP PCODE
      4  FSM P-11
      9  FSM P-11
```

| Command Line | <C:> | MX_SALES | Rec: EOF/10 | Ins | Caps |

Enter a dBASE III PLUS command.

Fig. 3.14. *Salespersons who have sold items in P-11 code.*

Step 6: List selectively by employee. Find the purchases that Doug Kornfeld sold. Type *LIST PDATE,PCODE,PNO,PAMT OFF FOR ESP = "DWK"*. Figure 3.15 shows what the screen displays.

The DISPLAY Command

Another command, DISPLAY, works much like LIST. Both DISPLAY and LIST present the data in a file. Like LIST, DISPLAY can derive new information from current data, and it can use a search condition to extract records selectively. Neither command uses the keyword FIELDS in expressing a field list.

Step 1: Use DISPLAY. Type the following commands:

GO 5
DISPLAY OFF

Step 2: Compare your result to figure 3.16.

```
. LIST PDATE,PCODE,PNO,PAMT OFF FOR ESP = "DWK"
PDATE    PCODE PNO    PAMT
06/15/85 H-27   1 4000.00
06/17/85 H-19   1 3523.17
06/25/85 P-14   1 8097.00
07/02/85 P-10   2  152.52
.
Command Line    ||<C:>||MX_SALES           ||Rec: EOF/10    ||Ins  ||  Caps
           Enter a dBASE III PLUS command.
```

Fig. 3.15. *Listing purchases by employee.*

```
. GO 5
. DISPLAY OFF
CFNAME   CLNAME     CPHONE   CNOTE PDATE    PCODE PNO    PAMT PPIF ESP
Harold   Stevens    543-9850 Memo  06/19/85 H-19   1 3523.17 .F.  FSM
.
Command Line    ||<C:>||MX_SALES           ||Rec: 5/10     ||Ins  ||  Caps
           Enter a dBASE III PLUS command.
```

Fig. 3.16. *Displaying a single record.*

The DISPLAY command offers a few convenient differences from LIST. LIST requires the scope RECORD # in the command, to restrict the listing to one record; DISPLAY does not. If the record is not specified, DISPLAY shows the current record as the default scope. To display all records, use ALL as a scope. DISPLAY ALL therefore is used to display all records.

Also, LIST extracts all records in the database, without a pause, and scrolls the records off the screen faster than you can read them. Thus, DISPLAY ALL is especially handy for examining records. DISPLAY ALL presents a screenful of records and pauses until you press any key but Esc. When the screen fills, the message Press any key to continue .... appears. Do not use DISPLAY ALL with TO PRINT, however. The printer will pause when the screen pauses, and the message Press any key to continue .... will be printed.

Que Tip: Type *LIST TO PRINT* to output all records to the printer. To output all records to the screen, type *DISPLAY ALL.*

▢ SUMMARY OF CONCEPTS
    PRESENTED IN LESSON 3

1. The LIST command displays all fields, except for memo fields, for all records. A memo field can be displayed if it is included in a field list.

2. You can suppress record number listings by using OFF in the command line.

3. Add TO PRINT to the LIST command to send the list to the printer. Redirect the list only if the printer is operational.

4. Most dBASE III Plus commands that retrieve or process records use a common set of qualifications, including field lists, scopes, and search conditions.

5. A search condition is the key to retrieving records selectively—that is, by the value of some field. Each search condition on a numeric, character, or date field is built by linking the field name to the search value with a relational operator. All search conditions begin with the keyword FOR.

6. Logical fields are searched by specifying just the name of the field, for true values, or .NOT. the name of the field, for false values.

7. New information can be calculated while fields are listed.

☐ LESSON 3
 EXERCISE

Use the verbs presented in this lesson to display the records in the second data file, SSBILLS, in a variety of ways.

Step 1: Open the second data file. Type *USE SSBILLS.*

Step 2: List the contents, suppressing record numbers. Type *LIST OFF.*

Step 3: Go to the middle record. Type *GO 3.*

Step 4: List the rest of the records. Type *LIST REST.*

Step 5: Extract a phone directory. List only the attention code and the vendor telephone fields. Enclose the prompt "VENDOR PHONE" between the two fields, and suppress the listing of the record numbers. Type *LIST VATTN,"VENDOR PHONE",VPHONE OFF.*

Step 6: List only the vendor whose name begins with *Trust.* Type *LIST VATTN,VNAME,VAMT FOR VNAME = "Trust".*

NOTES

4

Global Alterations and Deletions, and Date Arithmetic

Related sections in *dBASE III Plus Handbook*, 2nd Edition: Chapters 4, 5, and 7.

With dBASE III Plus, you can change any combination of fields and records, under certain conditions. You can make changes to all records and all fields at once, to just some fields in one record, or to several fields in several records. When you change more than one record at a time, the revisions are known as *global alterations*. The changes can save time, but beware: a mistake can wipe out a database.

In Lesson 4, you will use several commands to revise the database structure and content, notably the following:

- MODIFY STRUCTURE
- CHANGE
- REPLACE
- DELETE, RECALL, and PACK

Changing the Plan

Saltwater Sally's Sales Management System is now taking shape. The plan has been designed, and data has been entered to document each sale.

NOTES

Rarely is the first plan perfectly tailored to the needs of the user. New information often needs to be added, or items need to be deleted. The corresponding fields that retain the information subsequently must be added or deleted.

Before you begin to make changes, review the current plan.

Customer Data	*Field Name*
Customer first name	CFNAME
Customer last name	CLNAME
Telephone number	CPHONE
Additional customer notes	CNOTE

Sales Data	
Product code	PCODE
Purchase amount	PAMT
Number of items purchased	PNO
Date of purchase	PDATE
Paid-in-full marker	PPIF

Employee Data	
Initials of person selling product	ESP

Many changes could be made to improve the capability of the model. For example, adding a few fields could make the model far more powerful.

Only the phone number is presently available for contacting the customer. In this lesson, you will include an address to support mailings such as promotional announcements, mailing labels, and bills. Street, city, state, and ZIP fields will retain the postal information.

Taxes are inevitable. You will insert a field to retain the amount of sales tax paid by each customer for a purchase.

The last change you will make is to add a field for the amount of commission paid to each salesperson as a result of the purchase.

Here is an outline of the additions to be made to the model:

Customer	Street,city,state,ZIP
Purchase	Tax in dollars
Purchase	Date installed after purchase
Employee	Sales commission in dollars

NOTES

Adding this information greatly extends the capability of the sales system. Once again, you will use the MODIFY STRUCTURE command. (If MX_SALES is already the active database, omit Steps 1 and 2.)

Step 1: Specify the default drive and type *DO QPREP*. Select Lesson 4.

Step 2: Type *USE MX_SALES*.

Step 3: Put dBASE III Plus in MODIFY mode. Type *MODIFY STRUCTURE*. The screen shown in figure 4.1 appears.

```
                                            Bytes remaining:   3940

┌─────────────────┐┌─────────────┐┌──────────────┐┌────────────────────┐
│ CURSOR  <-- -->  ││   INSERT    ││   DELETE     ││ Up a field:    ↑   │
│ Char:    ← →     ││ Char:  Ins  ││ Char:   Del  ││ Down a field:  ↓   │
│ Word: Home End   ││ Field: ^N   ││ Word:   ^Y   ││ Exit/Save:     ^End│
│ Pan:    ^← ^→    ││ Help:  F1   ││ Field:  ^U   ││ Abort:         Esc │
└─────────────────┘└─────────────┘└──────────────┘└────────────────────┘

     Field Name  Type     Width  Dec        Field Name  Type     Width  Dec

  1  CFNAME    Character    8           9  PPIF      Logical      1
  2  CLNAME    Character   10          10  ESP       Character    3
  3  CPHONE    Character    8
  4  CNOTE     Memo        10
  5  PDATE     Date         8
  6  PCODE     Character    4
  7  PNO       Numeric      1     0
  8  PAMT      Numeric      7     2

 MODIFY STRUCTURE  <C:> MX_SALES              Field: 3/10              Caps
                          Enter the field name.
 Field names begin with a letter and may contain letters, digits and underscores
```

Fig. 4.1. *The MODIFY STRUCTURE screen.*

Step 4: Add the customer address fields. You can add fields at the bottom of the existing fields or between fields. Try to keep fields that store similar information together. First, add the additional customer fields. Open up a spot for insertion by placing the cursor on the CPHONE field. Press Ctrl and hold it down while pressing N. CPHONE moves down, and a space opens for the street field.

Add *CSTREET*, designate it as a character field, and give it a width of *15*. Remember from Lesson 1 to press the correct letter to designate a field type: C (character), N (numeric), D (date), L (logical), or M (memo).

NOTES

Press Ctrl-N. Another line opens up. Add *CCITY*, designate it as a character field, and give it a width of *15*. The cursor moves down to the CPHONE field again.

Press Ctrl-N to add another space. Enter *CST*, the customer's state of residence. Designate it as a character field with a width of *2*.

Use Ctrl-N to open up one last line. Add *CZIP*, a character field of *5*. Additions to the customer fields are now complete. Your screen should look like figure 4.2.

```
                                       Bytes remaining:    3983

  ┌─────────────────┬─────────────┬──────────────┬──────────────────────┐
  │ CURSOR  <-- -->  │   INSERT     │   DELETE      │ Up a field:      ↑   │
  │ Char:     ← →    │ Char:   Ins  │ Char:    Del  │ Down a field:    ↓   │
  │ Word: Home End   │ Field: ^N    │ Word:    ^Y   │ Exit/Save:      ^End │
  │ Pan:     ^← ^→   │ Help:   F1   │ Field:   ^U   │ Abort:          Esc  │
  └─────────────────┴─────────────┴──────────────┴──────────────────────┘

     Field Name  Type      Width  Dec         Field Name  Type      Width  Dec

  1  CFNAME      Character    8        9   PDATE      Date         8
  2  CLNAME      Character   10       10   PCODE      Character    4
  3  CSTREET     Character   15       11   PNO        Numeric      1      0
  4  CCITY       Character   15       12   PAMT       Numeric      7      2
  5  CST         Character    2       13   PPIF       Logical      1
  6  CZIP        Character    5       14   ESP        Character    3
  7  CPHONE      Character    8
  8  CNOTE       Memo        10

  MODIFY STRUCTURE|<C:>|MX_SALES          |Field: 8/14              |    Caps
                       Enter the field name.
  Field names begin with a letter and may contain letters, digits and underscores
```

Fig. 4.2. *Customer address fields added.*

Step 5: Add the purchase fields. Move the cursor down to PCODE and press Ctrl-N to open up a space. Enter *PINDATE*, the date on which the hot tub or pool is installed at the home of a purchaser. Press D for the date field. Now add the tax field. Move the cursor down to PPIF and press Ctrl-N. Add *PTAX* and designate it as a numeric field.

Look at the PAMT field. The tax field usually will be much smaller than the amount paid. The width, therefore, is 1 less than PAMT. Enter *6* as the width and *2* for the number of decimal places. The purchase information is now complete. Compare your screen with figure 4.3.

NOTES

```
                                             Bytes remaining:   3889

┌──────────────┬──────────────┬──────────────┬─────────────────────┐
│ CURSOR  <-- -->│   INSERT   │   DELETE     │ Up a field:    ↑     │
│ Char:    ← →   │ Char:  Ins │ Char:    Del │ Down a field:  ↓     │
│ Word: Home End │ Field: ^N  │ Word:    ^Y  │ Exit/Save:    ^End   │
│ Pan:    ^← ^→  │ Help:  F1  │ Field:   ^U  │ Abort:        Esc    │
└──────────────┴──────────────┴──────────────┴─────────────────────┘
```

	Field Name	Type	Width	Dec		Field Name	Type	Width	Dec
1	CFNAME	Character	8		9	PDATE	Date	8	
2	CLNAME	Character	10		10	PINDATE	Date	8	
3	CSTREET	Character	15		11	PCODE	Character	4	
4	CCITY	Character	15		12	PNO	Numeric	1	0
5	CST	Character	2		13	PAMT	Numeric	7	2
6	CZIP	Character	5		14	PTAX	Numeric	6	2
7	CPHONE	Character	8		15	PPIF	Logical	1	
8	CNOTE	Memo	10		16	ESP	Character	3	

```
MODIFY STRUCTURE|<C:>|MX_SALES          |Field: 15/16 |          | Caps
                   Enter the field name.
Field names begin with a letter and may contain letters, digits and underscores
```

Fig. 4.3. *Purchase information fields added.*

Step 6: Add the employee commission field. Move the cursor to the bottom of the field listings so that the blank field number 17 appears. Type *ECOMM* (employee commission), and designate the field as numeric with a width of 7 and 2 decimal places (see fig. 4.4).

Step 7: Save your work by pressing Ctrl-End (not to be confused with Ctrl-N). Press Return to confirm that you want to save your changes.

Step 8: Check your work by using the *LIST STRUCTURE* command. Add *TO PRINT* if a printer is in operation. dBASE III Plus prints the new structure (see fig. 4.5).

Global Alterations

Several new fields have been added to the database for each record, but no information is currently contained in the new fields. You now have a choice: you can either add the information one field at a time or use a dBASE III Plus shortcut called global alterations.

Global alterations are techniques and commands that allow you to update the database faster than one record at a time.

```
                                              Bytes remaining:    3882

┌─────────────────┬───────────────┬───────────────┬────────────────────────┐
│ CURSOR  <── ──> │   INSERT      │   DELETE      │ Up a field:       ↑    │
│ Char:     ← →   │ Char:   Ins   │ Char:   Del   │ Down a field:     ↓    │
│ Word: Home End  │ Field:  ^N    │ Word:   ^Y    │ Exit/Save:      ^End   │
│ Pan:    ^← ^→   │ Help:   F1    │ Field:  ^U    │ Abort:           Esc   │
└─────────────────┴───────────────┴───────────────┴────────────────────────┘

        Field Name   Type      Width  Dec         Field Name   Type      Width  Dec

     9  PDATE        Date        8          17   ECOMM         Numeric      7     2
    10  PINDATE      Date        8
    11  PCODE        Character   4
    12  PNO          Numeric     1     0
    13  PAMT         Numeric     7     2
    14  PTAX         Numeric     6     2
    15  PPIF         Logical     1
    16  ESP          Character   3

──────────────────────────────────────────────────────────────────────────────
MODIFY STRUCTURE │<C:>│MX_SALES          ║Field: 17/17  ║        ║    Caps
              Enter the number of decimal places.
  Decimal widths are 0 to 15 and must be at least 2 less than the field width.
```

Fig. 4.4. *Employee commission field added.*

```
Date of last update   : 07/08/87
Field  Field Name   Type      Width  Dec
   1   CFNAME       Character    8
   2   CLNAME       Character   10
   3   CSTREET      Character   15
   4   CCITY        Character   15
   5   CST          Character    2
   6   CZIP         Character    5
   7   CPHONE       Character    8
   8   CNOTE        Memo        10
   9   PDATE        Date         8
  10   PINDATE      Date         8
  11   PCODE        Character    4
  12   PNO          Numeric      1
  13   PAMT         Numeric      7     2
  14   PTAX         Numeric      6     2
  15   PPIF         Logical      1
  16   ESP          Character    3
  17   ECOMM        Numeric      7     2
** Total **                    119

──────────────────────────────────────────────────────────────────────────────
Command Line    ║<C:>║MX_SALES            ║Rec: 10/10  ║        ║   Caps
             Enter a dBASE III PLUS command.
```

Fig. 4.5. *Revised database structure.*

Step 1: Update with the CHANGE command. Type the following commands:

> GO TOP
> CHANGE FIELDS CSTREET,CCITY,CST,CZIP,PINDATE

Unlike the EDIT command, the CHANGE command displays only the fields to be changed (see fig. 4.6).

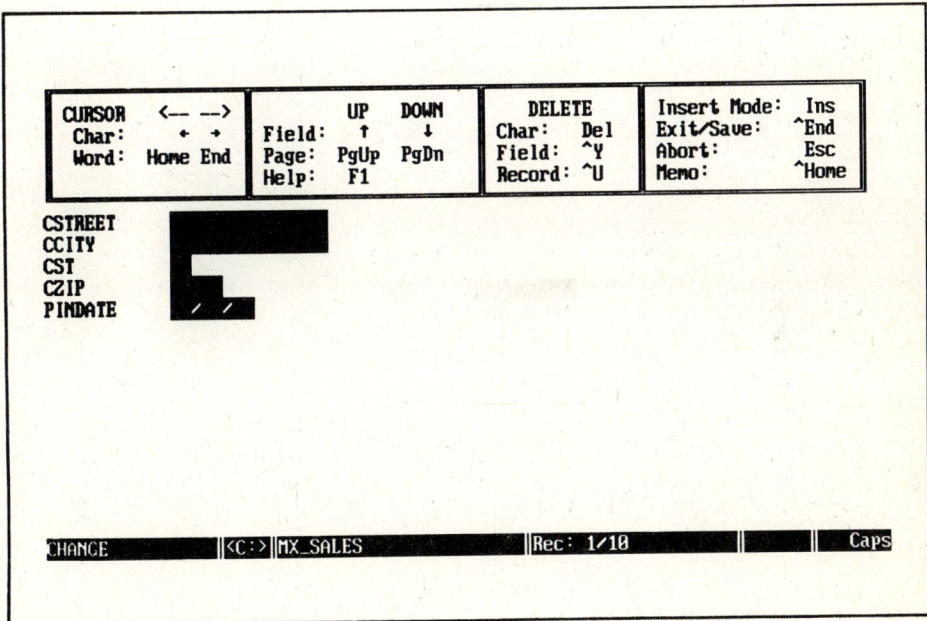

```
┌─────────────────────────────────────────────────────────────────────────┐
│                                                                           │
│  ┌──────────────────┐┌──────────────────┐┌─────────────┐┌──────────────┐│
│  │CURSOR  <── ──>   ││           UP  DOWN││   DELETE    ││Insert Mode: Ins││
│  │Char:    ←   →    ││Field:      ↑    ↓ ││Char:    Del ││Exit/Save:  ^End││
│  │Word:  Home End   ││Page:   PgUp  PgDn ││Field:  ^Y   ││Abort:      Esc ││
│  │                  ││Help:    F1        ││Record: ^U   ││Memo:      ^Home││
│  └──────────────────┘└──────────────────┘└─────────────┘└──────────────┘│
│                                                                           │
│  CSTREET    ████████████████                                              │
│  CCITY                                                                     │
│  CST                                                                       │
│  CZIP                                                                      │
│  PINDATE     /   /                                                        │
│                                                                           │
│                                                                           │
│                                                                           │
│  CHANGE        <C:> MX_SALES           Rec: 1/10              Caps         │
└─────────────────────────────────────────────────────────────────────────┘
```

Fig. 4.6. *Fields selected with CHANGE.*

Step 2: Enter the new data as outlined:

Record #	CSTREET	CCITY	CST	CZIP	PINDATE
1	1 Oak Street	Atlanta	GA	30332	06/23/85
2	22 Priscilla Ln.	Smyrna	GA	30080	06/25/85
3	87 Cul-de-Sac	Decatur	GA	30030	06/26/85
4	49 Blossom Ln.	Atlanta	GA	30327	06/26/85
5	6 Peachtree St.	Atlanta	GA	30326	06/27/85
6	92 Aqua Vita	Riverdale	GA	30274	06/27/85
7	190 Arden Way	Atlanta	GA	30302	06/27/85
8	227 Jefferson	Decatur	GA	30030	06/28/85
9	17 Hamilton Pl.	Cleveland	TN	37311	07/06/85
10	1000 Maple St.	Doraville	GA	30040	07/02/85

NOTES

As in EDIT mode, in CHANGE mode your work is saved automatically after the last record in the file is updated.

Mass Replacements

Aside from using CHANGE or EDIT, another way to alter records is to use the REPLACE command. CHANGE and EDIT work on one record at a time. REPLACE, on the other hand, alters a field for as many as all the records at a time. CHANGE and EDIT require that you page to each record to make alterations, but REPLACE works without even bringing records to the screen.

The "secret" to using REPLACE is to write a general formula for replacing a value (including a blank or a zero) with a new value. In the next steps, you will calculate the values for the PTAX field based on the purchase amounts multiplied by a fixed tax rate.

Use REPLACE to enter the amount of tax into each record. The tax rate in Saltwater Sally's area is five percent of the purchase amount. To enter the tax into the first record, complete the following steps:

Step 1: Move to the first record. Type *GO TOP*. The dot prompt appears.

Step 2: Issue the REPLACE command to enter the tax amount. Type *REPLACE PTAX WITH .05 * PAMT*. You will see the message 1 record replaced.

Note the use of the asterisk (*) to represent multiplication.

Step 3: Use the DISPLAY command to view the results. Type *DISPLAY PTAX*. The screen displays 200.00.

You could perform a series of ten individual replacements, but the global alteration shortcut is far more powerful. REPLACE with the ALL scope works globally and enables you to alter all the records at once.

Step 4: Use REPLACE ALL to enter all tax amounts. Type *REPLACE ALL PTAX WITH .05 * PAMT*. The screen displays 10 records replaced.

Step 5: Check your work. Type *LIST PAMT,PTAX*. Your screen should look like figure 4.7.

The REPLACE command has operated on all ten records, updating the PTAX fields to reflect 5% of the respective PAMT fields.

Step 6: Update the commissions. The commission amount, ECOMM, is 27 percent of sales. Use REPLACE to calculate the commission amount globally and to enter the result into each ECOMM field. Type *REPLACE ALL ECOMM WITH .27 * PAMT*. dBASE displays 10 records replaced.

```
. LIST PAMT,PTAX
Record#    PAMT    PTAX
       1  4000.00 200.00
       2  6600.35 330.02
       3  3523.17 176.16
       4  9042.00 452.10
       5  3523.17 176.16
       6  6600.35 330.02
       7  8097.00 404.85
       8  4000.00 200.00
       9  9042.00 452.10
      10   152.52   7.63
.
Command Line    ||<C:>||MX_SALES            |Rec: EOF/10    ||      || Caps

         Enter a dBASE III PLUS command.
```

Fig. 4.7. *Sales tax amounts calculated with REPLACE command.*

Step 7: Check your work by typing *LIST PAMT,ECOMM.* Figure 4.8 shows what appears on the screen.

```
, LIST PAMT,ECOMM
Record#    PAMT    ECOMM
      1  4000.00 1080.00
      2  6600.35 1782.09
      3  3523.17  951.26
      4  9042.00 2441.34
      5  3523.17  951.26
      6  6600.35 1782.09
      7  8097.00 2186.19
      8  4000.00 1080.00
      9  9042.00 2441.34
     10   152.52   41.18


Command Line    |<C:>|MX_SALES              |Rec: EOF/10          |          |   Caps
               Enter a dBASE III PLUS command.
```

Fig. 4.8. *Commissions entered with REPLACE.*

You can apply the REPLACE command selectively by building in a search condition. In the model, assume that commission rates vary by the size of the purchase amount—namely, that amounts above $4000 accrue a 35% commission. Apply a search condition to the REPLACE command and issue it again.

Step 8: Apply conditional replacements. Type *REPLACE ALL ECOMM WITH .35 * PAMT FOR PAMT > 4000.* Remember that the asterisk represents multiplication. The message 5 records replaced appears.

Step 9: Check your work. Type *LIST PAMT,ECOMM.* Your screen should look similar to figure 4.9.

All those records (numbers 2, 4, 6, 7, and 9) that met the condition (PAMT>4000) were changed from the first commission rate (27%) to the second rate (35%). Notice that the old information was replaced with the new and is gone forever.

Avoid REPLACE commands such as

REPLACE ALL ECOMM WITH 0

```
. LIST PAMT,ECOMM
Record#    PAMT    ECOMM
       1  4000.00 1080.00
       2  6600.35 2310.12
       3  3523.17  951.26
       4  9042.00 3164.70
       5  3523.17  951.26
       6  6600.35 2310.12
       7  8097.00 2833.95
       8  4000.00 1080.00
       9  9042.00 3164.70
      10   152.52   41.18
.
Command Line    <C:>  MX_SALES                Rec: EOF/10              Caps

      Enter a dBASE III PLUS command.
```

Fig. 4.9. *Commissions replaced conditionally.*

All calculated information about commissions would be "zeroed out" and would be gone forever. Remember, global alterations can make both desired and undesired updates quickly.

Deleting Records from a Database

Purchases sometimes are returned, although not frequently when the merchandise is the size of a swimming pool. The Sales Analysis system nevertheless requires a way to cancel a sale before installation. In cases like this, commands that delete records are necessary.

To illustrate, you will enter a new record into the database and then delete it. Suppose that Chris Connally purchases a hot tub but then learns that his boss has transferred him to El Paso. The tub has not been installed, and Connally requests a refund.

Step 1: Add Chris Connally's record. Type *APPEND* and enter the following sales data:

Record No.	11
CFNAME	Chris
CLNAME	Connally
CSTREET	43 Crown Ln.
CCITY	Jonesboro
CST	GA
CZIP	30236
CPHONE	954-0981
CNOTE	memo
PDATE	07/06/85
PINDATE	07/06/85
PCODE	H-19
PNO	1
PAMT	3523.17
PTAX	176.16
PPIF	t
ESP	LEM
ECOMM	951.26

Step 2: Exit APPEND with Ctrl-End, and delete the sale. The DELETE command flags a record for deletion. Like other commands, DELETE operates over a scope and can take a search condition. To move the record pointer to record 11 and mark the record for deletion, type these commands:

        GOTO 11
        DELETE

NOTES

Que Tip: Be warned! Global alterations alter many records quickly, for better or for worse. Before making such alterations, think!

The screen displays 1 record deleted.

Step 3: Check your work. Type *LIST CLNAME*. You should see the data in figure 4.10.

```
, LIST CLNAME
Record#  CLNAME
      1  Blair
      2  Connors
      3  Jones
      4  Aster
      5  Stevens
      6  Brown
      7  Clark
      8  Jones
      9  Abbott
     10  Hoffsmith
     11 *Connally
,
Command Line    ||<C:>||MX_SALES              |Rec: EOF/11        ||        ||  Caps
              Enter a dBASE III PLUS command.
```

Fig. 4.10. *Record 11 marked by DELETE command.*

dBASE III Plus does not actually delete the record, but marks it as a candidate for later, permanent removal. The deletion mark on the screen is the asterisk preceding the first field value.

Minds can change, and so can deletions. Suppose that Connally decides to continue installing the hot tub and to sell it with the house. To "un-delete," use the RECALL command, which has the opposite effect of the DELETE command.

Step 4: Type *RECALL RECORD 11* to un-delete a record. The screen displays 1 record recalled.

Step 5: Check your work by typing *LIST CLNAME*. Figure 4.11 shows what appears on the screen.

NOTES

```
. LIST CLNAME
Record#  CLNAME
      1  Blair
      2  Connors
      3  Jones
      4  Aster
      5  Stevens
      6  Brown
      7  Clark
      8  Jones
      9  Abbott
     10  Hoffsmith
     11  Connally
.
Command Line    ||<C:>||MX_SALES            ||Rec: EOF/11        ||      || Caps
        Enter a dBASE III PLUS command.
```

Fig. 4.11. *Record 11 recalled.*

Suppose that Connally changes his mind again. Now you want to permanently eliminate his record. This is the purpose of the PACK command.

> **Step 6:** Type *DELETE RECORD 11* to delete Connally's record permanently. dBASE displays 1 record deleted. Type *PACK*. The message 10 records copied appears.

> **Step 7:** Check your work. Type *LIST CLNAME*. You now have deleted record 11 permanently. Your screen should look like figure 4.12.

The DELETE ALL command marks all records for deletion. If a PACK command is given, dBASE eliminates all the records at a rate of several hundred per minute. A much more powerful command, ZAP, instantly and permanently does the job of the other two commands. However, it is primarily intended for programmers. Do not use the ZAP command!

Performing Date Arithmetic

Saltwater Sally's uses two date fields, PDATE and PINDATE. Data values stored as dates offer a helpful tool for answering questions such as, "How many days have cus-

NOTES

```
. LIST CLNAME
Record#  CLNAME
      1  Blair
      2  Connors
      3  Jones
      4  Aster
      5  Stevens
      6  Brown
      7  Clark
      8  Jones
      9  Abbott
     10  Hoffsmith
.
Command Line   ║<C:>║MX_SALES            ║Rec: EOF/10          ║        ║   Caps

       Enter a dBASE III PLUS command.
```

Fig. 4.12. *Record 11 deleted permanently with PACK.*

Que Tip: Beware of the ZAP! ZAP is equivalent to DELETE ALL and PACK. Issuing this command deletes all your records instantaneously!

tomers waited between purchase and installation?" or "How long has it been since Stevens purchased his pool?" In other words, date fields permit one date to be subtracted from another to find elapsed time. You also can add days to a date and calculate a new date.

Date arithmetic is commonly used to compare an entered date with today's date. In dBASE III Plus, today's date is conveniently available in what is called the date function. A *function* is a built-in formula that takes a data value or expression, processes it, and returns another value. The *date function* takes the date you type when you turn on your computer—the DOS or system date—and converts that date into a form compatible with dates stored in date fields. The date function is expressed as the word DATE, immediately followed by a left and right parentheses: DATE( ).

Two commands allow you to see the value currently stored in the date function. You can use the DISPLAY command: DISPLAY DATE( ). Another possibility is to use the WHAT IS? command. Unlike other dBASE III Plus commands, the WHAT IS? command is expressed by a question mark (?), not a command verb. The form for testing the date function, then, is ? DATE( ).

Like the DISPLAY command, the WHAT IS? command puts on the screen the current value for a field or the calculated value of a function. WHAT IS? also can be used as a

NOTES

substitute for a hand calculator. For instance, to calculate quickly how much tax to charge on a sale of $2942, type *? 2942 ∗ .05*, which asks, "What is 2942 times 5%?" WHAT IS? performs all the basic math operations listed in table 4.1.

Table 4.1
Math Operations Supported in dBASE III Plus

Operation	Symbol
Addition	+
Subtraction	-
Multiplication	∗
Division	/
Raising to a power	∗∗ or ^

One word of caution in writing complex math expressions (those that involve more than two numbers): group the terms of the expression into logical units using parentheses. The results can be deceptively incorrect otherwise.

Step 1: Use the WHAT IS? command with the DATE( ) function. Type *? DATE( )*. If you see Ø1/Ø1/8Ø, you probably forgot to enter a date at startup.

Step 2: Calculate with the DATE( ) function and a field. Determine the days that have elapsed between today's date and the date of payment for the first purchase (the first record). Type the following commands:

> GOTO 1
> ? DATE( )-PDATE

A number representing the difference between the current system date and the record 1 purchase date appears.

Step 3: View multiple calendar calculations. The LIST command can display the days elapsed between the purchase date and the installation date for all records. The calculated answer indicates how fast (or possibly how slow) the delivery and installation staff performed. Type *LIST CLNAME,PINDATE-PDATE*. Figure 4.13 shows what appears on the screen.

The difference, in days, between purchase and installation is listed beside the name of the customer.

```
. LIST CLNAME,PINDATE-PDATE
Record#  CLNAME      PINDATE-PDATE
       1 Blair                   8
       2 Connors                 9
       3 Jones                   9
       4 Aster                   8
       5 Stevens                 8
       6 Brown                   5
       7 Clark                   2
       8 Jones                   1
       9 Abbott                  5
      10 Hoffsmith               0
.
Command Line    |<C:>|MX_SALES              |Rec: EOF/10    |    |    | Caps
         Enter a dBASE III PLUS command.
```

Fig. 4.13. *Calculating days elapsed between purchase and installation.*

◻ SUMMARY OF CONCEPTS
PRESENTED IN LESSON 4

1. Any database, including the Saltwater Sally's sales model, can be altered with the MODIFY STRUCTURE command.

2. View the structure of the database by using LIST STRUCTURE. You can send the result to the printer by adding TO PRINT.

3. The REPLACE command alters a given field for one or more records. Use RE-PLACE ALL to update the database globally.

4. Mark outdated or unwanted records with the DELETE command. RECALL returns them to normal status. Permanently remove deleted records with the PACK command. Never issue ZAP.

5. Date fields permit date arithmetic. Days can be added to or subtracted from a date field to yield a new date. One date subtracted from another yields the difference in elapsed days.

6. The date function DATE( ), when issued, substitutes for DATE( ) the current date in DOS.

7. The WHAT IS? command (?) can be used as a calculator or as a fill-in for the DISPLAY command to display values for fields and functions.

NOTES

LESSON 4
EXERCISE

Modify the accounts payable data file, SSBILLS, to make it more useful. Follow these steps:

Step 1: Type *USE SSBILLS*.

Step 2: The structure of SSBILLS presently includes DATEIN, a date field to track the receipt date of the bill. Add DATEDUE, a field to monitor the date on which the bill is due. Type *MODIFY STRUCTURE*. Move the cursor down to just below DATEIN. Press Ctrl-N to open up a space for a new field. Enter *DATEDUE* as the name of the new field and designate it as a date field with a D in the field-type column. Save your work by pressing Ctrl-End.

Step 3: Check the modified structure. Type *LIST STRUCTURE*.

Step 4: Globally update the new field. Assume that all bills are due within 30 days of the received date. Type *REPLACE ALL DATEDUE WITH DATEIN + 30*.

Step 5: Check your work. Type *LIST DATEIN,DATEDUE*.

NOTES

5

Statistics Commands and Memory Variables

Related sections in *dBASE III Plus Handbook*, 2nd Edition: Chapters 6 and 7.

Financial information is critical to management of Saltwater Sally's. dBASE III Plus provides commands to "number-crunch" numeric fields: to summarize data into useful information for management. The results can be inspected immediately and saved to special slots in memory.

The objective in this lesson is to use the statistics and memory commands, specifically the following ones:

- COUNT
- SUM
- AVERAGE
- DISPLAY MEMORY

By using these commands, you can keep detailed accounts of Saltwater Sally's sales performance.

The Statistics Commands

Performance analysis is one of the necessary management chores that the sales information system should be able to help with. Performance analysis is concerned with getting answers to such questions as, "Which salespersons sold what kinds of units, and how many did they sell?"

NOTES

This question and others like it can be answered quickly using the three statistics commands: COUNT, SUM, and AVERAGE.

The COUNT Command

COUNT determines the number of records. Without a qualification, COUNT determines the total number of records in the data file. (If MX_SALES is already the active database, omit Steps 1 and 2.)

Step 1: Specify the default drive and type *DO QPREP*. Select Lesson 5.

Step 2: Type *USE MX_SALES*.

Step 3: Type *COUNT*, to determine the number of records. The screen displays 1Ø records.

The COUNT command by itself is not very useful; the total record count is available on the status bar. However, COUNT "shines" when used with a search condition.

Step 4: Apply a numeric conditional expression to COUNT. Determine the number of purchases in which the total amount of purchase was greater than $4000. Type *COUNT FOR PAMT>4000*. The screen displays 5 records.

One of COUNT's more useful functions is to determine sales by each employee. The ESP field registers the salesperson's initials. Counting for each salesperson yields the analysis needed.

Step 5: Summarize sales performance; use COUNT for each of the three salespersons.

Type *COUNT FOR ESP="DWK"*. The screen displays 4 records.

Type *COUNT FOR ESP="LEM"*. dBASE displays 3 records.

Type *COUNT FOR ESP="FSM"*. The message 3 records appears.

In terms of number of purchases, Doug has sold the most tubs and pools.

The messages that COUNT produces (the number of records counted) appear at the dot prompt. The results are shown immediately but disappear as the screen scrolls upward or if the screen is cleared.

Step 6: Type *CLEAR*, to clear the screen. The dot prompt reappears.

What would happen if you wanted to check the sales performance a little later? Once the commands are off the screen, the entire sequence of commands must be reissued.

NOTES

To prevent having to reissue commands, the results of statistics commands can be saved in pigeonholes in memory called *memory variables*. As many as 256 such spots can be reserved, and, like fields, each is given a name of up to ten letters. By convention, most users assign these memory variables names that begin with M for memory. Also like field variables, memory variables can store information as numeric, character, date, or logical data.

Step 7: Assign sales performance values to memory variables.

Type *COUNT FOR ESP="DWK" TO M_DWK.* You will see the response 4 records.

Type *COUNT FOR ESP="LEM" TO M_LEM.* The program responds, 3 records.

Last, type *COUNT FOR ESP="FSM" TO M_FSM,* and you should see 3 records.

Each of the COUNT commands has assigned the resulting value to the corresponding memory variable. The variable retains its value as long as dBASE is in operation or until you alter the variable.

Variables reside in memory until you request to use them. One of the easiest techniques for viewing all variables is to use a variant of DISPLAY.

Step 8: Type *DISPLAY MEMORY*, to view all memory variables. Your screen should look like figure 5.1.

The name of each memory variable is in the first column. The second column refers to public or private variables and is of interest to programmers. Next is the type of variable; in this case, all are numbers. The displayed value is next, and the last column is the number of digits for each number that dBASE retains in memory.

The SUM Command

Whereas COUNT tallies the number of records, SUM computes the sums of values in the numeric fields.

Step 1: Use the SUM command. Type *SUM.* dBASE III Plus displays the data in figure 5.2.

SUM without any other modifier gives the sum of all numeric fields for all records. You can use the SUM command with a field list qualifier to specify certain fields.

Step 2: Use a field list with SUM. Type *SUM PAMT,PTAX.* Your screen should look similar to figure 5.3.

```
. DISPLAY MEMORY
M_DWK       pub  N        4  (        4.00000000)
M_LEM       pub  N        3  (        3.00000000)
M_FSM       pub  N        3  (        3.00000000)
     3 variables defined,     27 bytes used
   253 variables available,  5973 bytes available
```

```
Command Line    ||<C:>||MX_SALES            ||Rec: EOF/10        ||        || Caps
```

Enter a dBASE III PLUS command.

Fig. 5.1. *Sales performance memory variables.*

```
. SUM
    10 records summed
  PNO     PAMT     PTAX     ECOMM
  11   54580.56  2729.04  17887.29
```

```
Command Line    ||<C:>||MX_SALES            ||Rec: EOF/10        ||        || Caps
```

Enter a dBASE III PLUS command.

Fig. 5.2. *Values of numeric fields summed.*

```
. SUM PAMT,PTAX
     10 records summed
     PAMT     PTAX
  54580.56   2729.04
'
Command Line    ║<C:>║MX_SALES            ║Rec: EOF/10      ║        ║   Caps
              Enter a dBASE III PLUS command.
```

Fig. 5.3. *Specific fields summed.*

Only the two fields included in the field list are tallied.

Data derived from a calculation in each record can be summed over several records. dBASE can calculate the tax, purchase amount, and commissions paid; the total paid per product; a yearly estimate of the total paid; and the total commission.

You can use existing field names in combination with the SUM command to yield combined totals. Table 5.1 lists these field names.

Table 5.1
Field Names Used with SUM To Yield Combined Totals

Field Name	Total Yielded
PAMT	Purchase amount per record
PTAX	Tax per record
PAMT + PTAX	Total of purchase and tax
ECOMM	Commission amount per record

Step 3: Type *SUM PAMT,PTAX,PAMT + PTAX,ECOMM,* to derive the combined totals of all records in specific fields. Compare your results with figure 5.4.

```
. SUM PAMT,PTAX,PAMT + PTAX,ECOMM
     10 records summed
       PAMT      PTAX    PAMT + PTAX      ECOMM
    54500.56    2729.04      57309.60   17887.29
```

```
Command Line    ||<C:>||MX_SALES              ||Rec: EOF/10     ||      ||    Caps
          Enter a dBASE III PLUS command.
```

Fig. 5.4. *Purchase amount plus tax summed.*

SUM calculated each of the purchase-amount-plus-tax totals in each record, and then SUM added the subtotals into a combined total. The gross proceeds for 10 sales are now known, as well as the commission.

Step 4: Save the summed information. Repeat the SUM command and transfer the amounts to memory variables. Type the following command (all on one line):

UM PAMT,PTAX,PAMT + PTAX,ECOMM TO MSUMAMT,MSUMTAX,MGROSS,MSUMCOMM

Your screen should display the data shown in figure 5.5.

```
. SUM PAMT,PTAX,PAMT + PTAX,ECOMM TO MSUMAMT,MSUMTAX,MGROSS,MSUMCOMM
     10 records summed
      PAMT       PTAX       PAMT + PTAX      ECOMM
   54500.56    2729.04        57309.60     17887.29

Command Line     ||<C:>||MX_SALES              ||Rec: EOF/10      ||       ||     Caps
               Enter a dBASE III PLUS command.
```

Fig. 5.5. *Totals stored in memory variables.*

dBASE now transfers the values into memory, along with the results of the COUNT commands.

Step 5: Determine sales, by employee. You also can use SUM to determine the amounts sold, by salesperson. Substitute SUM for the COUNT verb in the expressions used in Step 5 of the COUNT exercise.

Type *SUM PAMT FOR ESP="DWK" TO M_DWKSUM.*

Type *SUM PAMT FOR ESP="LEM" TO M_LEMSUM.*

Type *SUM PAMT FOR ESP="FSM" TO M_FSMSUM.*

Step 6: Check your work by typing *DISPLAY MEMORY.* Compare your screen with figure 5.6.

```
, DISPLAY MEMORY
M_DWK      pub  N         4  (            4.00000000)
M_LEM      pub  N         3  (            3.00000000)
MSUMAMT    pub  N     54580.56  (        54580.56000000)
M_FSM      pub  N         3  (            3.00000000)
MSUMTAX    pub  N      2729.04  (         2729.04000000)
MGROSS     pub  N     57309.60  (        57309.60000000)
MSUMCOMM   pub  N     17887.29  (        17887.29000000)
M_DWKSUM   pub  N     15772.69  (        15772.69000000)
M_LEMSUM   pub  N     17200.70  (        17200.70000000)
M_FSMSUM   pub  N     21607.17  (        21607.17000000)
    10 variables defined,      90 bytes used
   246 variables available,   5910 bytes available
```

```
Command Line    ||<C:>||MX_SALES              ||Rec: EOF/10   ||      ||    Caps

              Enter a dBASE III PLUS command.
```

Fig. 5.6. *Memory variables displayed.*

The AVERAGE Command

Just as the SUM command computes sums, the AVERAGE command computes averages.

Step 1: Average all fields. Type *AVERAGE*. The results shown in figure 5.7 appear.

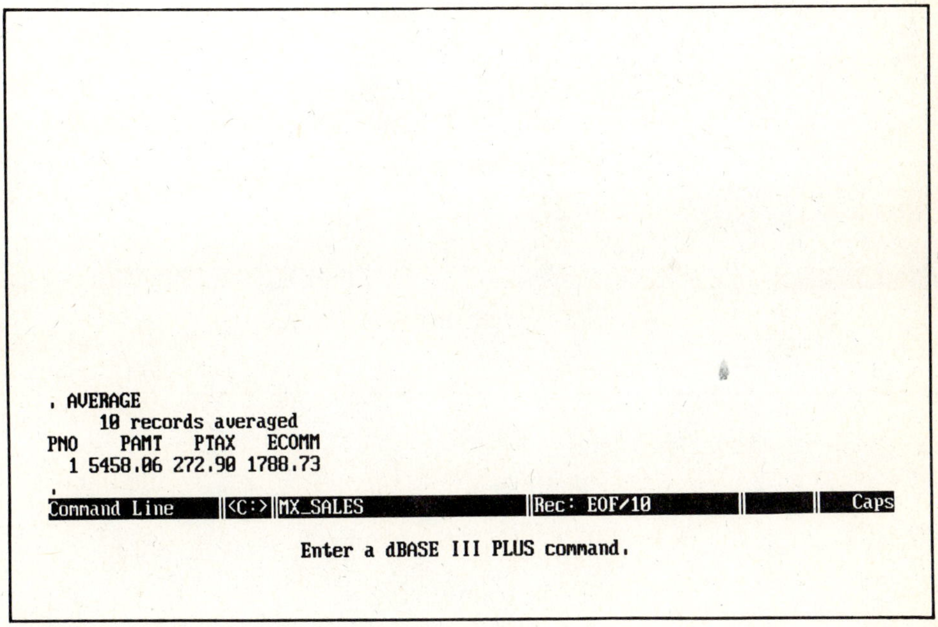

```
. AVERAGE
      10 records averaged
PNO    PAMT    PTAX   ECOMM
  1 5458.06 272.90 1788.73

Command Line   ||<C:>||MX_SALES               ||Rec: EOF/10          ||      || Caps

          Enter a dBASE III PLUS command.
```

Fig. 5.7. *Values of numeric fields averaged.*

Step 2: Assign the average payment and commission to memory variables. Type *AVERAGE PAMT,ECOMM TO MAVAMT, MAVCOMM.*

Step 3: Assign averages to variables, by salesperson.

Type *AVERAGE PAMT FOR ESP="DWK" TO MAV_DWK.*

Type *AVERAGE PAMT FOR ESP="LEM" TO MAV_LEM.*

Then type *AVERAGE PAMT FOR ESP="FSM" TO MAV_FSM.*

Step 4: Check your work. Type *DISPLAY MEMORY.* Compare your screen with figure 5.8.

```
. DISPLAY MEMORY
M_DWK       pub  N          4 (            4.00000000)
M_LEM       pub  N          3 (            3.00000000)
MSUMAMT     pub  N   54580.56 (        54580.56000000)
M_FSM       pub  N          3 (            3.00000000)
MSUMTAX     pub  N    2729.04 (         2729.04000000)
MGROSS      pub  N   57309.60 (        57309.60000000)
MSUMCOMM    pub  N   17887.29 (        17887.29000000)
M_DWKSUM    pub  N   15772.69 (        15772.69000000)
M_LEMSUM    pub  N   17200.70 (        17200.70000000)
M_FSMSUM    pub  N   21607.17 (        21607.17000000)
MAVAMT      pub  N    5458.06 (         5458.05600000)
MAVCOMM     pub  N    1788.73 (         1788.72900000)
MAV_DWK     pub  N    3943.17 (         3943.17250000)
MAV_LEM     pub  N    5733.57 (         5733.56666667)
MAV_FSM     pub  N    7202.39 (         7202.39000000)
    15 variables defined,       135 bytes used
   241 variables available,    5865 bytes available
.
Command Line    ||<C:>||MX_SALES               ||Rec: EOF/10       ||       || Caps

           Enter a dBASE III PLUS command.
```

Fig. 5.8. *All memory variables displayed.*

Memory Manipulation

Fifteen measurements of sales activity now are saved in memory and are retained until they are changed, until the power is turned off, or until you quit. If one of these happens, the memory is cleared.

Individual memory variables can be canceled from memory by issuing the RELEASE command. Type RELEASE and follow it with the names of the memory variables you no longer need. Separate variables with commas. If you want to clear all memory variables without leaving dBASE, you can give either the command CLEAR MEMORY or CLEAR ALL. CLEAR ALL also closes all open files and clears the screen.

Use the WHAT IS? command (?) to display or calculate data in memory variables. For instance, to find average sales for each employee, you can review the information stored in the memory variables beginning with MAV_ (Step 1), or you can calculate the averages by dividing the totals for each salesperson (the M_xxxSUM variables) by the number of sales for each salesperson (the M_xxx variables) (Step 2).

Step 1: Display average sales, by employee. Assume that AVERAGE information has been stored in memory variables. Separate numeric variables with commas. dBASE provides the answers on the line below. Type the following:

> ? MAV_DWK,MAV_LEM,MAV_FSM

The screen displays the following results:

> 3943.17   5733.57   7202.39

Step 2: Display average sales, by employee. Assume that only the SUM and COUNT data has been stored. Type the following (all on one line):

> ? M_DWKSUM / M_DWK, M_LEMSUM / M_LEM,
> M_FSMSUM / M_FSM

The following appears on the screen:

> 3943.17   5733.57   7202.39

Once in memory, information can be calculated, displayed, or retrieved in various ways.

SUMMARY OF CONCEPTS
PRESENTED IN LESSON 5

1. The dBASE III Plus statistics commands are COUNT, SUM, and AVERAGE. You can use a field list, a scope, and a search condition with all three statistics commands.

2. COUNT tallies the number of records.

3. SUM totals numeric fields.

4. AVERAGE determines averages.

5. You can use the statistics commands to transfer calculated values to memory variables: pigeonholes in memory that are given names and that retain the values.

6. DISPLAY MEMORY provides a listing of the memory variables currently assigned.

7. Remove memory variables with RELEASE, CLEAR MEMORY, or CLEAR ALL. Quitting dBASE also clears the memory.

■ LESSON 5
  EXERCISE

In this exercise, you will "number-crunch" the accounts payable file. You will determine important measurements of the large numeric bills, the total owed to vendors, and the average amount owed.

Step 1: Open up the data file SSBILLS. Type *USE SSBILLS*.

Step 2: Determine the number of bills in which more than $1000 is owed. Type *COUNT FOR VAMT > 1000*.

Step 3: Verify that the number of records displayed is correct by examining key fields of the large bills. Type *LIST VATTN,VAMT FOR VAMT > 1000 OFF*.

Step 4: Save the number of large bills to a memory variable. Type *COUNT FOR VAMT > 1000 TO M_BIGIOU*.

Step 5: Determine the total of the outstanding bills and store the result to a memory variable. Type *SUM VAMT TO M_ALLIOU*.

Step 6: Determine the average owed per bill and store the result to a memory variable. Type *AVERAGE VAMT TO M_AVIOU*.

Step 7: Check memory by typing *DISPLAY MEMORY*. If a printer is available, type *LIST MEMORY TO PRINT*.

NOTES

6

Labels and Reports

Related sections in *dBASE III Plus Handbook*, 2nd Edition: Chapters 2 and 8.

Many retrieval verbs, such as LIST and DISPLAY, enable you to direct data to a printer. Although the appearance of these printouts is adequate for most purposes, the format is not suitable for use in formal settings, such as in Saltwater Sally's Annual Report.

DISPLAY and LIST produce valuable information, but the output is in a raw, or unformatted, form. For more attractive presentation of data, dBASE III Plus offers these output formats:

- Multiple lines for each record, generally used for mailing labels (the LABEL format)

- One line per record, with top and bottom margins and headings (the REPORT format)

The data for each output format is funneled through dBASE III Plus into a *form file*. Just as a structure organizes a data file, a form organizes output. Think of a form as a style sheet, laying out the specifications for the label or report—for example, the number of labels to print across the page, the field to be reported in the first column, the report title, and so on. Forms need to be designed only once (then saved to the disk as a file). If a saved form needs to be changed, it can be modified just as a database can.

In this lesson, you will learn the following:

- How to design form files using CREATE LABEL or CREATE REPORT

- How to print labels and reports using LABEL FORM or REPORT FORM

NOTES

Designing the Label Form File

Saltwater Sally's wants to send promotional materials to its customers. Use the follow-ing steps to create a label form file to produce the labels. (If MX_SALES is already the active database, omit Steps 1 and 2.)

Step 1: Set the default drive, and type *DO QPREP*. Select Lesson 6.

Step 2: Type *USE MX_SALES*.

Step 3: Create the label form file. Type *CREATE LABEL*. The screen displays `Enter label file name:`.

Step 4: Enter the file name. Type *MX_CUSTL*. Figure 6.1 shows what appears on the screen.

```
┌─────────────────────────────────────────────────────────────────────────┐
│ Options            Contents            Exit   08:54:03 am                  │
│ ┌──────────────────────────────────────────────────┐                      │
│ │ Predefined size:      3 1/2 x 15/16 by 1          │                      │
│ │                                                   │                      │
│ │ Label width:          35                          │                      │
│ │ Label height:         5                           │                      │
│ │ Left margin:          0                           │                      │
│ │ Lines between labels: 1                           │                      │
│ │ Spaces between labels: 0                          │                      │
│ │ Labels across page:   1                           │                      │
│ └──────────────────────────────────────────────────┘                      │
│                                                                           │
│ ┌──────────┬──────────────────┬──────────────────┬────────────────────┐  │
│ │CURSOR: <-- -->│ Delete char: Del │ Insert row:    ^N │ Insert:    Ins   │  │
│ │Char:    ← →   │ Delete word: ^T  │ Toggle menu:   F1 │ Zoom in:  ^PgDn  │  │
│ │Word: Home End │ Delete row:  ^U  │ Abandon:      Esc │ Zoom out: ^PgUp  │  │
│ └──────────┴──────────────────┴──────────────────┴────────────────────┘  │
│ CREATE LABEL    <C:> MX_CUSTL.LBL          Opt: 1/7              Caps      │
│       Position selection bar - ↑↓,  Select - ↵,  Leave menu - ↔,           │
│       Select a standard label size: (Width x Height by Number across).     │
└─────────────────────────────────────────────────────────────────────────┘
```

Fig. 6.1. *CREATE LABEL screen, Options submenu.*

The CREATE LABEL menu in dBASE III Plus is an extension of the Assistant and works in much the same way as other Assistant menus. The menu, across the top of the screen, includes three options:

NOTES

Options   Specifies the dimensions of the labels, how the
                    labels are to be spaced, and how many fit across a
                    page (see fig. 6.1)

Contents   Specifies which fields, memory variables, character
                    strings, functions, and so on will appear on each line
                    of the labels (see fig. 6.2)

Exit   Specifies to either save or abandon the label design

```
 Options                        Contents                  Exit  09:03:23 am

                            Label contents 1:
                                          2:
                                          3:
                                          4:
                                          5:




 CURSOR:   <-- -->  Delete char: Del  Insert row:       ^N  Insert:     Ins
 Char:      ←  →    Delete word: ^T   Toggle menu:      F1  Zoom in:  ^PgDn
 Word:    Home End  Delete row:  ^U   Abandon:         Esc  Zoom out: ^PgUp

 CREATE LABEL    |<C:>|MX_CUSTL.LBL            |Opt: 1/5            |     Caps
           Position selection bar - ↑↓,  Select - ◄┘,  Leave menu - ↔,
        Enter a field/expression list to be displayed on the indicated label line.
```

Fig. 6.2. *CREATE LABEL screen, Contents submenu.*

Because data processing labels are available in standard sizes, dBASE III Plus provides several predefined sizes you can select from. The default size shown in figure 6.1
(3 1/2 × 15/16 by 1) allows for four printed lines (15/16 of an inch at 6 lines per inch)
with room for one line between labels. Each line permits up to 35 characters (3 1/2
inches at 10 characters per inch) with no spaces at either margin. The labels are printed
1 across.

If your labels require another size, you can cycle through the other predefined sizes
simply by pressing Return. If you are not happy with the predefined sizes, move the cursor down to the option you need to change, activate it by pressing Return, and type in
the new value.

NOTES

A check of the database structure shows that the customer names and addresses will fit easily on the default size label. The only changes to make are to print the labels two across, to decrease the label height to 4, and to delete the line between labels.

Step 5: Select the correct label size. With the **Predefined size:** option selected, press the Return key once to change the label dimension to 3 1/2 × 15/16 by 2.

Notice that the **Labels across page:** option and the **Spaces between labels:** option change automatically.

Step 6: Change the height of the labels. Press the down-arrow key to move to the **Label height:** option, press Return to activate it, and enter the number *4*.

Step 7: Change the number of lines between labels. Move down to the **Lines between labels:** option and change it to *0* in the same way as in Step 6 (see fig. 6.3).

```
 Options                    Contents             Exit  11:02:01 am

  Predefined size:         3 1/2 x 15/16 by 2

  Label width:              35
  Label height:             4
  Left margin:              0
  Lines between labels:     0
  Spaces between labels:    2
  Labels across page:       2




 CURSOR:   <-- -->    Delete char: Del   Insert row:      ^N    Insert:      Ins
  Char:     ←   →     Delete word: ^T    Toggle menu:     F1    Zoom in:  ^PgDn
  Word:   Home End    Delete row:  ^U    Abandon:        Esc    Zoom out: ^PgUp

 CREATE LABEL   <C:> MX_CUSTL.LBL           Opt: 1/?                      Caps
          Position selection bar - ↑↓,  Select - ←┘,  Leave menu - ↔,
          Select a standard label size: (Width x Height by Number across).
```

Fig. 6.3. *Changing the predefined label size.*

NOTES

Step 8: Specify the customer first name and last name as the contents for the first line. Use the right-arrow key to move to the **Contents** option. With the highlighted selection bar on **Label contents 1:**, press Return to activate this line. When the triangle appears, type *CFNAME,CLNAME* (see fig. 6.4). Finally, press Return again to lock in the contents. The triangle disappears.

```
Options                    Contents              Exit  10:48:46 am

                  Label contents 1: ▶CFNAME,CLNAME
                                2:
                                3:
                                4:
                                5:


 CURSOR:  <--  -->  Delete char: Del  Insert row:      ^N   Insert:     Ins
 Char:     ←    →   Delete word: ^T   Toggle menu:     F1   Zoom in:  ^PgDn
 Word:   Home End   Delete row:  ^U   Abandon:        Esc   Zoom out: ^PgUp

 CREATE LABEL   |<C:>|MX_CUSTL.LBL            |Opt: 1/5   |    |    | Caps
           Enter an expression.  F10 for a field menu.  Finish with ↵ .
       Enter a field/expression list to be displayed on the indicated label line.
```

Fig. 6.4. *Entering contents for first label line.*

Invariably, people forget the names of the fields in their database. When (not if) this happens to you in designing labels, you can use the F10 key on an active contents line to bring up a list of fields in the current database. The field list contains its own highlighted selection bar. Move it to the field you want to enter and press Return; that field is entered on the contents line. If you use the field list box only for reference, press Esc to return the cursor to the contents line.

Step 9: Specify the customer address as the second contents line. Move the selection bar down to **Label contents 2:** and press Return. Press the F10 key (see fig. 6.5). Move the selection bar down to the **CSTREET** field and press Return. Lock in the contents by pressing Return again.

```
Options                    Contents                Exit  10:49:25 am

      CFNAME              Label contents 1:  CFNAME,CLNAME
      CLNAME                            2:
      CSTREET                           3:
      CCITY                             4:
      CST                               5:
      CZIP
      CPHONE
      CNOTE
      PDATE
      PINDATE
      PCODE
      PNO

 CURSOR:    <-- -->  Delete ch  Field Name        Type      Width  Decimal
 Char:       ←  →    Delete wo
 Word:    Home  End  Delete ro  MX_SALES->CSTREET  Character   15

 CREATE LABEL    <C:> MX_CUSTL.LBL           Opt: 3/17                  Caps
            Position selection bar - ↑↓.  Select - ↵.  Leave menu - ↔.
        Enter a field/expression list to be displayed on the indicated label line.
```

Fig. 6.5. *Using field list to enter a field on contents line.*

Step 10: Specify the city, state, and ZIP code as the contents for the third label line. Move the selection bar down to **Label contents 3:**, press Return, type *CCITY,CST,CZIP*, and press Return again. Your screen should look like figure 6.6.

```
 Options                      Contents              Exit  10:50:11 am

                     Label contents 1:  CFNAME,CLNAME
                                    2:  CSTREET
                                    3:  CCITY,CST,CZIP
                                    4:
                                    5:




 CURSOR:   <-- -->   Delete char: Del   Insert row:      ^N   Insert:      Ins
   Char:    +   +    Delete word: ^T    Toggle menu:     F1   Zoom in:   ^PgDn
   Word:  Home End   Delete row:  ^U    Abandon:        Esc   Zoom out:  ^PgUp

 CREATE LABEL    <C:> MX_CUSTL.LBL          Opt: 3/5                      Caps
            Position selection bar - ↑↓,  Select - ←┘,  Leave menu - ↔,
      Enter a field/expression list to be displayed on the indicated label line.
```

Fig. 6.6. *Completed label contents.*

Step 11: Move the main menu selection bar to **Exit** (see fig. 6.7). Press the Return key with the **Save** option highlighted in the box.

Issuing and Modifying the Label Form File

The LABEL command, like LIST and DISPLAY, can take optionally both a scope and a search condition. To issue labels, designate the verb LABEL, the keyword FORM, and the name of the form file. TO PRINT also can be added to the command to redirect the information to a printer. In the following exercises, you can add TO PRINT if a printer is available.

Step 1: Issue LABEL FORM. Type *LABEL FORM MX_CUSTL*. Compare your screen to figure 6.8.

```
  Options                    Contents                    Exit  09:06:09 am
                                                         ┌──────────┐
                                                         │ Save     │
                                                         │ Abandon  │
                                                         └──────────┘




┌──────────────────┬───────────────────┬─────────────────┬──────────────────┐
│CURSOR:  <-- -->  │ Delete char: Del  │ Insert row:   ^N │ Insert:    Ins   │
│ Char:    ←  →    │ Delete word: ^T   │ Toggle menu:  F1 │ Zoom in:  ^PgDn  │
│ Word:  Home End  │ Delete row:  ^U   │ Abandon:     Esc │ Zoom out: ^PgUp  │
└──────────────────┴───────────────────┴─────────────────┴──────────────────┘
 CREATE LABEL    <C:> MX_CUSTL.LBL           Opt: 1/2               Caps
            Position selection bar - ↑↓,  Select - ←┘,  Leave menu - ↔,
                       Exit and save changes.
```

Fig. 6.7. *CREATE LABEL screen, Exit submenu.*

```
 . LABEL FORM MX_CUSTL
 James Blair              Francis Connors
 1 Oak Street             22 Priscilla Ln
 Atlanta GA 30332         Smyrna GA 30080

 Thomas Jones            Sam Aster
 87 Cul-de-Sac           49 Blossom Ln.
 Decatur GA 30030        Atlanta GA 30327

 Harold Stevens          Molly Brown
 6 Peachtree St.         92 Aqua Vita
 Atlanta GA 30326        Riverdale GA 30274

 John Clark              Susan Jones
 190 Arden Way           227 Jefferson
 Atlanta GA 30302        Decatur GA 30030

 William Abbott          Barbara Hoffsmith
 17 Hamilton Pl.         1000 Maple St.
 Cleveland TN 37311      Doraville GA 30040

 .
 Command Line    <C:> MX_SALES           Rec: EOF/10             Caps
            Enter a dBASE III PLUS command.
```

Fig. 6.8. *Labels generated with MX_CUSTL.*

The LABEL command precisely formats each record and field on the page. Fields that follow one another on the same line, such as city and state, are separated by one space. You can design and use many different form files with one data file.

Step 2: Issue LABEL FORM with a numeric condition. To promote a new portable spa, Sally's wants to target big purchasers for a special reception. Issue labels only for customers who paid more than $7500. Type *LABEL FORM MX_CUSTL FOR PAMT > 7500*. Compare your result to figure 6.9.

```
. LABEL FORM MX_CUSTL FOR PAMT > 7500
Sam Aster                    John Clark
49 Blossom Ln.               190 Arden Way
Atlanta GA 30327             Atlanta GA 30302

William Abbott
17 Hamilton Pl.
Cleveland TN 37311


Command Line    <C:> MX_SALES              Rec: EOF/10              Caps
              Enter a dBASE III PLUS command.
```

Fig. 6.9. *Customer labels for big purchasers.*

Step 3: Issue LABEL FORM with a character condition. Sally's also wants to target customers by city. Issue labels according to the content of the CCITY field. Remember that character expressions must be enclosed in quotation marks. Type *LABEL FORM MX_CUSTL FOR CCITY = 'Atlanta'*. dBASE generates labels for the four Atlanta residents (see fig. 6.10).

Step 4: Modify the label. Alter the form file to print the addresses on 3-up (3-across) labels. Enter MODIFY mode by typing *MODIFY LABEL*. The screen displays Enter label file name:. Type *MX_CUSTL*. Your original LABEL FORM should appear.

```
. LABEL FORM MX_CUSTL FOR CCITY = 'Atlanta'
James Blair                    Sam Aster
1 Oak Street                   49 Blossom Ln.
Atlanta GA 30332               Atlanta GA 30327

Harold Stevens                 John Clark
6 Peachtree St.                190 Arden Way
Atlanta GA 30326               Atlanta GA 30302

.
Command Line    ||<C:>||MX_SALES              ||Rec: EOF/10

        Enter a dBASE III PLUS command.
```

Fig. 6.10. *Customer labels for Atlanta residents.*

Step 5: Revise the label form file. Make the revisions to the layout as illustrated in figure 6.11. The labels to be used are *3* across, and slightly narrower than the original format (*25* instead of 35 in width). Each of the 3 labels in a row is separated by *2* spaces. Save your work by moving to **Exit** and pressing Return with **Save** highlighted.

```
┌──────────────────────────────────────────────────────────────────────┐
│ Options              Contents              Exit  11:38:13 am           │
│ ┌──────────────────────────────────────────────────┐                  │
│ │ Predefined size:      3 1/2 x 15/16 by 3          │                  │
│ │                                                    │                  │
│ │ Label width:          25                           │                  │
│ │ Label height:         4                            │                  │
│ │ Left margin:          0                            │                  │
│ │ Lines between labels: 0                            │                  │
│ │ Spaces between labels: 2                           │                  │
│ │ Labels across page:   3                            │                  │
│ └──────────────────────────────────────────────────┘                  │
│                                                                        │
│                                                                        │
│ ┌────────────────┬─────────────────┬──────────────┬─────────────────┐ │
│ │CURSOR: <-- -->│Delete char: Del │Insert row:  ^N│Insert:    Ins   │ │
│ │Char:    ← →   │Delete word: ^T  │Toggle menu: F1│Zoom in:  ^PgDn  │ │
│ │Word: Home End │Delete row:  ^U  │Abandon:    Esc│Zoom out: ^PgUp  │ │
│ └────────────────┴─────────────────┴──────────────┴─────────────────┘ │
│ MODIFY LABEL   <C:> MX_CUSTL.LBL        Opt: 2/7              Caps     │
│         Position selection bar - ↑↓, Select - ←┘, Leave menu - ↔,      │
│             Enter the number of characters in the label width.         │
└──────────────────────────────────────────────────────────────────────┘
```

Fig. 6.11. *Modified label form file.*

Step 6: Use the SAMPLE option of LABEL FORM to align labels correctly in your printer. Asterisks are printed, instead of field values, and you can adjust the labels until they are correctly positioned. Type *LABEL FORM MX_CUSTL SAMPLE*. Figure 6.12 shows what appears on the screen.

Step 7: Issue the labels by pressing N (for No) at the question Do you want more samples? (Y/N). Compare your results to figure 6.13.

Designing the Report Form File

Reports, like labels, require a form file to design the report specifications. Report form files, unlike label form files, are designed to print fields for one record on one line.

```
. LABEL FORM MX_CUSTL SAMPLE
************************    ************************    ************************
************************    ************************    ************************
************************    ************************    ************************
************************    ************************    ************************
Do you want more samples? (Y/N)
Command Line    ||<C:>||MX_SALES              |Rec: EOF/10       ||      ||  Caps
```
Enter a dBASE III PLUS command.

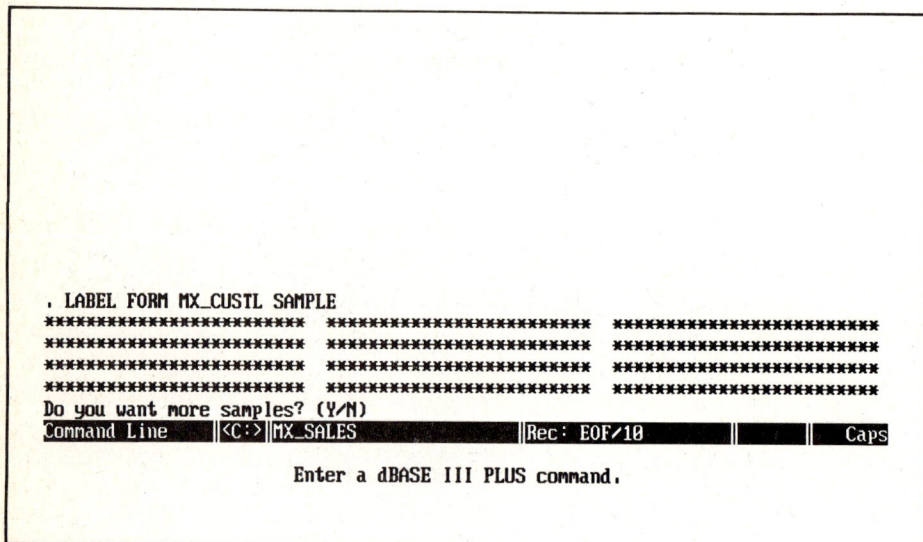

Fig. 6.12. *Printing sample labels.*

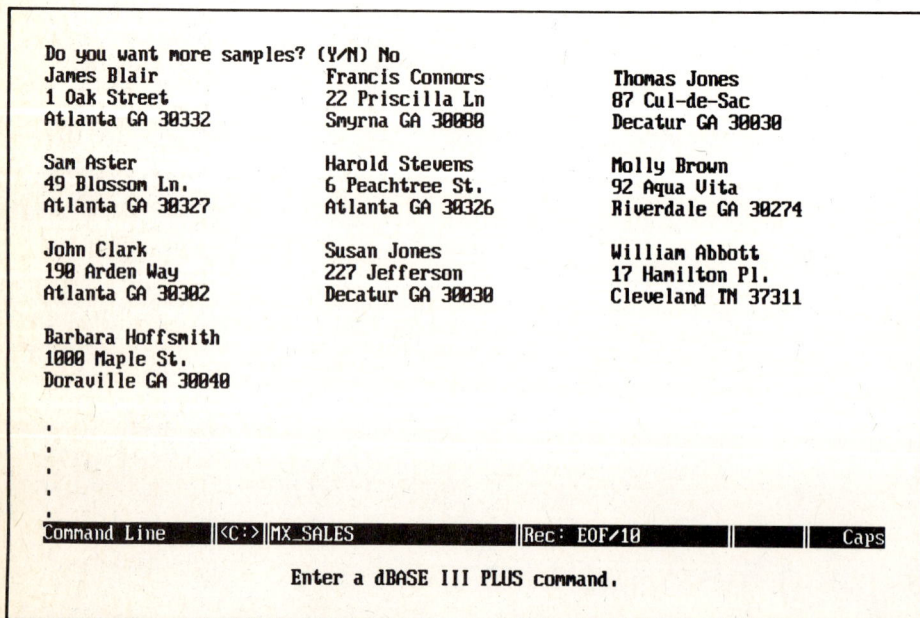

```
Do you want more samples? (Y/N) No
James Blair              Francis Connors          Thomas Jones
1 Oak Street             22 Priscilla Ln          87 Cul-de-Sac
Atlanta GA 30332         Smyrna GA 30080          Decatur GA 30030

Sam Aster                Harold Stevens           Molly Brown
49 Blossom Ln.           6 Peachtree St.          92 Aqua Vita
Atlanta GA 30327         Atlanta GA 30326         Riverdale GA 30274

John Clark               Susan Jones              William Abbott
190 Arden Way            227 Jefferson            17 Hamilton Pl.
Atlanta GA 30302         Decatur GA 30030         Cleveland TN 37311

Barbara Hoffsmith
1000 Maple St.
Doraville GA 30040

.
.
.
Command Line    ||<C:>||MX_SALES              |Rec: EOF/10       ||      ||  Caps
```
Enter a dBASE III PLUS command.

Fig. 6.13. *Three-across labels.*

Report specifications include page numbers, the current date, a report title appearing at the top of every page of the report, column headings, division of the records into groups and subgroups, and subtotals and totals of numeric fields (see fig. 6.14). With the exception of grouping and subgrouping, all the specifications are discussed in this lesson. Grouping is considered in Lesson 8.

```
Page
Date
                        Report Title

Heading           Heading        Heading
Column 1          Column 2       Column 4

**Group A

Field1 data       Field2 data    Field3 data    {for Record 1
Field1 data       Field2 data    Field3 data    {for Record 2
                                 _____
**Subtotal                       XXXXXXXX.XX    {for Group A

**Group B

Field1 data       Field2 data    Field3 data    {for Record 3
Field1 data       Field2 data    Field3 data    {for Record 4
                                 _____
**Subtotal                       XXXXXXXX.XX    {for Group B
                                 _____
        **Total                  XXXXXXXX.XX
```

Fig. 6.14. *Generalized report format.*

Saltwater Sally's from time to time needs polished-looking reports for its shareholders and directors. These reports present the same information that the retrieve and statistics commands produce, but in a more acceptable format for these people. The format itself is specified in a report form file, which is defined with the CREATE REPORT command.

> **Step 1:** Create a sales report form file. Type *CREATE REPORT*. The screen displays
> Enter report file name:.

> **Step 2:** Enter the name of the form file. Type *SALES*. The REPORT main menu appears with the **Options** submenu in view (see fig. 6.15).

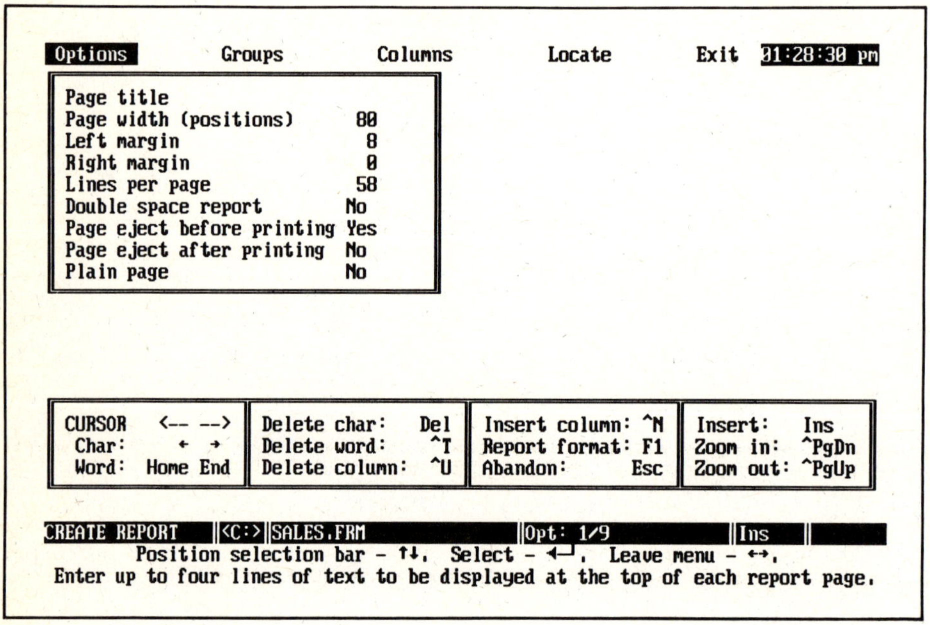

```
 Options        Groups        Columns        Locate        Exit  01:28:30 pm
┌──────────────────────────────────┐
│ Page title                       │
│ Page width (positions)      80   │
│ Left margin                  8   │
│ Right margin                 0   │
│ Lines per page              58   │
│ Double space report         No   │
│ Page eject before printing  Yes  │
│ Page eject after printing   No   │
│ Plain page                  No   │
└──────────────────────────────────┘




┌─────────────────────┬──────────────────────┬──────────────────────┬────────────────────┐
│ CURSOR   <-- -->    │ Delete char:    Del  │ Insert column: ^N    │ Insert:     Ins    │
│ Char:     ←   →     │ Delete word:    ^T   │ Report format: F1    │ Zoom in:   ^PgDn   │
│ Word:  Home End     │ Delete column:  ^U   │ Abandon:       Esc   │ Zoom out:  ^PgUp   │
└─────────────────────┴──────────────────────┴──────────────────────┴────────────────────┘

CREATE REPORT   |<C:>|SALES.FRM                |Opt: 1/9        |Ins |
          Position selection bar - ↑↓, Select - ←┘, Leave menu - ←→,
  Enter up to four lines of text to be displayed at the top of each report page,
```

Fig. 6.15. *CREATE REPORT screen, Options submenu.*

The CREATE REPORT menu in dBASE III Plus operates in the same manner as the CREATE LABEL menu and other Assistant menus. The menu includes the following options:

Options   Specifies how the report will be sized, paged, and identified. It also determines on which page the report will begin and end.

Groups   Determines grouping and subgrouping information for the report

Columns   Specifies what is reported in each column of the report by heading and field contents. Also determines whether totals are printed for the column. One screen is filled out for each column in the report.

Locate   Eases movement to previously defined columns, for quicker editing (not directly concerned with report specifications)

Exit   Specifies to either save or abandon the report specifications

Step 3: Enter a title for the report. Activate the **Page title** option by pressing Return. A four-line box appears to the right, into which you type the title. On two lines, type this title:

> Sales at Saltwater Sally's
> Hot Tubs and Pools

Do not be concerned about centering the title; dBASE will handle that task automatically. Your screen should look like figure 6.16. When you finish, lock in the title by pressing Ctrl-End.

Step 4: Change the lines per page setting. Press the down-arrow key to move the selection bar to the **Lines per page** option, press the Return key, enter the number *55*, and press Return again. Your screen should now look like figure 6.17.

Step 5: Move the menu selection bar to the **Columns** option. The **Columns** submenu appears along with the Report Format window (see fig. 6.18).

As columns are defined in the report, the format for the report is sketched in the Report Format window. This window appears when the **Columns** submenu is called to the screen, and it replaces the help block. It keeps a running total of the room that a report requires and the room that remains. If you need the help block again, it can be toggled on and off the screen with the F1 key.

```
 Options        Groups        Columns         Locate        Exit  01:29:37 pm
 Page title                  ⟩
 Page width (positions)      88
 Left margin                  8
 Right margin                 8
 Lines per page              58
 Double space report         No          Sales at Saltwater Sally's
 Page eject before printing  Yes         Hot Tubs and Pools
 Page eject after printing   No
 Plain page                  No

 CURSOR   <-- -->   Delete char:    Del   Insert column: ^N   Insert:    Ins
 Char:     ←   →    Delete word:    ^T    Report format: F1   Zoom in:  ^PgDn
 Word:   Home End   Delete column:  ^U    Abandon:       Esc   Zoom out: ^PgUp

 CREATE REPORT    <C:> SALES.FRM              Opt: 1/9           Ins
               Enter report title. Exit - Ctrl-End.
    Enter up to four lines of text to be displayed at the top of each report page.
```

Fig. 6.16. *Entering the report title.*

```
 Options        Groups        Columns         Locate        Exit  01:37:24 pm
 Page title                  Sales at
 Page width (positions)      88
 Left margin                  8
 Right margin                 8
 Lines per page              55
 Double space report         No
 Page eject before printing  Yes
 Page eject after printing   No
 Plain page                  No

 CURSOR   <-- -->   Delete char:    Del   Insert column: ^N   Insert:    Ins
 Char:     ←   →    Delete word:    ^T    Report format: F1   Zoom in:  ^PgDn
 Word:   Home End   Delete column:  ^U    Abandon:       Esc   Zoom out: ^PgUp

 CREATE REPORT    <C:> SALES.FRM              Opt: 5/9           Ins
            Position selection bar - ↑↓. Select - ↵. Leave menu - ↔.
               Enter the number of lines to display on each page.
```

Fig. 6.17. *Title and options set.*

```
 Options        Groups       │Columns│      Locate        Exit  01:40:25 pm
                      ┌──────────────────────────────────┐
                      │ Contents                         │
                      │ Heading                          │
                      │ Width                 0          │
                      │ Decimal places                   │
                      │ Total this column                │
                      └──────────────────────────────────┘



         ┌─Report Format──────────────────────────────────────────────────────┐
         │>>>>>>>>─────────────────────────────────────────────────────────────│
         │                                                                      │
         │                                                                      │
         │                                                                      │
         └──────────────────────────────────────────────────────────────────────┘

  CREATE REPORT   ║<C:>║SALES.FRM              │Column: 1         ║Ins ║
        Position selection bar - ↑↓.  Select - ←┘.  Prev/Next column - PgUp/PgDn.
        Enter a field or expression to display in the indicated report column.
```

Fig. 6.18. *CREATE REPORT screen, Columns submenu.*

Currently, the Report Format window shows an eight-character "chevron" (>>>>>>>>)
in the upper left corner. These chevrons are an indication that the **Left margin** is currently set at 8 (refer to fig. 6.15). Seventy-two spaces of the 80 positions specified in the
Page width (positions) are still available.

Note also that the fourth panel of the status bar identifies the number of the column
currently being defined. Move to different columns of the report by using the PgDn and
PgUp keys.

Step 6: Specify the first column to hold the customer's last name. Activate the **Contents** line by pressing Return and entering the field CLNAME. The field can
be entered by simply typing it, or it can be entered by pressing the F10 key,
selecting **CLNAME** from the list that appears to the left, and pressing Return. Figure 6.19 illustrates the second method. In either case, lock in the
contents by pressing Return again.

```
 Options          Groups        Columns         Locate        Exit  02:03:19 pm
        ┌──────────────────────┌─────────────────────────────────────────────┐
        │ CFNAME               │ Contents        ████████████████             │
        │ CLNAME               │ Heading                                      │
        │ CSTREET              │ Width                  0                      │
        │ CCITY                │ Decimal places                               │
        │ CST                  │ Total this column                            │
        │ CZIP                 └─────────────────────────────────────────────┘
        │ CPHONE
        │ CNOTE                 ┌──────────────────────────────────────────────┐
        │ PDATE                 │ Field Name            Type      Width  Decimal│
        └──────────────────────│                                               │
       ┌─Report Format─────────│ MX_SALES─>CLNAME      Character   10          │
       >>>>>>>>─────────────────└───────────────────────────────────────────────────────────
       │
       │
       │
       │
       └──────────────────────────────────────────────────────────────────────
 CREATE REPORT   |<C:>|SALES.FRM                    |Column: 1           |Ins
           Position selection bar - ↑↓.  Select - ◄┘.  Leave menu - ↔.
           Enter a field or expression to display in the indicated report column.
```

Fig. 6.19. *Entering a field from the field list.*

Step 7: Enter a column heading for the customer's last name. Move the selection bar down to the **Heading** line, press Return, and type up to a four-line heading in the box that appears. Type the following heading on two lines:

> CUSTOMER'S
> LAST NAME

Your screen should look like figure 6.20. Press Ctrl-End to lock in the heading.

```
 Options          Groups        Columns         Locate      Exit  02:13:27 pm
                         ┌─────────────────────────────────────────┐
                         │ Contents        CLNAME                   │
                         │ Heading       ▐                          │
                         │ Width           10                       │
                         │ Decimal places                           │
                         │ Total this column                        │
                         └─────────────────────────────────────────┘
                                    ┌──────────────────────────────┐
                                    │CUSTOMER'S                     │
                                    │LAST NAME                      │
                                    │                               │
                                    │                               │
                                    └──────────────────────────────┘
   ┌Report Format───────────────────────────┐
   │>>>>>>>>       ──────────────────────────────────────────────────
   │
   │
   │         XXXXXXXXXX
   └

 CREATE REPORT   │<C:>│SALES.FRM            │Column: 1        │Ins │   Caps
                      Enter column heading.  Exit - Ctrl-End.
            Enter up to four lines of text to display above the indicated column.
```

Fig. 6.20. *Entering a column heading.*

Notice that the **Width** line is set at 10, the width of the CLNAME field. If the heading turns out to require more space than this, the width can be increased accordingly. Also, the heading entry now includes a semicolon (;), which acts as a line break between the first and second lines of the heading box. The semicolon will not appear on the printed report. Notice also that the Report Format window has been updated with the new specifications for column 1 (see fig. 6.21).

```
 Options           Groups         Columns          Locate        Exit  02:14:12 pm

                         ┌────────────────────────────────────────────────┐
                         │ Contents            CLNAME                      │
                         │ Heading             CUSTOMER'S:LAST NAME        │
                         │ Width               10                          │
                         │ Decimal places                                 │
                         │ Total this column                              │
                         └────────────────────────────────────────────────┘




     ┌Report Format────────────────────────────────────────────────────────────┐
     │>>>>>>>>CUSTOMER'S ───────────────────────────────────────────────────────│
     │        LAST NAME                                                          │
     │                                                                           │
     │                                                                           │
     │      ┌────────────────────────────────────────────────────────────────┐  │
     │      │ XXXXXXXXXX                                                       │  │
     │      └────────────────────────────────────────────────────────────────┘  │

  CREATE REPORT   <C:> SALES.FRM              Column: 1          Ins      Caps
     Position selection bar - ↑↓.  Select - ↵.  Prev/Next column - PgUp/PgDn.
     Enter up to four lines of text to display above the indicated column.
```

Fig. 6.21. *Specifications for column 1 (CLNAME).*

Step 8: Specify the second column to report the customer's first name. Press PgDn to move to the second column position. The status bar's fourth panel will identify the blank entry box as Column: 2. Type the contents and heading as follows, and compare your screen to figure 6.22:

Contents	*CFNAME*
Heading	*FIRST*
	NAME

```
  Options           Groups        Columns        Locate        Exit  07:36:16 am
                            ┌────────────────────────────────────────────┐
                            │ Contents          CFNAME                    │
                            │ Heading           FIRST:NAME                │
                            │ Width             8                         │
                            │ Decimal places                             │
                            │ Total this column                          │
                            └────────────────────────────────────────────┘



   ┌─Report Format─────────────────────────────────────────────────────────┐
   │ >>>>>>>CUSTOMER'S FIRST    ──────────────────────────────────────────── │
   │        LAST NAME   NAME                                                 │
   │                                                                         │
   │                                                                         │
   ├─────────────────────────────────────────────────────────────────────── │
   │        XXXXXXXXXX XXXXXXX                                               │
   └─────────────────────────────────────────────────────────────────────── ┘
  CREATE REPORT    ║<C:>║SALES.FRM        ║Column: 2          ║       ║ Caps
       Position selection bar - ↑↓,  Select - ↵,  Prev/Next column - PgUp/PgDn.
       Enter up to four lines of text to display above the indicated column.
```

Fig. 6.22. *Specifications for column 2 (CFNAME).*

Step 9: Specify column 3 for the customer's phone number. Press PgDn to move to column 3, and type the following (see fig. 6.23):

Contents	*CPHONE*
Heading	*PHONE*
	NO.

Step 10: Specify column 4 for the purchase date. Press PgDn to move to column 4, and type the following (see fig. 6.24):

Contents	*PDATE*
Heading	*PURCH.*
	DATE

```
Options        Groups       Columns        Locate       Exit  07:38:49 am
                         ┌─────────────────────────────────────────────┐
                         │ Contents          CPHONE                     │
                         │ Heading           PHONE:NO.                   │
                         │ Width             8                          │
                         │ Decimal places                              │
                         │ Total this column                           │
                         └─────────────────────────────────────────────┘

       ┌─Report Format──────────────────────────────────────────────────┐
       │>>>>>>>CUSTOMER'S FIRST    PHONE    ─────────────────────────────│
       │       LAST NAME  NAME     NO.                                   │
       │                                                                 │
       ├─────────────────────────────────────────────────────────────── │
       │      XXXXXXXXXX XXXXXXX XXXXXXX                                  │
       └─────────────────────────────────────────────────────────────────┘
CREATE REPORT    <C:> SALES.FRM           Column: 3              Caps
       Position selection bar - ↑↓.  Select - ←┘.  Prev/Next column - PgUp/PgDn.
       Enter up to four lines of text to display above the indicated column.
```

Fig. 6.23. *Specifications for column 3 (CPHONE).*

```
Options        Groups       Columns        Locate       Exit  08:05:11 am
                         ┌─────────────────────────────────────────────┐
                         │ Contents          PDATE                      │
                         │ Heading           PURCH.:DATE                 │
                         │ Width             8                          │
                         │ Decimal places                              │
                         │ Total this column                           │
                         └─────────────────────────────────────────────┘

       ┌─Report Format──────────────────────────────────────────────────┐
       │>>>>>>>CUSTOMER'S FIRST    PHONE    PURCH.  ──────────────────────│
       │       LAST NAME  NAME     NO.      DATE                         │
       │                                                                 │
       ├─────────────────────────────────────────────────────────────── │
       │      XXXXXXXXXX XXXXXXX XXXXXXX mm/dd/yy                         │
       └─────────────────────────────────────────────────────────────────┘
CREATE REPORT    <C:> SALES.FRM           Column: 4              Caps
       Position selection bar - ↑↓.  Select - ←┘.  Prev/Next column - PgUp/PgDn.
       Enter up to four lines of text to display above the indicated column.
```

Fig. 6.24. *Specifications for column 4 (PDATE).*

Step 11: Specify column 5 for the purchase code. Press PgDn to move to column 5, and type the following (see fig. 6.25):

Contents	*PCODE*
Heading	*PURCH.*
	CODE

```
 Options          Groups         Columns        Locate       Exit  08:14:22 an
                         ┌─────────────────────────────────────────────────┐
                         │ Contents            PCODE                        │
                         │ Heading             PURCH.:CODE                   │
                         │ Width               6                            │
                         │ Decimal places                                   │
                         │ Total this column                                │
                         └─────────────────────────────────────────────────┘


   ┌─Report Format───────────────────────────────────────────────────────────
   │>>>>>>CUSTOMER'S FIRST    PHONE   PURCH.   PURCH. ------------------------
   │      LAST NAME   NAME    NO.     DATE     CODE
   │
   │
   ├───────────────────────────────────────────────────────────────────────
   │     XXXXXXXXXX XXXXXXX XXXXXXX mm/dd/yy XXXX

 CREATE REPORT    |<C:>|SALES.FRM              |Column: 5       ||        | Caps
       Position selection bar - ↑↓.  Select - ↵.  Prev/Next column - PgUp/PgDn.
       Enter up to four lines of text to display above the indicated column.
```

Fig. 6.25. *Specifications for column 5 (PCODE).*

Step 12: Specify column 6 for the purchase amount. Press PgDn to move to column 6, and type the following:

Contents	*PAMT*
Heading	*PURCH.*
	AMOUNT

Because PAMT is a numeric field, dBASE assumes that you want totals for it. Make sure that the **Width** is set wide enough to accommodate the total figure. Generally, it's a good idea to increase the width one position more than the length of the field. Move to the **Width** line, activate it, and enter *8*. Compare your screen with figure 6.26.

```
Options          Groups          Columns          Locate          Exit  08:25:22 am
                    ┌──────────────────────────────────────────────────────┐
                    │ Contents           PAMT                               │
                    │ Heading            PURCH.;AMOUNT                       │
                    │ Width              8                                  │
                    │ Decimal places     2                                  │
                    │ Total this column  Yes                                │
                    └──────────────────────────────────────────────────────┘



  ┌─Report Format─────────────────────────────────────────────────────────────┐
  │CUSTOMER'S FIRST   PHONE     PURCH.   PURCH. PURCH.   ──────────────────     │
  │LAST NAME  NAME    NO.       DATE     CODE   AMOUNT                          │
  │                                                                            │
  │                                                                            │
  │XXXXXXXXXX XXXXXXX XXXXXXX mm/dd/yy XXXX      ####.##                        │
  └────────────────────────────────────────────────────────────────────────────┘

CREATE REPORT   ‖<C:>‖SALES.FRM              ‖Column: 6      ‖        ‖    Caps
   Position selection bar – ↑↓.  Select – ←┘.  Prev/Next column – PgUp/PgDn.
   Enter a field or expression to display in the indicated report column.
```

Fig. 6.26. *Specifications for column 6 (PAMT).*

Step 13: Save the completed report format. Move the main menu selection bar to **Exit**, and press the Return key with the **Save** option highlighted.

Issuing and Modifying the Report Form File

The form file has now been entered, and you are ready to issue the report. The command syntax to issue the report consists of the verb (REPORT), the keyword FORM, the name of the form file (SALES), and (optionally) TO PRINT.

Step 1: Issue the report by typing *REPORT FORM SALES*. Figure 6.27 shows what appears on the screen.

```
. REPORT FORM SALES
     Page No.      1
     07/10/87
                           Sales at Saltwater Sally's
                             Hot Tubs and Pools

     CUSTOMER'S FIRST    PHONE    PURCH.   PURCH.    PURCH.
     LAST NAME  NAME     NO.      DATE     CODE      AMOUNT


     Blair      James    351-8923 06/15/85 H-27      4000.00
     Connors    Francis  975-0807 06/16/85 H-22      6600.35
     Jones      Thomas   971-9412 06/17/85 H-19      3523.17
     Aster      Sam      371-2341 06/18/85 P-11      9042.00
     Stevens    Harold   543-9050 06/19/85 H-19      3523.17
     Brown      Molly    876-1252 06/22/85 H-22      6600.35
     Clark      John     351-1118 06/25/85 P-14      8097.00
     Jones      Susan    370-4726 06/27/85 H-27      4000.00
     Abbott     William  875-2212 07/01/85 P-11      9042.00
     Hoffsmith  Barbara  542-1199 07/02/85 P-10       152.52
     *** Total ***
                                                    54580.56
```

Fig. 6.27. *The printed report.*

dBASE prints the correct page number and date, followed by the report title and field headings. The program also prints the selected fields for all 10 records.

The REPORT FORM command also has the flexibility to produce the report for only selected records in the database and to modify the appearance of the report in certain respects. See Lesson 8 for details.

NOTES

A report that has been created is not cast in stone. Getting the spacing of a report right is often a matter of trial and error. You easily can modify a report through the MODIFY REPORT command. This command allows changes of any type to the report form: changing an option or column specification, adding a new column, or deleting an existing column.

Step 2: Modify the SALES form file by increasing the widths of the phone number and purchase data fields. Type *MODIFY REPORT SALES*, and move the main menu selection bar to **Locate** by pressing L (see fig. 6.28). Move the submenu selection bar down to **CPHONE** and press Return.

You are now in the **Columns** submenu for column 3, able to change any of its settings.

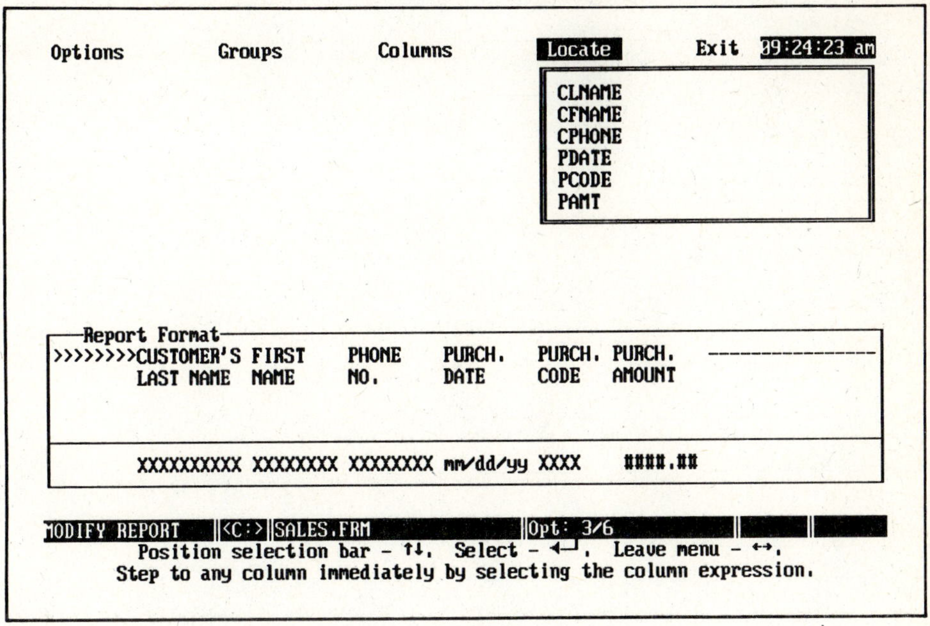

Fig. 6.28. *MODIFY REPORT screen, Locate submenu.*

Step 3: Change the width of the phone number column. Move the selection bar down to the **Width** line, and press Return. Type the new value of *10*, and close with another Return.

Step 4: Change the width of the purchase date column. Press PgDn to move to the next field, and change the **Width** of column 4 (PDATE) to *10*.

NOTES

Notice that the spacing between columns in the Report Format window changes to reflect the new column widths (see fig. 6.29).

```
 Options          Groups         Columns        Locate       Exit  09:28:45 am
                              ┌─────────────────────────────────────────┐
                              │ Contents            PDATE                │
                              │ Heading             PURCH.:DATE          │
                              │ Width               10                   │
                              │ Decimal places                          │
                              │ Total this column                       │
                              └─────────────────────────────────────────┘


 ┌─Report Format──────────────────────────────────────────────────────────┐
 │>>>>>>>>CUSTOMER'S FIRST    PHONE      PURCH.    PURCH. PURCH.  ───────────│
 │        LAST NAME  NAME     NO.        DATE      CODE   AMOUNT            │
 │                                                                         │
 │                                                                         │
 │        XXXXXXXXXX XXXXXXXX XXXXXXXX   mm/dd/yy  XXXX   ####.##          │
 └─────────────────────────────────────────────────────────────────────────┘
 MODIFY REPORT   ‖<C:>‖SALES.FRM              ‖Column: 4    ‖     ‖      ‖
       Position selection bar - ↑↓,  Select - ◄┘,  Prev/Next column - PgUp/PgDn.
              Enter the number of characters for the column width.
```

Fig. 6.29. *Modified report format.*

Step 5: Save the modified report form. Move to the **Exit** option on the main menu and, with **Save** highlighted, press Return.

Step 6: Run the modified report. Type *REPORT FORM SALES*. The screen will look as it does in figure 6.30.

```
. REPORT FORM SALES
        Page No.       1
        07/10/87
                               Sales at Saltwater Sally's
                                   Hot Tubs and Pools

        CUSTOMER'S  FIRST    PHONE      PURCH.    PURCH.    PURCH.
        LAST NAME   NAME     NO.        DATE      CODE      AMOUNT


        Blair       James    351-8923   06/15/85  H-27      4000.00
        Connors     Francis  975-0807   06/16/85  H-22      6600.35
        Jones       Thomas   971-9412   06/17/85  H-19      3523.17
        Aster       Sam      371-2341   06/18/85  P-11      9042.00
        Stevens     Harold   543-9850   06/19/85  H-19      3523.17
        Brown       Molly    876-1252   06/22/85  H-22      6600.35
        Clark       John     351-1118   06/25/85  P-14      8097.00
        Jones       Susan    370-4726   06/27/85  H-27      4000.00
        Abbott      William  875-2212   07/01/85  P-11      9042.00
        Hoffsmith   Barbara  542-1199   07/02/85  P-10       152.52
        *** Total ***

                                                           54580.56
```

Fig. 6.30. *Modified sales report.*

☐ SUMMARY OF CONCEPTS
PRESENTED IN LESSON 6

1. You design form files to output information in a polished format. After you design form files, you can save them for later use.

2. Label form files configure data into a mailing label format.

3. Report form files produce reports with page settings, headings, and page identifications.

4. To create a label form file, type CREATE LABEL and the name of the form. Modify the label form file with MODIFY LABEL.

5. To create a report form file, type CREATE REPORT and the name of the form. Modify the report form file by using MODIFY REPORT.

6. Issue the LABEL command by typing LABEL FORM and the form file name. You can add TO PRINT if a printer is available, and you can add SAMPLE to test the alignment.

7. Issue the REPORT command by typing REPORT FORM and the form file name. Adding TO PRINT is optional.

NOTES

■ LESSON 6
  EXERCISE

Generate labels according to specific conditions.

Step 1: Print labels for customers who purchased more than $2000 worth of materials. Type *LABEL FORM MX_CUSTL FOR PAMT > 2000.*

Step 2: Print labels for customers who purchased more than $9000 worth of materials. Type *LABEL FORM MX_CUSTL FOR PAMT > 9000.*

Step 3: Print labels for customers who are not residents of Atlanta. Type *LABEL FORM MX_CUSTL FOR CCITY <> "Atlanta".*

Direct the output to an available printer, and also experiment with the dBASE III Plus label adjustment option. Add *TO PRINT SAMPLE* to the LABEL FORM command.

NOTES

7

Indexing and Searching

Related sections in *dBASE III Plus Handbook*, 2nd Edition: Chapters 5 and 6.

Retrieval verbs present records on the screen in the order that they were entered into the database. Many situations, though, call for a different, more logical order: for instance, an alphabetical listing of customers or a ranking of purchases by amount.

Two dBASE III Plus commands are used to reorder records logically: SORT and INDEX. The SORT command produces a duplicate data file that differs from the original only in that it lists records in the sorted order. The original file is still maintained on disk. (For more information on the SORT command, refer to the *dBASE III Plus Handbook*, 2nd Edition.)

Although SORT does the job, INDEX is far more versatile. INDEX, unlike SORT, does not produce another data file. Instead, INDEX produces a special index file, or lookup file, that serves the same purpose as the index of a book. The *index file* is a reference that stores not the entire database but only the information necessary to locate the data in the desired order. An index file is therefore much smaller than the related data file.

In this lesson, you will learn these skills:

- To rearrange the order of the records with INDEX
- To search for a record using a search based on a key phrase

NOTES

Indexing a Database

The MX_SALES database shows the need for some type of indexing. The current order of presentation serves no real advantage. In this set of exercises, you will use the INDEX command to present records in a more logical order. (If MX_SALES is already the active database, omit Steps 1 and 2.)

Step 1: Type *DO QPREP* at the dot prompt. Select Lesson 7.

Step 2: Type *USE MX_SALES.*

Step 3: Type *LIST CLNAME,CFNAME* to see the original order. Figure 7.1 shows the result; the first and last names are extracted in no useful order.

```
. LIST CLNAME,CFNAME
Record#  CLNAME      CFNAME
      1  Blair       James
      2  Connors     Francis
      3  Jones       Thomas
      4  Aster       Sam
      5  Stevens     Harold
      6  Brown       Molly
      7  Clark       John
      8  Jones       Susan
      9  Abbott      William
     10  Hoffsmith   Barbara


Command Line      <C:> MX_SALES              Rec: EOF/10           Caps
            Enter a dBASE III PLUS command.
```

Fig. 7.1. *Records listed in original order.*

Step 4: Generate an index based on alphabetical order of the customers' last names. Write the ordering information to an index file named LNAME_OR (the last-name order index). Type *INDEX ON CLNAME TO LNAME_OR.* The screen displays

        100% indexed   10 Records indexed

NOTES

Step 5: Check your work. Type *LIST CLNAME,CFNAME*. Notice the record numbers (see fig. 7.2). dBASE retrieves records in the new order (alphabetical by last name) rather than in the original order.

```
. LIST CLNAME,CFNAME
Record#  CLNAME     CFNAME
     9   Abbott     William
     4   Aster      Sam
     1   Blair      James
     6   Brown      Molly
     7   Clark      John
     2   Connors    Francis
    10   Hoffsmith  Barbara
     3   Jones      Thomas
     8   Jones      Susan
     5   Stevens    Harold
```

Command Line ||<C:>||MX_SALES ||Rec: EOF/10 || || Caps

Enter a dBASE III PLUS command.

Fig. 7.2. *Records listed in alphabetical order by last name.*

Step 6: Suppress the index and check your work. Type

CLOSE INDEX
LIST CLNAME,CFNAME

The CLOSE INDEX command deactivates the index. The index file is still on the disk drive, but it is no longer active. Your screen once again should display the records in original order as shown in figure 7.1.

Using the INDEX command creates an index. Once it has been created, an index does not have to be created again. However, it does have to be linked to the database before it can affect the order of presentation. Linking is done with the SET INDEX TO command. Use this command followed by the index file name whenever the index order is needed during a work session or whenever the index must be updated. The only time the SET INDEX TO command is not needed is during the work session when the index file is created.

NOTES

Step 7: Reactivate the existing index. Type these commands:

> SET INDEX TO LNAME_OR
> LIST CLNAME,CFNAME

You have activated the index LNAME_OR. Your screen again should display the records in alphabetical order by last name as shown in figure 7.2. Type *CLOSE INDEX* to suppress the index.

Notice the two records with the last name of Jones. Thomas Jones is listed before Susan Jones. When you have duplicate last names, you can use the first name as a secondary index key and alphabetize according to last name and then first name.

Step 8: Write the index to CLFNA_OR (customer's last and first name order). Type *INDEX ON CLNAME + CFNAME TO CLFNA_OR*. The screen displays

    100% indexed   10 Records indexed

Step 9: Check your work by typing *LIST CLNAME,CFNAME*. The two Jones listings are now in the correct order (see fig. 7.3).

```
. LIST CLNAME,CFNAME
Record#  CLNAME    CFNAME
      9  Abbott    William
      4  Aster     Sam
      1  Blair     James
      6  Brown     Molly
      7  Clark     John
      2  Connors   Francis
     10  Hoffsmith Barbara
      8  Jones     Susan
      3  Jones     Thomas
      5  Stevens   Harold

Command Line    ||<C:>||MX_SALES              ||Rec: EOF/10      ||      || Caps

          Enter a dBASE III PLUS command.
```

Fig. 7.3. *The two Jones listings in alphabetically order by first name.*

NOTES

Step 10: Arrange the records by the size of the purchase amount. Type *INDEX ON PAMT TO AMT_OR.* The screen displays

100% indexed   10 Records indexed

Step 11: Check your work by typing *LIST CLNAME,PAMT.* The records are now arranged by purchase amount, from smallest to largest (see fig. 7.4).

```
. LIST CLNAME,PAMT
Record#  CLNAME      PAMT
    10   Hoffsmith   152.52
     3   Jones      3523.17
     5   Stevens    3523.17
     1   Blair      4000.00
     8   Jones      4000.00
     2   Connors    6600.35
     6   Brown      6600.35
     7   Clark      8097.00
     4   Aster      9042.00
     9   Abbott     9042.00
```

Command Line	‖<C:>‖MX_SALES	‖Rec: EOF/10	‖	‖ Caps

Enter a dBASE III PLUS command.

Fig. 7.4. *Records listed by purchase amount in ascending order.*

Step 12: Reverse the payment index. Type *INDEX ON - PAMT TO AMT1_OR.* The screen displays the message

100% indexed   10 Records indexed

Step 13: Check your work. Type *LIST CLNAME,PAMT.* Compare your screen to figure 7.5.

Inserting the minus sign in the INDEX command reverses the order of the numerical index generated. The record order is now arranged from the largest payment to the smallest payment. Reversed, or descending, indexes are not possible with character fields.

```
. LIST CLNAME,PAMT
Record#  CLNAME       PAMT
      4  Aster      9042.00
      9  Abbott     9042.00
      7  Clark      8097.00
      2  Connors    6600.35
      6  Brown      6600.35
      1  Blair      4000.00
      8  Jones      4000.00
      3  Jones      3523.17
      5  Stevens    3523.17
     10  Hoffsmith   152.52
```

```
Command Line    |<C:>|MX_SALES              |Rec: EOF/10       |    | Caps
                   Enter a dBASE III PLUS command.
```

Fig. 7.5. *Records listed by purchase amount in descending order.*

You can routinely activate and deactivate several indexes. Therefore, you sometimes might forget which index is currently active. dBASE provides a method that lets you view the name of the active index and the selected order.

Step 14: Determine the active index. Type *DISPLAY STATUS*. Your screen should display the currently active data file, index file, and memo file information (see fig. 7.6).

```
. DISPLAY STATUS

Currently Selected Database:
Select area: 1, Database in Use: C:MX_SALES.dbf    Alias: MX_SALES
     Master index file:  C:AMT1_OR.ndx  Key: -PAMT
            Memo file:   C:MX_SALES.dbt

File search path:
Default disk drive: C:
Print destination:  PRN:
Margin =      0
Current work area =    1

Press any key to continue...
Command Line    |<C:>|MX_SALES           |Rec: 4/10        |         | Caps
         Enter a dBASE III PLUS command.
```

Fig. 7.6. *File information from DISPLAY STATUS.*

Follow the screen directions; press any key to continue. The current set conditions (ON or OFF) will appear as well as the current assignments of the function keys (see fig. 7.7).

Another command, DIR, lists all the existing database files in the directory. To search for the index files, use DIR and the specification *.NDX. NDX is the file extension that dBASE assigns an index file, and the asterisk stands for any file name. Together with the DIR command, they list all the index files.

Step 15: Check the directory for index files. Type *DIR *.NDX*. A list of the index files in your directory appears on the screen (see fig. 7.8).

```
ALTERNATE  - OFF    DELETED    - OFF    FIXED      - OFF    SAFETY      - ON
BELL       - OFF    DELIMITERS - OFF    HEADING    - ON     SCOREBOARD  - ON
CARRY      - OFF    DEVICE     - SCRN   HELP       - ON     STATUS      - ON
CATALOG    - OFF    DOHISTORY  - OFF    HISTORY    - ON     STEP        - OFF
CENTURY    - OFF    ECHO       - OFF    INTENSITY  - ON     TALK        - ON
CONFIRM    - OFF    ESCAPE     - ON     MENU       - ON     TITLE       - ON
CONSOLE    - ON     EXACT      - OFF    PRINT      - OFF    UNIQUE      - OFF
DEBUG      - OFF    FIELDS     - OFF

Programmable function keys:
F2  - assist;
F3  - list;
F4  - dir;
F5  - display structure;
F6  - display status;
F7  - display memory;
F8  - display;
F9  - append;
F10 - edit;
.
```

| Command Line | <C:> | MX_SALES | Rec: 4/10 | | Caps |

```
       Enter a dBASE III PLUS command.
```

Fig. 7.7. *Condition settings and function key assignments from DISPLAY STATUS.*

```
. DIR *.NDX
LNAME_OR.NDX        CLFNA_OR.NDX        AMT_OR.NDX          AMT1_OR.NDX

    4096 bytes in     4 files.
3538944 bytes remaining on drive.
.
```

| Command Line | <C:> | MX_SALES | Rec: 4/10 | | Caps |

```
       Enter a dBASE III PLUS command.
```

Fig. 7.8. *Directory listing of index files.*

Indexes often become corrupted. A major source of corruption is power fluctuation. Errors are reported, or records that you *know* exist are not displayed. If you have any doubts about an index's integrity, regenerate or rebuild the index. To rebuild the current index, use the REINDEX command.

> ***Step 16:*** REINDEX the file. Type the following commands:
>
>> SET INDEX TO CLFNA_OR
>> REINDEX
>
> The following message appears:
>
>> `Rebuilding index - B:CLFNA_OR.ndx`
>>
>> `100% indexed`   `10 Records indexed`

Another way you may corrupt an index is by adding records to a data file while the index is deactivated. If 10 purchases were added now, the CLFNA_OR index would reorganize the names correctly, because CLFNA_OR is activated. However, the payment index, AMT1_OR, would not reflect the new additions.

One way around this difficulty is to set multiple indexes with a single SET INDEX TO command. Just list all the indexes after the command and separate them with commas. All the indexes will be updated as changes are made to the database, but only the first named index—the *master index*—controls the order of presentation.

> **Que Tip:** If you are ever in doubt about the correct operation of an index, index the data file again.

> ***Step 17:*** Deactivate the current index by typing *CLOSE INDEX*. The dot prompt appears.

Searching a Database

A formal report can include more information than what you need to answer a specific question. Often just a single record is enough. To retrieve that one record, you have to locate it and then display it. Both the FIND and LOCATE commands require a search condition, but they differ in how that search condition is written. The FIND command searches an index file (FIND is discussed in the next section). The LOCATE command searches the database on a record-by-record basis and can be used with or without an index. The following steps illustrate the use of the LOCATE command.

> ***Step 1:*** LOCATE a record for 2 items purchased. Type *LOCATE FOR PNO = 2.* The screen displays
>
>> `Record =      10`

NOTES

LOCATE starts at the top of the database and checks each record, one after another, for one whose PNO field has the value 2. When it finds the first such record, the record pointer marks it as the current record, and LOCATE terminates.

Step 2: Check your work by typing *DISPLAY CLNAME,PNO*. The screen displays the record that meets the condition:

```
Record# CLNAME              PNO
     1Ø Hoffsmith             2
```

Step 3: LOCATE with a character expression. Search for the first purchase for which Lucy Murray (initials LEM) was the salesperson. Type *LOCATE FOR ESP = "LEM"*. dBASE displays the message

```
Record =      2
```

Step 4: Check your work by typing *DISPLAY CLNAME,ESP*. The screen displays the record that meets the condition:

```
Record# CLNAME              ESP
      2 Connors              LEM
```

Because Lucy Murray made at least one other sale, other records also meet the condition. LOCATE, however, searches only for the first record. Another command, CONTINUE, continues the search.

Step 5: Continue the search by typing *CONTINUE*. The screen displays

```
Record =      6
```

Step 6: Check your work by typing *DISPLAY CLNAME,ESP*. The screen displays the next record that meets the condition:

```
Record# CLNAME              ESP
      6 Brown                LEM
```

Step 7: Continue the search. Type *CONTINUE*. dBASE III Plus displays this message:

```
Record =      8
```

Step 8: Check your work by typing *DISPLAY CLNAME,ESP*. The screen displays the next record that meets the condition:

```
Record# CLNAME              ESP
      8 Jones                LEM
```

Step 9: Continue to search. Type *CONTINUE*. The screen displays the message End of LOCATE scope.

NOTES

Using FIND for an Instant Search

The FIND command offers two significant advantages over LOCATE. First, FIND works faster because it goes to a record directly, without doing a sequential search of each record in the database. FIND does this by searching an index file for the location of the record. A second advantage is that the search condition can be abbreviated to just the data value. You do not have to give the field name.

> *Step 1:* Try to find Mr. Clark's purchase record. Type *FIND Clark.* Figure 7.9 shows the resulting error message.

```
. FIND Clark
Database is not indexed.
    ?
FIND Clark
Command Line      <C:> MX_SALES                 Rec: 9/10
                       Do you want some help? (Y/N)
                       Enter a dBASE III PLUS command.
```

Fig. 7.9. *Result of FIND without an active index.*

The data file must be indexed on the field containing the search phrase. Before you use the FIND command, you must activate the index by the last name and first name fields, which you established earlier.

> *Step 2:* Activate the index. Type *SET INDEX TO CLFNA_OR.*

> *Step 3:* Issue the FIND command on the indexed database. Type *FIND Clark.* Panel four of the status bar displays Rec: 7/10, and the dot prompt appears.

NOTES

Step 4: Check your work by typing *DISPLAY CLNAME*. The screen displays the record that meets the condition:

```
Record# CLNAME
      7 Clark
```

The response is nearly instantaneous, whether the data file is large or small.

Step 5: FIND with uppercase and lowercase phrases. Type *FIND JONES*. The screen displays the message No find.

The FIND command works only if the phrases match, letter by letter. That is, FIND is case sensitive. Type the search phrase in mixed format (first letter capitalized and the rest lowercase).

Step 6: Enter a search phrase in mixed case. Type *FIND Jones*. The record pointer moves to record 8, and the dot prompt appears.

Step 7: Check your work by typing *DISPLAY CLNAME,CFNAME*. dBASE displays the first record that meets the condition:

```
Record# CLNAME              CFNAME
      8 Jones               Susan
```

No equivalent exists for CONTINUE with the FIND command, nor is such an equivalent necessary to find the next occurrence of Jones. Because the index is generated by last name, any other Jones must be "sorted" in sequence just after the first Jones. Use the SKIP command to move the record pointer to the next Jones (see Lesson 2).

Step 8: Skip through an indexed database. Type *SKIP*. When the dot prompt appears, type *DISPLAY CLNAME,CFNAME*. The screen displays the next Jones in the alphabetical list—Thomas Jones:

```
Record# CLNAME              CFNAME
      3 Jones               Thomas
```

SUMMARY OF CONCEPTS
PRESENTED IN LESSON 7

1. Unless you specify otherwise, records are retrieved in the original order in which they were entered.

2. The INDEX command generates a file that looks up each record in some logical order from a larger data file.

3. You generate an index by issuing the INDEX ON command, the name of the field or fields that control the order, TO, and the name of the index file.

4. Break ties by using more than one field in the index expression: CLNAME + CFNAME.

5. Use the INDEX command to sort numeric fields. Reverse the sort order by using a minus sign with INDEX.

6. Use DISPLAY STATUS often to report the active data and index files.

7. DIR lists the available database files. DIR *.NDX lists all the index files.

8. REINDEX regenerates the active index file.

9. LOCATE searches the data file, one record at a time, for the first record that matches the search condition.

10. FIND with a search condition instantly retrieves the first record that has a field containing the condition.

11. LOCATE can be used on any data file but can be relatively slow for large data files. FIND works more quickly but requires that the data file be indexed on the same field that you want to use FIND on. For instance, you must INDEX on the last name field if you want to FIND last names.

LESSON 7
EXERCISE

Practice organizing and searching the accounts payable data file.

Step 1: Open the database by typing *USE SSBILLS*.

Step 2: Organize by the amount Saltwater Sally's owes its vendors. Order (INDEX) by the amount field (VAMT), and save the ordering information to an index file named AMT_OR (ordered by amount). Type *INDEX ON VAMT TO AMT_OR*. Check your work by typing *LIST VNAME,VAMT*.

Step 3: Reverse the order of listing by amount. Insert a minus sign in the INDEX command to reverse the numeric sort order. Type *INDEX ON - VAMT TO OAMT_OR*. Check the work again with the LIST command.

Step 4: Close the index by typing *CLOSE INDEX*. Check your work. The file lists in the original sort order.

Step 5: Search record by record for large amounts (amounts larger than $1000). Type *LOCATE FOR VAMT > 1000*. If a record is found, type *CONTINUE* to search again. Use CONTINUE until dBASE announces that all records have been searched.

Step 6: Index on the company name field (VNAME) and save to another index file, NAME_OR (name order). Type *INDEX ON VNAME TO NAME_OR*. Check your work by typing *LIST VNAME,VATTN*.

Step 7: Check the current data and index files. Type *DISPLAY STATUS*. Read each line carefully.

NOTES

8

Producing Polished Products

Related sections in *dBASE III Plus Handbook*, 2nd Edition: Chapters 2 and 8.

The REPORT command can work with both an optional scope and a search condition. Both greatly expand the power of dBASE III Plus to provide focused information.

Reports have several other useful features. In this lesson, you will use these features to develop management reports for Saltwater Sally's information system.

In this lesson, you will

- Issue conditional reports
- Create other reports
- Issue reports with subtotals
- Issue reports from memo fields

Conditional Reports

Follow these steps to first prepare your files for work and then to issue a conditional report. (If MX_SALES is already the active database, omit Steps 1 and 2.)

Step 1: Type *DO QPREP* at the dot prompt. Select Lesson 8.

Step 2: Type *USE MX_SALES*. The screen displays the dot prompt.

NOTES

Step 3: Type *REPORT FORM SALES* to view the entire Sales Report you created in Lesson 6.

Step 4: Limit the report. Type *REPORT FORM SALES FOR CCITY = 'Atlanta'.* Figure 8.1 shows the result.

```
. REPORT FORM SALES FOR CCITY = 'Atlanta'
         Page No.      1
         07/10/87
                                Sales at Saltwater Sally's
                                  Hot Tubs and Pools

         CUSTOMER'S FIRST    PHONE      PURCH.     PURCH.    PURCH.
         LAST NAME  NAME     NO.        DATE       CODE      AMOUNT


           Blair      James    351-8923   06/15/85   H-27     4000.00
           Aster      Sam      371-2341   06/18/85   P-11     9042.00
           Stevens    Harold   543-9858   06/19/85   H-19     3523.17
           Clark      John     351-1118   06/25/85   P-14     8097.00
         *** Total ***

                                                            24662.17
```

Fig. 8.1. *A conditional report listing customers in Atlanta.*

Because you specified CCITY = 'Atlanta', dBASE printed only the names of the customers who reside in Atlanta. A total of four purchases were summed.

Conditional expressions can be developed for numeric, character, logical, and date fields. The conditional field does not have to be printed in the report in order to control selection of the records to be reported.

Step 5: Do conditional reporting with an unreported field. Type *REPORT FORM SALES FOR ESP = 'LEM'.* Figure 8.2 shows what appears on the screen.

Any condition that can be applied to other retrieval commands (LIST, DISPLAY ALL) can be applied to REPORT. You can use one report form to extract data under many different conditions.

```
. REPORT FORM SALES FOR ESP ='LEM'
       Page No,     1
       07/10/87
                               Sales at Saltwater Sally's
                                  Hot Tubs and Pools

       CUSTOMER'S FIRST      PHONE       PURCH,     PURCH,     PURCH,
       LAST NAME  NAME       NO,         DATE       CODE       AMOUNT


       Connors    Francis    975-0807    06/16/85   H-22        6600,35
       Brown      Molly      876-1252    06/22/85   H-22        6600,35
       Jones      Susan      370-4726    06/27/85   H-27        4000,00
       *** Total ***
                                                              17200,70
```

Fig. 8.2. *A conditional report listing sales made by Lucy Murray.*

A report that does not display its conditions presents a problem. Look at figure 8.2. Under what conditions was the REPORT command issued? Does the report identify the salesperson? If you looked at this report six months from now, how could you tell what the report represents?

dBASE III Plus's HEADING option comes in handy here. If you add a supplementary heading when you issue the report, the heading clarifies the terms upon which the report was issued.

Step 6: Use HEADING with a conditional report. Specify that the report should print only the sales made by Lucy Murray. Type *REPORT FORM SALES FOR ESP ='LEM' HEADING "Lucy Murray's Sales"*. Figure 8.3 shows the result.

```
. REPORT FORM SALES FOR ESP ='LEM' HEADING "Lucy Murray's Sales"
       Page No.      1             Lucy Murray's Sales
       07/18/87
                             Sales at Saltwater Sally's
                               Hot Tubs and Pools

       CUSTOMER'S FIRST    PHONE      PURCH.    PURCH.    PURCH.
       LAST NAME  NAME     NO.        DATE      CODE      AMOUNT


       Connors    Francis  975-8807   06/16/85  H-22      6600.35
       Brown      Molly    876-1252   06/22/85  H-22      6600.35
       Jones      Susan    370-4726   06/27/85  H-27      4000.00
       *** Total ***
                                                          17200.70
```

Fig. 8.3. *Conditional report with heading added.*

The condition upon which the report was printed is now evident. Never forget to use the HEADING feature when you report only a portion of your data file.

NOTES

Other Reports

Different forms can select different data from the same database. Saltwater Sally's sales information system requires at least two other reports: a detailed financial report and a listing of the customer memos.

The Detailed Financial Report

The next report you will create provides the financial details of the sales, stating clearly the amount paid, the tax paid, and the commission. The report form will be called SALEFIN. To create and build the form, you will use the same method you used to build the general sales form.

Step 1: Type *CREATE REPORT SALEFIN* to enter the CREATE REPORT mode. You will see the main menu with the **Options** submenu.

Step 2: Enter the report title and options as shown in figure 8.4.

```
┌──────────────────────────────────────────────────────────────────────┐
│                                                                        │
│  ▐Options▌      Groups       Columns        Locate      Exit ▐11:56:55 am▌│
│  ┌─────────────────────────────┐                                       │
│  │ Page title              ▐    │                                       │
│  │ Page width (positions)  80   │  ┌──────────────────────────────┐    │
│  │ Left margin              8   │  │SALTWATER SALLY'S SALES SYSTEM │    │
│  │ Right margin             0   │  │DETAILED FINANCIAL REPORT      │    │
│  │ Lines per page          55   │  │                              │    │
│  │ Double space report     No   │  └──────────────────────────────┘    │
│  │ Page eject before printing Yes│                                       │
│  │ Page eject after printing  No │                                       │
│  │ Plain page              No   │                                       │
│  └─────────────────────────────┘                                       │
│                                                                        │
│  ┌──────────────┬─────────────────┬────────────────────┬─────────────┐ │
│  │ CURSOR <── ──>│ Delete char: Del│ Insert column: ^N  │ Insert:  Ins│ │
│  │ Char:   ← →   │ Delete word:  ^T│ Report format: F1  │ Zoom in: ^PgDn│ │
│  │ Word: Home End│ Delete column:^U│ Abandon:     Esc   │ Zoom out:^PgUp│ │
│  └──────────────┴─────────────────┴────────────────────┴─────────────┘ │
│  ▐CREATE REPORT▌  ▐<C:>▌SALEFIN.FRM      ▐Opt: 1/9▌      ▐Ins▌    ▐Caps▌│
└──────────────────────────────────────────────────────────────────────┘
```

Fig. 8.4. *Title and options for SALEFIN report.*

NOTES

Step 3: Skip the **Groups** option. Move the selection bar directly to the **Columns** option.

Step 4: Add column contents and column headers. Add the report columns according to the specifications in table 8.1. Each column number is filled out on a separate screen. When you finish entering each field, PgDn to the next screen. Note that dBASE enters a default width. Override the widths as specified. Save the form by moving to **Exit** and pressing Return on the **Save** option.

The completed report form will look like figure 8.5.

```
  Options          Groups        Columns          Locate        ┌─Exit─┐ 11:36:57
                                                                 │ Save    │
                                                                 │ Abandon │
                                                                 └─────────┘








  ┌─Report Format─────────────────────────────────────────────────────────────
  │>>>>>>>CUSTOMER'S PURCH.    PURCH NO. AMT       TAX       PD IN SLS SALES  ----
  │       LAST NAME  DATE      CODE  === PAID      PAID      FULL? PER COMM
  │       ========= ====       ====      ====      ====      ===== === ====
  ├──────────────────────────────────────────────────────────────────────────
  │       XXXXXXXXXX mm/dd/yy XXXX     #  ####.## ###.## .L.   XXX ####.##

  ┌CREATE REPORT ──┤<C:>│SALEFIN.FRM            │Opt: 1/2          │Ins   │ Caps
            Position selection bar - ↑↓,  Select - ◄┘,  Leave menu - ↔,
                               Exit and save changes.
```

Fig. 8.5. *Completed report form for SALEFIN report.*

Step 5: Check your work by typing *REPORT FORM SALEFIN.* Figure 8.6 shows the resulting report.

The report form has been built and saved. One more modification is desired: to report subtotals of the report based on each salesperson's individual performance. To accomplish this task, use the **Groups** option in MODIFY REPORT mode.

Table 8.1
Data for SALEFIN Report Form

Column Number	Column Contents	Column Header	Width	Total # Decimals	(Y/N)
1	CLNAME	CUSTOMER'S LAST NAME =========	10		
2	PDATE	PURCH. DATE ====	8		
3	PCODE	PURCH CODE ====	5		
4	PNO	NO. ===	4	0	Y
5	PAMT	AMT PAID ====	8	2	Y
6	PTAX	TAX PAID ====	7	2	Y
7	PPIF	PD IN FULL? =====	5		
8	ESP	SLS PER ===	3		
9	ECOMM	SALES COMM ====	8	2	Y

```
. REPORT FORM SALEFIN
      Page No.    1
      07/10/87
                              SALTWATER SALLY'S SALES SYSTEM
                              DETAILED FINANCIAL REPORT

      CUSTOMER'S PURCH.   PURCH   NO.      AMT      TAX PD IN SLS      SALES
      LAST NAME  DATE     CODE    ===      PAID     PAID FULL? PER     COMM
      ========= ====      ====    ===      ====     ==== ===== ===     ====


      Blair      06/15/85 H-27     1    4000.00   200.00  .T.  DWK    1000.00
      Connors    06/16/85 H-22     1    6600.35   330.02  .T.  LEM    2310.12
      Jones      06/17/85 H-19     1    3523.17   176.16  .T.  DWK     951.26
      Aster      06/18/85 P-11     1    9042.00   452.10  .F.  FSM    3164.70
      Stevens    06/19/85 H-19     1    3523.17   176.16  .F.  FSM     951.26
      Brown      06/22/85 H-22     1    6600.35   330.02  .F.  LEM    2310.12
      Clark      06/25/85 P-14     1    8097.00   404.85  .F.  DWK    2833.95
      Jones      06/27/85 H-27     1    4000.00   200.00  .T.  LEM    1000.00
      Abbott     07/01/85 P-11     1    9042.00   452.10  .T.  FSM    3164.70
      Hoffsmith  07/02/85 P-10     2     152.52     7.63  .T.  DWK      41.18
      *** Total ***
                                  11 54580.56 2729.04             17887.29
```

Fig. 8.6. *The SALEFIN report.*

Step 6: Modify the report. Type *MODIFY REPORT SALEFIN* and press G. At the **Group on expression** line in the **Groups** submenu (see fig. 8.7), enter *ESP*, the field upon which to break the report into groups. Enter the **Group heading** as illustrated in the figure. Save the modification by moving to **Exit** and pressing Return on the **Save** option.

Step 7: Check your work. Do not use the TO PRINT option unless you have lots of paper. Type *REPORT FORM SALEFIN*. Figure 8.8 shows a printout of the modified SALEFIN report.

What happened? The report breaks every time the value of ESP changes as the report record pointer moves from one record to the next. The ESP field changes from "DWK" to "LEM" to "FSM", according to the salesperson. REPORT issues a subtotal every time the salesperson changes from the one previously reported.

REPORT FORM cannot organize a file into groups; the INDEX command does. Use INDEX ON to organize the file by the salesperson's initials. All ESP values will be grouped together, and only three subtotals (one for each salesperson) will be reported.

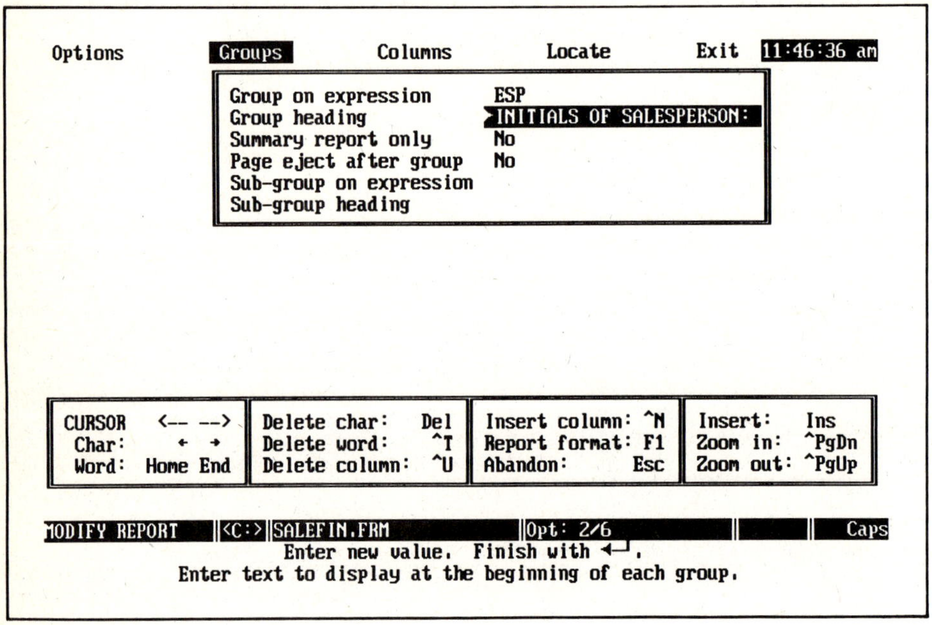

```
 Options          Groups          Columns          Locate          Exit  11:46:36 am
              ┌──────────────────────────────────────────────┐
              │ Group on expression      ESP                  │
              │ Group heading           ▶INITIALS OF SALESPERSON:│
              │ Summary report only      No                   │
              │ Page eject after group   No                   │
              │ Sub-group on expression                       │
              │ Sub-group heading                             │
              └──────────────────────────────────────────────┘



  ┌──────────────────────┬─────────────────────────┬────────────────────────┬──────────────────────┐
  │ CURSOR   <-- -->     │ Delete char:    Del     │ Insert column: ^N      │ Insert:     Ins      │
  │ Char:      ←   →     │ Delete word:    ^T      │ Report format: F1      │ Zoom in:   ^PgDn     │
  │ Word:  Home End      │ Delete column:  ^U      │ Abandon:       Esc     │ Zoom out:  ^PgUp     │
  └──────────────────────┴─────────────────────────┴────────────────────────┴──────────────────────┘

 ╞MODIFY REPORT ║<C:>║SALEFIN.FRM        ║Opt: 2/6        ║        ║ Caps
                    Enter new value.  Finish with ←┘.
              Enter text to display at the beginning of each group.
```

Fig. 8.7. *MODIFY REPORT screen, Groups option.*

```
                    SALTWATER SALLY'S SALES SYSTEM
                      DETAILED FINANCIAL REPORT

CUSTOMER'S  PURCH.    PURCH.   NO.      AMT     TAX PD IN SLS    SALES
LAST NAME   DATE      CODE     ===     PAID    PAID FULL? PER     COMM
=========   ====      ====     ===     ====    ==== ===== ===    ====


** INITIALS OF SALESPERSON: DWK
  Blair     06/15/85 H-27      1   4000.00  200.00 .T.   DWK  1080.00
** Subtotal **
                                1   4000.00  200.00            1080.00


** INITIALS OF SALESPERSON: LEM
  Connors   06/16/85 H-22      1   6600.35  330.02 .T.   LEM  2310.12
** Subtotal **
                                1   6600.35  330.02            2310.12


** INITIALS OF SALESPERSON: DWK
  Jones     06/17/85 H-19      1   3523.17  176.16 .T.   DWK   951.26
** Subtotal **
                                1   3523.17  176.16             951.26


** INITIALS OF SALESPERSON: FSM
  Aster     06/18/85 P-11      1   9042.00  452.10 .F.   FSM  3164.70
  Stevens   06/19/85 H-19      1   3523.17  176.16 .F.   FSM   951.26
** Subtotal **
                                2  12565.17  628.26            4115.96


** INITIALS OF SALESPERSON: LEM
  Brown     06/22/85 H-22      1   6600.35  330.02 .F.   LEM  2310.12
** Subtotal **
                                1   6600.35  330.02            2310.12


** INITIALS OF SALESPERSON: DWK
  Clark     06/25/85 P-14      1   8097.00  404.85 .F.   DWK  2833.95
** Subtotal **
                                1   8097.00  404.85            2833.95


** INITIALS OF SALESPERSON: LEM
  Jones     06/27/85 H-27      1   4000.00  200.00 .T.   LEM  1080.00
** Subtotal **
                                1   4000.00  200.00            1080.00


** INITIALS OF SALESPERSON: FSM
  Abbott    07/01/85 P-11      1   9042.00  452.10 .T.   FSM  3164.70
** Subtotal **
                                1   9042.00  452.10            3164.70


** INITIALS OF SALESPERSON: DWK
  Hoffsmith 07/02/85 P-10      2    152.52    7.63 .T.   DWK    41.18

** Subtotal **
                                2    152.52    7.63              41.18
*** Total ***
                               11  54580.56 2729.04           17887.29
```

Fig. 8.8. *Printout of the SALEFIN report with a grouping expression.*

NOTES

Step 8: Prepare to issue a subtotaled report. Type these commands:

INDEX ON ESP TO TEMP
REPORT FORM SALEFIN

The screen displays

100% indexed   10 Records indexed

The report is organized by salesperson into three subtotals (see fig. 8.9).

```
                    SALTWATER SALLY'S SALES SYSTEM
                     DETAILED FINANCIAL REPORT

CUSTOMER'S  PURCH.   PURCH   NO.      AMT      TAX PD IN SLS    SALES
LAST NAME   DATE     CODE    ===     PAID     PAID FULL? PER    COMM
=========   ====     ====    ===     ====     ==== ===== ===    ====


** INITIALS OF SALESPERSON: DWK
  Blair     06/15/85 H-27    1   4000.00   200.00 .T.    DWK   1080.00
  Jones     06/17/85 H-19    1   3523.17   176.16 .T.    DWK    951.26
  Clark     06/25/85 P-14    1   8097.00   404.85 .F.    DWK   2833.95
  Hoffsmith 07/02/85 P-10    2    152.52     7.63 .T.    DWK     41.18
** Subtotal **
                            5  15772.69   788.64               4906.39

** INITIALS OF SALESPERSON: FSM
  Aster     06/18/85 P-11    1   9042.00   452.10 .F.    FSM   3164.70
  Stevens   06/19/85 H-19    1   3523.17   176.16 .F.    FSM    951.26
  Abbott    07/01/85 P-11    1   9042.00   452.10 .T.    FSM   3164.70
** Subtotal **
                            3  21607.17  1080.36               7280.66

** INITIALS OF SALESPERSON: LEM
  Connors   06/16/85 H-22    1   6600.35   330.02 .T.    LEM   2310.12
  Brown     06/22/85 H-22    1   6600.35   330.02 .F.    LEM   2310.12
  Jones     06/27/85 H-27    1   4000.00   200.00 .T.    LEM   1080.00
** Subtotal **
                            3  17200.70   860.04               5700.24
*** Total ***
                           11  54580.56  2729.04              17887.29
```

Fig. 8.9. *The SALEFIN report indexed by salesperson into three subtotals.*

The financial report is now working properly. Three salespersons yield three subtotals, one for each. The grand total is at the bottom for all numeric fields for which a total was designated in the form.

Que Tip: To report subtotals by category, enter a field in the **Group on expression** line of your report and organize (index) the data file on the field before reporting.

NOTES

The Customer Notes Report

The next report you will create prints CNOTES, the memo field that retains the customers' observations or the entries of the salespersons. Like the other fields you have printed, memo fields can be printed with the REPORT FORM command.

Step 1: Establish the report form. Type *CREATE REPORT CUSTNOTE.* You will see the **Options** submenu.

Step 2: Enter the options shown in figure 8.10.

```
┌─────────────────────────────────────────────────────────────────────────┐
│ Options          Groups        Columns        Locate      Exit 08:29:42 am│
│ ┌─────────────────────────────────┐                                       │
│ │Page title                    ▐  │                                       │
│ │Page width (positions)     80    │ ┌───────────────────────────────────┐ │
│ │Left margin                 8    │ │SALTWATER SALLY'S SALES SYSTEM     │ │
│ │Right margin                0    │ │ADDITIONAL CUSTOMER NOTES          │ │
│ │Lines per page             55    │ │                                   │ │
│ │Double space report        No    │ │                                   │ │
│ │Page eject before printing Yes   │ └───────────────────────────────────┘ │
│ │Page eject after printing  No    │                                       │
│ │Plain page                 No    │                                       │
│ └─────────────────────────────────┘                                       │
│                                                                           │
│ ┌───────────────────┬─────────────────────┬─────────────────────┬────────┐│
│ │CURSOR   <-- -->   │Delete char:    Del  │Insert column: ^N    │Insert:    Ins││
│ │Char:     ← →      │Delete word:    ^T   │Report format: F1    │Zoom in:  ^PgDn││
│ │Word:  Home End    │Delete column:  ^U   │Abandon:       Esc   │Zoom out: ^PgUp││
│ └───────────────────┴─────────────────────┴─────────────────────┴────────┘│
│ CREATE REPORT    <C:> CUSTNOTE.FRM         Opt: 1/9                  Caps  │
│               Enter report title.  Exit - Ctrl-End.                       │
│   Enter up to four lines of text to be displayed at the top of each report page.│
└─────────────────────────────────────────────────────────────────────────┘
```

Fig. 8.10. *Title and options for CUSTNOTE report.*

Step 3: Skip the **Groups** option. Press C to move to the **Columns** option.

Step 4: Add column contents and column headers as indicated in table 8.2. The completed report form should look as it does in figure 8.11. Save the completed form by moving to **Exit** and pressing Return on the **Save** option.

```
   Options          Groups          Columns          Locate          Exit  08:40:37
                                                                    ┌──────────┐
                                                                    │ Save     │
                                                                    │ Abandon  │
                                                                    └──────────┘




   ┌─Report Format─────────────────────────────────────────────────────────────┐
   │>>>>>>>CUSTOMER'S FIRST     PURCH.    CUSTOMER                               │
   │       LAST NAME  NAME      DATE      NOTES                                  │
   │       ========= ====      ====      =====                                   │
   ├────────────────────────────────────────────────────────────────────────────┤
   │                                                                            │
   │       XXXXXXXXXX XXXXXXXX mm/dd/yy MMMMMMMMMMMMMMMMMMMMMMMMMMMMMMMMMMMMMMMM  │
   └────────────────────────────────────────────────────────────────────────────┘
   ╞═══════════════════════════════════════════════════════════════════════════╡
   │CREATE REPORT   ║<C:>║CUSTNOTE.FRM              Opt: 1/2              ║  Caps │
        Position selection bar - ↑↓,  Select - ↵,  Leave menu - ↔,
                        Exit and save changes.
```

Fig. 8.11. *Completed report form for CUSTNOTE report.*

Table 8.2
Data for CUSTNOTE Report Form

Column Contents	Column Header	Width	# Decimals	Total (Y/N)
CLNAME	CUSTOMER'S LAST NAME =========	10		
CFNAME	FIRST NAME ====	8		
PDATE	PURCH. DATE ====	8		
CNOTE	CUSTOMER NOTES =====	40		

Step 5: Check your work by typing *REPORT FORM CUSTNOTE.* Figure 8.12 shows the resulting report.

The customer notes report is now completed. All notes were wordwrapped into the report; none of the words were broken mid-word on a line. dBASE always breaks lines between words if possible.

```
                    SALTWATER SALLY'S SALES SYSTEM
                     ADDITIONAL CUSTOMER NOTES

CUSTOMER'S  FIRST     PURCH.    CUSTOMER
LAST NAME   NAME      DATE      NOTES
==========  ====      ====      =====


Blair       James     06/15/85  The customer agreed that our prices were
                                higher, but our tubs were of better
                                quality.
Jones       Thomas    06/17/85  Customer is purchasing a vacation home
                                in six months.  Give him a call about
                                sale at that time.
Clark       John      06/25/85  Customer wishes to install deck. Give
                                contractor a call.
Hoffsmith   Barbara   07/02/85  Customer remarked that the price for the
                                55 gallon drums of pool cleaner was the
                                lowest price in town.

Aster       Sam       06/18/85
Stevens     Harold    06/19/85
Abbott      William   07/01/85
Connors     Francis   06/16/85
Brown       Molly     06/22/85
Jones       Susan     06/27/85
```

Fig. 8.12. *The CUSTNOTE report.*

☐ SUMMARY OF CONCEPTS
PRESENTED IN LESSON 8

1. The REPORT command can take both a scope and a search condition. Reports can be generated over a designated number of records under a given condition.

2. You easily can develop other report forms to yield new reports.

3. To retrieve memo fields, use the REPORT command. You can stipulate any width. dBASE wordwraps the notes according to the width you specify.

4. The REPORT command has a subtotals feature. The report breaks and subtotals by category, but only if the file is indexed by the category.

LESSON 8
EXERCISE

You have constructed polished reports for sales information. Now create reports for the bills file.

Step 1: Open up the bills file by typing *USE SSBILLS.*

Step 2: Create a general report about the bills. Type *CREATE REPORT GENBILLS.* The **Options** submenu should appear.

Step 3: Enter the title and page options as shown in figure 8.13.

```
 Options          Groups        Columns        Locate       Exit  08:52:44
 ┌───────────────────────────────┐
 │ Page title                 ▌  │   ┌──────────────────────────────────┐
 │ Page width (positions)   80   │   │ BILLS OWED BY SALTWATER SALLY'S  │
 │ Left margin               8   │   │ GENERAL REPORT                   │
 │ Right margin              0   │   │                                  │
 │ Lines per page           55   │   │                                  │
 │ Double space report      No   │   └──────────────────────────────────┘
 │ Page eject before printing Yes│
 │ Page eject after printing  No │
 │ Plain page               No   │
 └───────────────────────────────┘

 ┌──────────────────┬──────────────────┬──────────────────┬──────────────────┐
 │ CURSOR  <-- -->  │ Delete char: Del │ Insert column: ^N│ Insert:    Ins   │
 │ Char:    ← →     │ Delete word: ^T  │ Report format: F1│ Zoom in:  ^PgDn  │
 │ Word: Home End   │ Delete column:^U │ Abandon:    Esc  │ Zoom out: ^PgUp  │
 └──────────────────┴──────────────────┴──────────────────┴──────────────────┘

 CREATE REPORT   ‖<C:>‖GENBILLS.FRM        Opt: 1/9               Caps
                  Enter report title.  Exit - Ctrl-End.
 Enter up to four lines of text to be displayed at the top of each report page.
```

Fig. 8.13. *Title and page options for GENBILLS report.*

Step 4: Move to the **Columns** option.

Step 5: Add column contents and column headers as shown in table 8.3, and save the form.

Step 6: Check your work. Type *REPORT FORM GENBILLS.* Compare your screen to figure 8.14.

Table 8.3
Data for GENBILLS Report Form

Column Contents	Column Header	Width	# Decimals	Total (Y/N)
VNAME	VENDOR NAME ======	10		
VATTN	DIRECT TO: ======	15		
VPHONE	TELE- PHONE =====	8		
VBILLNO	BILL NO. ====	5	0	N
DATEIN	DATE REC. ====	8		
DATEDUE	DATE DUE ====	8		
VAMT	AMOUNT OF BILL =======	10	2	Y
VPIF	BILL PAID? =====	5		

```
                    BILLS OWED BY SALTWATER SALLYS
                         GENERAL REPORT
VENDOR          DIRECT          TELE-     BILL DATE    DATE          AMOUNT BILL
NAME            TO:             PHONE     NO.  REC.    DUE          OF BILL PAID?
======          ======          =====     ==== ====    ====         ======= =====

Aquarius        Mr. James Smith 283-2123   323 06/19/85 07/19/85    1923.20 .F.
Pool Supp.
Tidewater       Ms. C. Maid     593-9200  3453 06/29/85 07/29/85    1284.32 .F.
Tillie's
Acme            Mr. Sam Lyons   932-1253   121 07/02/85 08/01/85     842.23 .F.
Chlorine
Southern        Business Office 953-4243  2131 07/03/85 08/02/85     112.00 .F.
Bell
Trust           Mr. Roger Bix   312-3292     3 07/05/85 08/04/85     634.00 .F.
Realty Co.
*** Total ***
                                                                    4795.75
```

Fig. 8.14. *The GENBILLS report.*

NOTES

9

Automation (or Let dBASE Do the Typing)

Related sections in *dBASE III Plus Handbook*, 2nd Edition: Chapters 5, 7, 9, and 11.

In this lesson, you will learn about automating dBASE commands. dBASE III Plus can save and reissue the repetitive commands that you type at the keyboard, sparing you the work of extra keystrokes. In this lesson, you will learn:

- How to write and set a filter

- How to save a filter in a query file

- How to write and save a field list in a view file

- How to use MODIFY COMMAND to build program files

- How to build programs that perform repetitive operations, interact with the operator, and branch to different actions at the user's request

- How to create memory variables in programs

- How to manage screen display within a program

- How to use dBASE III Plus date functions

NOTES

Automating Commands

Some keyboard commands can be "finger breakers." Look at some commands you typed in the previous lessons:

    LIST CLNAME,PAMT,PNO,"SELLING PRICE PER ITEM",PAMT/PNO
    LIST ALL CLNAME,PAMT FOR PAMT/PNO = (152.52 / 2)
    CHANGE ALL FIELDS CSTREET,CCITY,CST,CZIP,PINDATE
    SUM PAMT,PTAX,PAMT + PTAX,ECOMM
    REPORT FORM SALES FOR ESP ='LEM' HEADING "Lucy Murray's
      Sales"

dBASE III Plus offers methods that can save your fingers the tedium of retyping the same commands and qualifications over and over. These methods include building *global qualifications*, such as field lists and search conditions, that affect not a single command but all retrieval commands. A global field list is set up with the command SET FIELDS TO; a global search condition is set up with the command SET FILTER TO.

Another general labor-saving method is to write a *program*, or *command file*. A program consists of a series of dBASE commands that can be executed together as a set. The program is written using the dBASE III Plus word processor, saved to a program file, and executed with the DO command plus the name of the program file.

Programs save you time keying in commands for standard or routine applications that you otherwise would have to repeat each time the application ran. For instance, if every month you must total and report commissions for each salesperson, a program can save you time retyping all the commands, and it also can assure that the application is done consistently each time it runs. Programs also offer you the flexibility to develop applications that can be operated by someone with little direct knowledge of dBASE III Plus.

In this lesson you will look first at how to set global qualifications and then how to write a simple program to automate the calculation of the salesperson's performance that you detailed in Lesson 5.

Setting a Field List

Assume that you are running a reporting project to compare different purchase transactions. The project will require numerous retrievals and reports from the database, but only for those fields that summarize the purchase data. With the SET FIELDS TO command, you can focus on just the fields you need.

Step 1: Type *DO QPREP*. Select Lesson 9.

Step 2: Type *USE MX_SALES*.

NOTES

Step 3: Set a field list. Type *SET FIELDS TO PDATE,PINDATE,PCODE,PNO,PAMT,PTAX,PPIF* and press Return.

Step 4: Display with a field list set. Type *DISPLAY ALL* (see fig. 9.1). Note that without specifying a field list with DISPLAY, only the purchase information fields are presented. All other fields in the database are hidden from view.

```
. DISPLAY ALL
Record#  PDATE     PINDATE   PCODE PNO    PAMT   PTAX PPIF
      1  06/15/85  06/23/85  H-27   1  4000.00 200.00 .T.
      2  06/16/85  06/25/85  H-22   1  6600.35 330.02 .T.
      3  06/17/85  06/26/85  H-19   1  3523.17 176.16 .T.
      4  06/18/85  06/26/85  P-11   1  9042.00 452.10 .F.
      5  06/19/85  06/27/85  H-19   1  3523.17 176.16 .F.
      6  06/22/85  06/27/85  H-22   1  6600.35 330.02 .F.
      7  06/25/85  06/27/85  P-14   1  8097.00 404.85 .F.
      8  06/27/85  06/28/85  H-27   1  4000.00 200.00 .T.
      9  07/01/85  07/06/85  P-11   1  9042.00 452.10 .T.
     10  07/02/85  07/02/85  P-10   2   152.52   7.63 .T.

Command Line   ‖<C:>‖MX_SALES              Rec: EOF/10   ‖       Caps

                Enter a dBASE III PLUS command.
```

Fig. 9.1. *Displaying records with a field list set.*

Step 5: List the structure of the database with fields set. Type *LIST STRUCTURE*. Notice that the set fields are marked with a greater-than sign (>) (see fig. 9.2).

Step 6: Try running the SALES report form. Type *REPORT FORM SALES*. The SALES report form defines columns with fields not set up with SET FIELDS TO. Thus, dBASE returns the message Syntax error in field expression, indicating that dBASE did not recognize a field name defined in the report form.

If you want to create a new report form, dBASE will restrict your column definitions to only those fields in the SET FIELDS TO list.

```
Structure for database: C:MX_SALES.dbf
Number of data records:      10
Date of last update   : 07/11/87
Field  Field Name  Type       Width   Dec
    1  CFNAME      Character      8
    2  CLNAME      Character     10
    3  CSTREET     Character     15
    4  CCITY       Character     15
    5  CST         Character      2
    6  CZIP        Character      5
    7  CPHONE      Character      8
    8  CNOTE       Memo          10
    9 >PDATE       Date           8
   10 >PINDATE     Date           8
   11 >PCODE       Character      4
   12 >PNO         Numeric        1
   13 >PAMT        Numeric        7     2
   14 >PTAX        Numeric        6     2
   15 >PPIF        Logical        1
   16  ESP         Character      3
   17  ECOMM       Numeric        7     2
** Total **                    119
```

Fig. 9.2. *LIST STRUCTURE with field list.*

Step 7: Clear the fields list. Type *CLEAR FIELDS* to cancel the effect of the SET FIELDS TO command.

Setting a Database Filter

Now try another scenario. Assume that your report project is going to focus on purchases made in June to customers in Georgia. You will be running a number of different retrieval commands, and it would be nice not to have to write the same search condition for each command. The way out of the retyping dilemma is to use a *filter*, a condition that separates the desired records from the full database. The SET FILTER TO command sets the filter.

Step 1: Enter a database filter. Type *SET FILTER TO CST = 'GA' .AND. CMONTH(PDATE) = 'June'.*

In this case the search condition is *compound*, or *multiple*. That is, it combines two independent conditions—one for the city and one for the purchase month. The link between the two is made with .AND., a *logical operator*. The .AND. operator indicates that both conditions must be true for the record to be retrieved. Another operator, .OR., would be used if either of the two conditions could be met. A third operator, .NOT., is used to exclude records on a certain condition. For instance, a multiple search condition to retrieve all Georgia records except those from Atlanta would be FOR CST = 'GA' .AND..NOT. CCITY = 'Atlanta'.

You recall that the PDATE field records the complete purchase date, including day, month, and year. Because you often will want to retrieve records based on only part of the full date, dBASE III Plus contains a number of date functions that extract just the part of the date you need. These date functions are listed in table 9.1. In the parentheses, you enclose the name of a date expression, which can be either a date field in the database or a date memory variable.

Table 9.1
dBASE III Plus Date Extraction Functions

Date Functions Returning Numeric Values

DAY( )	Day of the month
DOW( )	Day of the week
MONTH( )	Number of the month
YEAR( )	Number of the year

Date Functions Returning Character Values

CDOW( )	Name of the day of the week
CMONTH( )	Name of the month

NOTES

Step 2: Display all records for the CST and PDATE fields. Type *DISPLAY ALL CST,PDATE*. Verify that only those records that match the filter are presented (see fig. 9.3).

```
. DISPLAY ALL CST,PDATE
Record#  CST PDATE
      1   GA  06/15/85
      2   GA  06/16/85
      3   GA  06/17/85
      4   GA  06/18/85
      5   GA  06/19/85
      6   GA  06/22/85
      7   GA  06/25/85
      8   GA  06/27/85
.
Command Line   ||<C:>||MX_SALES              Rec: EOF/10          ||        Caps
                 Enter a dBASE III PLUS command.
```

Fig. 9.3. *DISPLAY ALL with a filter.*

Step 3: DISPLAY STATUS with the filter set. Type *DISPLAY STATUS* and verify that the filter is set for the database (see. fig. 9.4).

Step 4: Run the SALES report form file with the filter set. Type *REPORT FORM SALES HEADING 'Purchases within Georgia'.* Compare your screen with figure 9.5.

Step 5: Turn off the filter. Type *SET FILTER TO* without specifying a new filter.

Making Filters and Field Lists Permanent

Filters and field lists set up using SET FIELDS TO and SET FILTER TO last only until they are closed or until the work session ends. At the next work session, you would have to reenter the SET commands. To get around this difficulty, dBASE III Plus offers

```
. DISPLAY STATUS

Currently Selected Database:
Select area:  1, Database in Use: C:MX_SALES.dbf     Alias: MX_SALES
              Memo file:    C:MX_SALES.dbt
Filter: CST = 'GA' .AND. CMONTH(PDATE) = 'June'

File search path:
Default disk drive: C:
Print destination:  PRN:
Margin =      0
Current work area =     1


Press any key to continue...
Command Line     |<C:>|MX_SALES                   Rec: EOF/10      |          Caps

            Enter a dBASE III PLUS command.
```

Fig. 9.4. *DISPLAY STATUS with a filter.*

```
. REPORT FORM SALES HEADING 'Purchases within Georgia'
      Page No.    1            Purchases within Georgia
      07/11/87
                         Sales at Saltwater Sally's
                            Hot Tubs and Pools

      CUSTOMER'S FIRST     PHONE     PURCH.    PURCH.    PURCH.
      LAST NAME  NAME      NO.       DATE      CODE      AMOUNT


      Blair      James     351-8923  06/15/85  H-27      4000.00
      Connors    Francis   975-8807  06/16/85  H-22      6600.35
      Jones      Thomas    971-9412  06/17/85  H-19      3523.17
      Aster      Sam       371-2341  06/18/85  P-11      9042.00
      Stevens    Harold    543-9850  06/19/85  H-19      3523.17
      Brown      Molly     876-1252  06/22/85  H-22      6600.35
      Clark      John      351-1118  06/25/85  P-14      8097.00
      Jones      Susan     370-4726  06/27/85  H-27      4000.00
      *** Total ***
                                                        45386.04

Command Line     |<C:>|MX_SALES                   Rec: EOF/10      |

            Enter a dBASE III PLUS command.
```

Fig. 9.5. *REPORT FORM SALES with a filter.*

a way to save the settings permanently to disk files. A filter can be saved to a query file (through CREATE QUERY), and a field list can be saved to a view file (through CREATE VIEW). Each of these CREATE commands calls up an Assistant menu similar to the CREATE REPORT and CREATE LABEL menus. Once you have created a view file or a query file, you need only to SET VIEW TO or SET QUERY TO the name you gave the file when you created it.

Step 1: Create a query file to store a search condition for June records in Georgia. Type *CREATE QUERY* and at the prompt Enter view file name: type *GA_JUNE*. The CREATE QUERY screen appears (see fig. 9.6).

```
┌─────────────────────────────────────────────────────────────────────────┐
│ ▌Set Filter▐          Nest          Display          Exit  ▌12:36:30 pm▐ │
│ ┌──────────────────────────────────────────┐                             │
│ │ Field Name                               │                             │
│ │ Operator                                 │                             │
│ │ Constant/Expression                      │                             │
│ │ Connect                                  │                             │
│ ├──────────────────────────────────────────┤                             │
│ │ Line Number          1                   │                             │
│ └──────────────────────────────────────────┘                             │
│ ┌──────┬────────┬────────────┬─────────────────────┬──────────┐          │
│ │ Line │ Field  │ Operator   │ Constant/Expression │ Connect  │          │
│ ├──────┼────────┼────────────┼─────────────────────┼──────────┤          │
│ │  1   │        │            │                     │          │          │
│ │  2   │        │            │                     │          │          │
│ │  3   │        │            │                     │          │          │
│ │  4   │        │            │                     │          │          │
│ │  5   │        │            │                     │          │          │
│ │  6   │        │            │                     │          │          │
│ │  7   │        │            │                     │          │          │
│ └──────┴────────┴────────────┴─────────────────────┴──────────┘          │
│ ▌CREATE QUERY▐  ▌<C:>▐▌GA_JUNE.QRY▐        ▌Opt: 1/2▐          ▌Caps▐     │
│        Position selection bar - ↑↓,  Select - ↵,  Leave menu - ↔,         │
│           Select a field name for the filter condition.                  │
└─────────────────────────────────────────────────────────────────────────┘
```

Fig. 9.6. *CREATE QUERY screen.*

Step 2: Set up the filter. Activate the **Field Name** line by highlighting that option and pressing Return. Then move the selection bar down to the **CST** field (see fig. 9.7). Press Return.

Step 3: Select an operator for the condition. Activate the **Operator** line, and press Return on the = **Matches** option (see fig. 9.8).

```
 Set Filter            Nest           Display            Exit  04:39:14 am
┌──────────────────────────────────────┐  ┌─────────────┐
│ Field Name          ⟩                │  │ CFNAME      │
│ Operator                             │  │ CLNAME      │
│ Constant/Expression                  │  │ CSTREET     │
│ Connect                              │  │ CCITY       │
│                                      │  │ CST         │
│ Line Number         1                │  │ CZIP        │
└──────────────────────────────────────┘  │ CPHONE      │
                                           │ CNOTE       │
┌──────────────────────────────────┐  ┌── │ PDATE       ┌──────────────┐
│ Field Name       Type    Width Decimal│a│ PINDATE     │ Connect      │
│                                   │  │  │ PCODE       │              │
│ MX_SALES->CST    Character   2    │  │  │ PNO         │              │
│                                   │  │  │ PAMT        │              │
│ 3                                 │  │  │ PTAX        │              │
│ 4                                 │  │  │ PPIF        │              │
│ 5                                 │  │  │ ESP         │              │
│ 6                                 │  │  │ ECOMM       │              │
│ 7                                 │  │  └─────────────┘              │
└──────────────────────────────────┘

 CREATE QUERY    <B:> GA_JUNE.QRY         Opt: 5/16              Caps
         Position selection bar - ↑↓.  Select - ↵.  Leave menu - ↔.
                Select a field name for the filter condition.
```

Fig. 9.7. *Entering a field name on the QUERY screen.*

```
 Set Filter            Nest           Display            Exit  04:42:42 am
┌──────────────────────────────────────┐  ┌──────────────────────────┐
│ Field Name          CST              │  │ =  Matches               │
│ Operator            ⟩                │  │ <> Does not match        │
│ Constant/Expression                  │  │    Begins with           │
│ Connect                              │  │    Does not begin with   │
│                                      │  │    Ends with             │
│ Line Number         1                │  │    Does not end with     │
└──────────────────────────────────────┘  │ $  Contains              │
                                           │    Does not contain      │
┌──────────────────────────────────────┐  │    Is contained in       │
│ Line  Field      Operator       Co │  │    Is not contained in   │
│                                    │  │ >  Comes after           │
│ 1     CST                          │  │ >= Comes after or matches│
│ 2                                  │  │ <  Comes before          │
│ 3                                  │  │ <= Comes before or matches│
│ 4                                  │  └──────────────────────────┘
│ 5                                  │
│ 6                                  │
│ 7                                  │
└──────────────────────────────────────┘

 CREATE QUERY    <B:> GA_JUNE.QRY         Opt: 1/14              Caps
         Position selection bar - ↑↓.  Select - ↵.  Leave menu - ↔.
              Select a comparison operator for the filter condition.
```

Fig. 9.8. *Entering an operator on the QUERY screen.*

Step 4: Enter the search expression. Activate the **Constant/Expression** line and type *'GA'*. Press Return to lock in the expression (see fig. 9.9).

```
┌─────────────────────────────────────────────────────────────────────────┐
│ ▆Set Filter▆          Nest          Display         Exit  ▆01:16:28 pm▆   │
│ ┌───────────────────────────────────────────────┐                        │
│ │ Field Name          CST                        │                        │
│ │ Operator            Matches                     │                        │
│ │ Constant/Expression 'GA'                        │                        │
│ │ Connect                                         │                        │
│ │ ─────────────────────────────────────────────  │                        │
│ │ Line Number         1                           │                        │
│ └───────────────────────────────────────────────┘                        │
│                                                                           │
│  ┌──────┬───────────┬──────────────┬─────────────────────┬───────────┐   │
│  │ Line │ Field     │ Operator     │ Constant/Expression │ Connect   │   │
│  ├──────┼───────────┼──────────────┼─────────────────────┼───────────┤   │
│  │ 1    │ CST       │ Matches      │ 'GA'                │           │   │
│  │ 2    │           │              │                     │           │   │
│  │ 3    │           │              │                     │           │   │
│  │ 4    │           │              │                     │           │   │
│  │ 5    │           │              │                     │           │   │
│  │ 6    │           │              │                     │           │   │
│  │ 7    │           │              │                     │           │   │
│  └──────┴───────────┴──────────────┴─────────────────────┴───────────┘   │
│ ▆CREATE QUERY▆  ▆<B:>▆▆GA_JUNE.QRY▆      ▆Opt: 1/5▆      ▆       ▆ ▆Caps▆ │
│        Position selection bar - ↑↓.  Select - ◄┘.  Leave menu - ↔.        │
│          Select a field name for the filter condition.                    │
└─────────────────────────────────────────────────────────────────────────┘
```

Fig. 9.9. *Entering a search expression on the QUERY screen.*

Step 5: Connect the second condition. Activate the **Connect** line and select the option **Combine with .AND.** (see fig. 9.10).

Step 6: Enter the second condition. Activate the **Field Name** and select the **PDATE** field. Select >= **More than or equal** for the **Operator**. Type the **Constant/Expression** as *CTOD('6/1/85')*. Your screen should resemble figure 9.11.

Step 6 is unusual in two respects. First, the CREATE QUERY screen accepts only the straight field name. Where you earlier typed the condition CMONTH(PDATE) in setting a filter from the dot prompt, the CREATE QUERY screen will not allow CMONTH or any other function. To get around this problem, the date filter for June is written with a lower bound and an upper bound. Selected records must be greater than or equal to June 1, 1985, and less than or equal to June 30, 1985. The second condition specified in Step 6 sets the lower bound. You will set the upper bound in Step 7.

```
┌─────────────────────────────────────────────────────────────────────┐
│  Set Filter            Nest         Display          Exit  04:49:14 am│
│  ┌─────────────────────────────────┐ ┌─────────────────────────────┐ │
│  │ Field Name         CST          │ │ No combination              │ │
│  │ Operator           Matches      │ │ Combine with .AND.          │ │
│  │ Constant/Expression 'GA'        │ │ Combine with .OR.           │ │
│  │ Connect                    ↗     │ │ Combine with .AND..NOT.     │ │
│  │                                 │ │ Combine with .OR..NOT.      │ │
│  │ Line Number        1            │ └─────────────────────────────┘ │
│  └─────────────────────────────────┘                                 │
│                                                                       │
│  ┌──────┬────────┬────────────────┬─────────────────────┬──────────┐ │
│  │ Line │ Field  │ Operator       │ Constant/Expression │ Connect  │ │
│  ├──────┼────────┼────────────────┼─────────────────────┼──────────┤ │
│  │ 1    │ CST    │ Matches        │ 'GA'                │          │ │
│  │ 2    │        │                │                     │          │ │
│  │ 3    │        │                │                     │          │ │
│  │ 4    │        │                │                     │          │ │
│  │ 5    │        │                │                     │          │ │
│  │ 6    │        │                │                     │          │ │
│  │ 7    │        │                │                     │          │ │
│  └──────┴────────┴────────────────┴─────────────────────┴──────────┘ │
│                                                                       │
│  CREATE QUERY    ‖<B:>‖GA_JUNE.QRY        ‖Opt: 2/5‖      ‖  ‖ Caps   │
│       Position selection bar – ↑↓,  Select – ◄─┘,  Leave menu – ↔,    │
│         Select a logical connector for the filter condition.          │
└─────────────────────────────────────────────────────────────────────┘
```

Fig. 9.10. *Connecting a second condition.*

```
┌─────────────────────────────────────────────────────────────────────┐
│  Set Filter            Nest         Display          Exit  05:16:55 am│
│  ┌─────────────────────────────────┐                                 │
│  │ Field Name         PDATE        │                                 │
│  │ Operator           More than or equal                             │
│  │ Constant/Expression CTOD('6/1/85')                                │
│  │ Connect                         │                                 │
│  │                                 │                                 │
│  │ Line Number        2            │                                 │
│  └─────────────────────────────────┘                                 │
│                                                                       │
│  ┌──────┬────────┬────────────────────┬─────────────────┬──────────┐ │
│  │ Line │ Field  │ Operator           │ Constant/Expression│ Connect │ │
│  ├──────┼────────┼────────────────────┼─────────────────┼──────────┤ │
│  │ 1    │ CST    │ Matches            │ 'GA'            │ .AND.    │ │
│  │ 2    │ PDATE  │ More than or equal │ CTOD('6/1/85') │          │ │
│  │ 3    │        │                    │                 │          │ │
│  │ 4    │        │                    │                 │          │ │
│  │ 5    │        │                    │                 │          │ │
│  │ 6    │        │                    │                 │          │ │
│  │ 7    │        │                    │                 │          │ │
│  └──────┴────────┴────────────────────┴─────────────────┴──────────┘ │
│                                                                       │
│  CREATE QUERY    ‖<B:>‖GA_JUNE.QRY        ‖Opt: 4/5‖      ‖  ‖ Caps   │
│       Position selection bar – ↑↓,  Select – ◄─┘,  Leave menu – ↔,    │
│         Select a logical connector for the filter condition.          │
└─────────────────────────────────────────────────────────────────────┘
```

Fig. 9.11. *CREATE QUERY screen after completing the second condition.*

Second is the use of the CTOD function in the **Constant/Expression**. CTOD (character to date) is a function that converts a date expressed in character form (within quotation marks) to a date in true date form. This function is necessary, because there is no other way to key a value directly as a date.

Step 7: Enter the upper date bound. Activate the **Connect** line and select **Combine with .AND.** Enter the field **PDATE** as the **Field Name**. Select <= **Less than or equal** for the **Operator**. Type the **Constant/Expression** as *CTOD('6/30/85')*. Your screen should resemble figure 9.12.

```
┌─────────────────────────────────────────────────────────────────────────┐
│ ▐Set Filter▌         Nest          Display         Exit ▐05:20:18 am▌     │
│  ┌──────────────────────────────────────────────────────┐                │
│  │ Field Name          PDATE                             │                │
│  │ Operator            Less than or equal                │                │
│  │ Constant/Expression CTOD('6/30/85')                   │                │
│  │ Connect                                               │                │
│  │                                                       │                │
│  │ Line Number         3                                 │                │
│  └──────────────────────────────────────────────────────┘                │
│                                                                           │
│  ┌──────┬────────┬─────────────────┬──────────────────┬──────────┐       │
│  │ Line │ Field  │ Operator        │ Constant/Expression │ Connect │       │
│  ├──────┼────────┼─────────────────┼──────────────────┼──────────┤       │
│  │ 1    │ CST    │ Matches         │ 'GA'             │ .AND.    │       │
│  │ 2    │ PDATE  │ More than or equal │ CTOD('6/1/85') │ .AND.    │       │
│  │ 3    │ PDATE  │ Less than or equal │ CTOD('6/30/85') │         │       │
│  │ 4    │        │                 │                  │          │       │
│  │ 5    │        │                 │                  │          │       │
│  │ 6    │        │                 │                  │          │       │
│  │ 7    │        │                 │                  │          │       │
│  └──────┴────────┴─────────────────┴──────────────────┴──────────┘       │
│                                                                           │
│ ▐CREATE QUERY▌ ▐<B:>▌GA_JUNE.QRY         ▐Opt: 4/5▌           ▐Caps▌       │
│     Position selection bar - ↑↓,  Select - ◄┘,  Leave menu - ↔,           │
│        Select a logical connector for the filter condition.               │
└─────────────────────────────────────────────────────────────────────────┘
```

Fig. 9.12. *CREATE QUERY screen after completing the third condition.*

You now have completed the specification of the filter. To check your work while still in CREATE QUERY, you can use the **Display** option.

Step 8: Display records with the filter. Use the right-arrow key to move the main menu selection bar to the **Display** option, and press Return. When the first record appears at the left, press the F1 key to see all the fields (see fig. 9.13). You can PgDn to see other records in the database that meet the filter conditions.

```
  Set Filter              Nest           Display          Exit  05:25:09 am
  CFNAME     James
  CLNAME     Blair
  CSTREET    1 Oak Street
  CCITY      Atlanta
  CST        GA
  CZIP       30332
  CPHONE     351-8923
  CNOTE      memo
  PDATE      06/15/85
  PINDATE    06/23/85
  PCODE      H-27
  PNO        1
  PAMT       4000.00
  PTAX       200.00
  PPIF       T
  ESP        DWK
  ECOMM      1000.00




  CREATE QUERY    <B:> GA_JUNE.QRY           Rec: 1/10                 Caps
  Next/Previous record - PgDn/PgUp.  Toggle query form - F1.  Leave option - ←→.
           Display records in the database that meet the query condition.
```

Fig. 9.13. *Displaying records in the CREATE QUERY screen.*

Step 9: Save the query specifications. Move from **Display** to the **Exit** submenu. Press the Return key with **Save** highlighted.

Step 10: Display the status. Type *DISPLAY STATUS* to verify that the filter has been set (see fig. 9.14).

```
. DISPLAY STATUS

Currently Selected Database:
Select area:  1, Database in Use: B:MX_SALES.dbf    Alias: MX_SALES
          Memo file:   B:MX_SALES.dbt
Filter: CST= 'GA'  .AND.PDATE>= CTOD('6/1/85') .AND.PDATE<= CTOD('6/30/85')

File search path:
Default disk drive: B:
Print destination:  PRN:
Margin =     0
Current work area =    1

Press any key to continue...
Command Line     ||<B:>||MX_SALES                 ||Rec: 1/10        ||       ||    Caps
             Enter a dBASE III PLUS command.
```

Fig. 9.14. *Displaying the status with a query file set.*

Close an open query file by using the command SET FILTER TO. It also will be closed automatically if you issue either CLOSE DATABASES or CLEAR ALL. To reopen a query file, use the command SET FILTER TO FILE and give the name of the file. Query files are stored on disk under the given name and the file extension .QRY. Therefore, to do a directory listing of all the query files on disk, type the command *DIR *.QRY*.

Step 11: Close the query file. Type *SET FILTER TO*.

Creating a View File

A view file is one of the handiest dBASE III Plus finger-saving tools. It sets up specifications for a number of different types of dBASE III Plus files and command qualifications, including these:

NOTES

- Database files
- Index files
- Format files
- Field lists
- Search conditions
- Database relations

Notice that with respect to the search condition, a view file can achieve the same result as setting a filter from the dot prompt. In other words, a view file substitutes for a separate query file. Format files are covered in Lesson 11, and database relations are covered in Lesson 12.

Assume in the following steps that you are setting up a view file in your files to include not only the MX_SALES database but all the indexes to the file, the purchase field list, and a filter to restrict records to purchases in Georgia in June.

Step 1: Clear all current settings. Type *CLEAR ALL.*

Step 2: Begin defining the view file screen. Type *CREATE VIEW.* At the prompt Enter view file name: type *SALES.* The CREATE VIEW menu will appear as in figure 9.15.

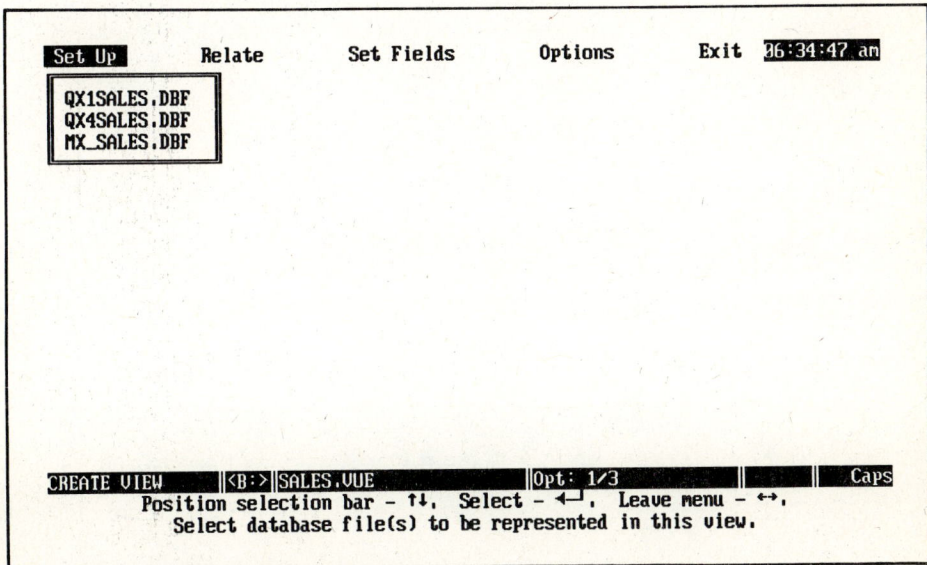

```
 Set Up        Relate      Set Fields      Options      Exit  06:34:47 am
┌───────────────┐
│ QX1SALES.DBF  │
│ QX4SALES.DBF  │
│ MX_SALES.DBF  │
└───────────────┘




 CREATE VIEW      <B:> SALES.VUE          Opt: 1/3               Caps
      Position selection bar - ↑↓,  Select - ←┘,  Leave menu - ←→,
      Select database file(s) to be represented in this view.
```

Fig. 9.15. *CREATE VIEW menu.*

NOTES

The CREATE VIEW screen is menu driven, as are other dBASE III Plus file creation screens. It operates in the same manner as other such screens.

Step 3: Select a database. Move the **Set Up** submenu selection bar to **MX_SALES.DBF**, and press Return. A submenu with the names of index files appears to the right.

Step 4: Select indexes. With the view file you are setting up, only the AMT_OR and AMT1_OR indexes are important. You might recall from Lesson 7 that both of these files index the PAMT field, AMT_OR in ascending order and AMT1_OR in descending order. Move the selection bar in the index submenu to **AMT_OR** and press Return. This now becomes the master index for the database. Move the selection bar to **AMT1_OR**, and select it. Notice that both indexes are marked with an arrow (see fig. 9.16).

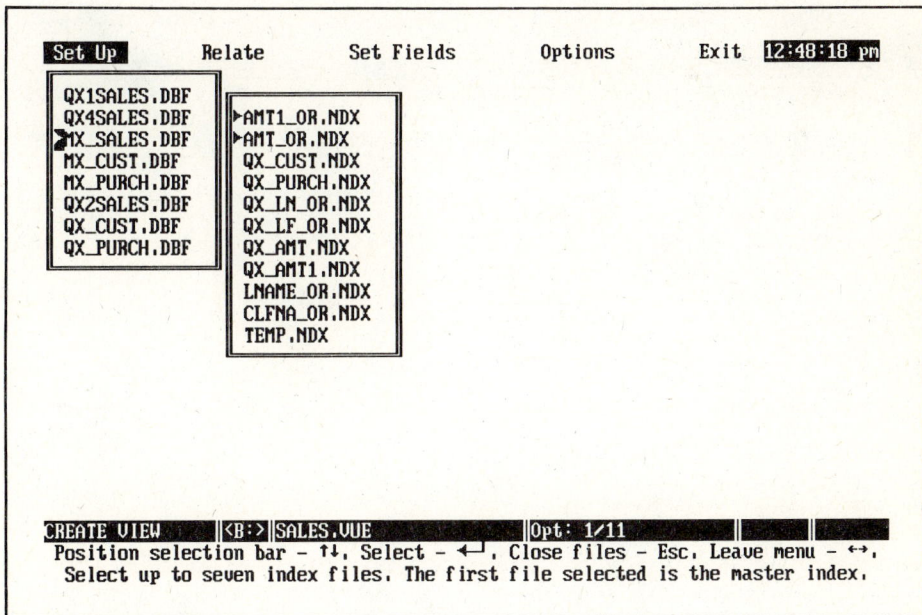

```
 Set Up         Relate        Set Fields        Options        Exit  12:48:18 pm

 QX1SALES.DBF
 QX4SALES.DBF   ►AMT1_OR.NDX
▶MX_SALES.DBF   ►AMT_OR.NDX
 MX_CUST.DBF     QX_CUST.NDX
 MX_PURCH.DBF    QX_PURCH.NDX
 QX2SALES.DBF    QX_LN_OR.NDX
 QX_CUST.DBF     QX_LF_OR.NDX
 QX_PURCH.DBF    QX_AMT.NDX
                 QX_AMT1.NDX
                 LNAME_OR.NDX
                 CLFNA_OR.NDX
                 TEMP.NDX




 CREATE VIEW    <B:> SALES.VUE            Opt: 1/11
 Position selection bar - ↑↓, Select - ↵, Close files - Esc, Leave menu - ↔,
 Select up to seven index files. The first file selected is the master index.
```

Fig. 9.16. *Selecting indexes for the view file.*

Step 5: Set a field list for the view file. Press the left-arrow key to leave the index submenu. At the main menu, press the right-arrow key until the **Set Fields** submenu drops down, identifying the selected database, **MX_SALES.DBF** (see fig. 9.17).

```
    Set Up        Relate       Set Fields      Options       Exit  06:36:34 am
                               MX_SALES.DBF




















CREATE VIEW      <B:> SALES.VUE                Opt: 1/1                  Caps
          Position selection bar - ↑↓,  Select - ↵,  Leave menu - ↔,
                Select a database from which to choose fields.
```

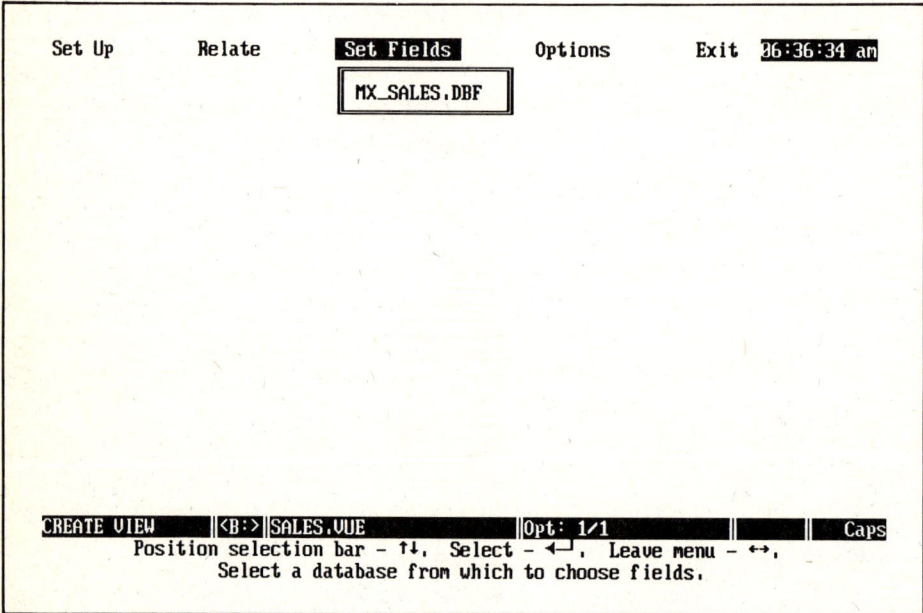

Fig. 9.17. *CREATE VIEW menu, Set Fields submenu.*

Step 6: Select the fields for the view file. Press Return to activate the **Set Fields** submenu. All the fields in the database appear in a submenu on the left side of the screen. All the fields currently are marked with arrows, indicating that they all will be selected for the list. Deselect those that are not needed in the view file. Highlight each in turn and press Return:

> **CFNAME, CLNAME, CSTREET, CCITY, CST, CZIP, CPHONE, CNOTE, ESP, ECOMM**

When you are finished, your screen should resemble figure 9.18.

```
Set Up          Relate          Set Fields        Options        Exit   06:41:55 am
                                 MX_SALES.DBF

 CFNAME
 CLNAME
 CSTREET
 CCITY
 CST
 CZIP
 CPHONE
 CNOTE
►PDATE
►PINDATE
►PCODE
►PNO
►PAMT
►PTAX                Field Name          Type        Width  Decimal
►PPIF
 ESP                 MX_SALES->CFNAME    Character     8
 ECOMM

CREATE VIEW     ‖<B:>‖SALES.VUE              ‖Opt: 1/17                 ‖        ‖ Caps
              Position selection bar - ↑↓.  Select - ←⏎.  Leave menu - ↔.
Select the fields to include in this view.  Marked fields are already selected.
```

Fig. 9.18. *Selected fields for the view file.*

Step 7: Define a filter for the view file. Press the right-arrow key to move to the **Options** submenu, and activate the **Filter:** option. Type *CST='GA' .AND. CMONTH(PDATE) = 'June'.* The submenu line is not long enough to reveal the complete entry line, but the submenu will scroll, and everything you type will be recorded. Press the Return key to lock in the filter. The completed submenu resembles figure 9.19.

Step 8: Save the view file. Move to the **Exit** submenu, and press Return with **Save** highlighted.

Step 9: Review the status. Type *DISPLAY STATUS*. Notice that all the files and qualifications defined in the view file are currently active (see fig. 9.20).

```
   Set Up        Relate        Set Fields       Options      Exit  10:08:08 am
                                               ┌─────────────────────────────
                                               │ Filter:  CST='GA' .AND.CMONTH(
                                               │ Format:
                                               └─────────────────────────────




  CREATE VIEW      <B:> SALES.VUE              Opt: 1/2                   Caps
           Position selection bar - ↑↓, Select - ◄─┘, Leave menu - ←→,
           Enter a logical expression to filter the records in this view.
```

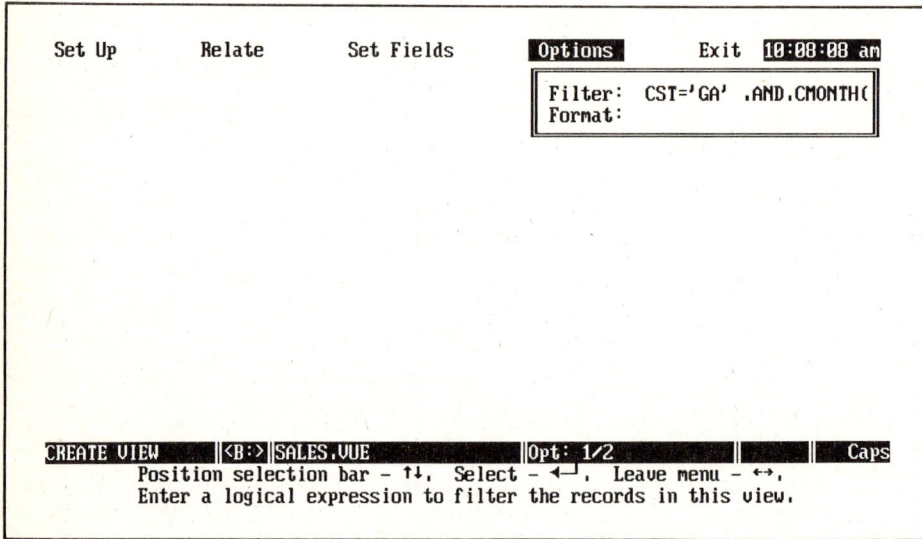

Fig. 9.19. *Defining filter for the view file.*

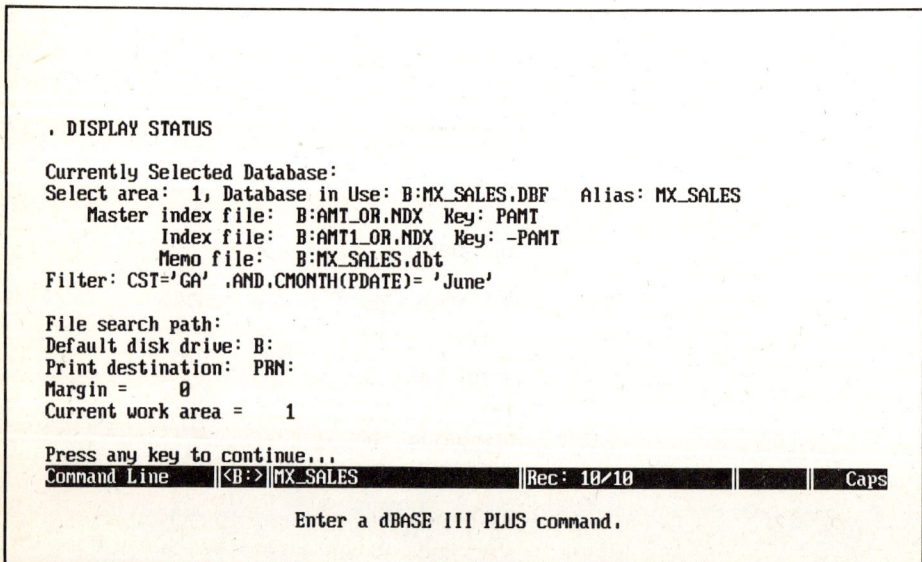

```
  . DISPLAY STATUS

  Currently Selected Database:
  Select area:  1, Database in Use: B:MX_SALES.DBF    Alias: MX_SALES
      Master index file:  B:AMT_OR.NDX  Key: PAMT
             Index file:  B:AMT1_OR.NDX  Key: -PAMT
              Memo file:  B:MX_SALES.dbt
  Filter: CST='GA' .AND.CMONTH(PDATE)= 'June'

  File search path:
  Default disk drive: B:
  Print destination:  PRN:
  Margin =      0
  Current work area =    1

  Press any key to continue...
  Command Line    <B:> MX_SALES              Rec: 10/10              Caps
                 Enter a dBASE III PLUS command.
```

Fig. 9.20. *DISPLAY STATUS with view file set.*

Step 10: Close the view file. Type *CLOSE DATABASES*. All settings are canceled.

To reopen the view file, use the command SET VIEW TO and give the name of the file.

Writing Programs

dBASE III Plus programs provide an important means of automating series of commands. The commands themselves for the most part include the same commands you are used to writing from the dot prompt. However, some commands are valid only within programs. These commands control the execution of the program, telling it what to do when and if certain conditions hold true. Understanding these control commands is critical to writing any but the most simple programs.

Programs also include a means for making notes to yourself on what a part of the program sets out to do. Programs are written in the dBASE III Plus command language, which is close to but not exactly English. After some period of time between writing and modifying, it can be difficult to remember what a section of program code was intended to do.

A note to yourself within the program makes it much easier to jog your memory and ultimately much easier to make corrections and changes. Notes or comments in programs are identified with an asterisk (*) as the first character in the line, with the command verb NOTE preceding the comment itself, or following two ampersands (&&) anywhere within a line. Get into the habit of *commenting* your programs liberally. The extra time it costs will pay for itself sooner than you might think.

In the next steps, you will begin your programming experience by writing a program that calculates and reports the summary statistics for the performance of Saltwater Sally's salespeople. In Lesson 5, you entered a series of commands, nine in all, that did the following:

- Calculated the number of sales for each salesperson (COUNT FOR ESP = 'XXX')

- Calculated the total sales for each salesperson (SUM PAMT FOR ESP = 'XXX')

- Calculated the average sales for each salesperson (AVERAGE PAMT FOR ESP = 'XXX')

These commands had to be repeated for each salesperson by substituting the salesperson's initials for the 'XXX' in the formulas. You can see that if the number of salespeople grew, generating the data would get tedious quickly. A simple program can help speed up the process.

Programs in dBASE III Plus generally are written with the same word processor you used to enter memo fields (see the section "Adding Information to the Database" in Lesson 1). They also can be written using a conventional word processor that can write so-called ASCII files. The workbook uses the dBASE word processor exclusively.

NOTES

The dBASE III Plus word processor is called into play by issuing the command MODIFY COMMAND along with the name of the file the program is to be stored to on disk. Program files in dBASE III Plus are automatically stored with the file extension .PRG. You do not have to provide a file extension.

Step 1: Start writing a program file named MX_PERF, standing for **M**y e**X**ercise **PERF**ormance, to summarize the sales performance of Saltwater Sally's salespersons. At the dot prompt, type *MODIFY COMMAND MX_PERF*. The screen that results is illustrated in figure 9.21.

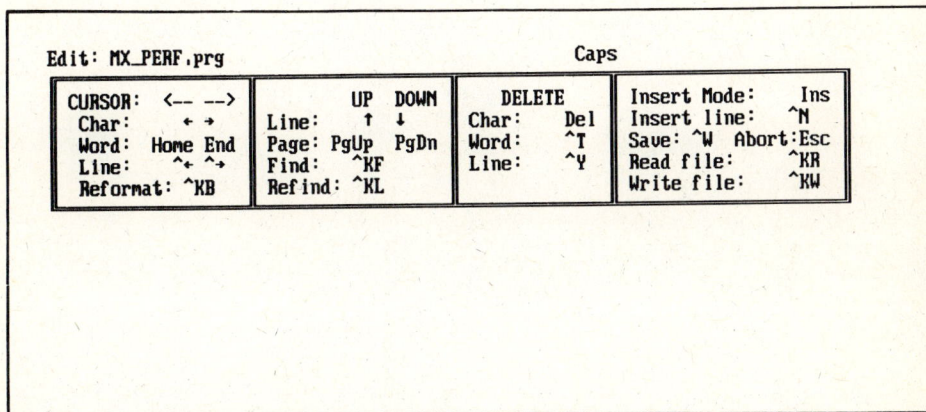

```
Edit: MX_PERF.prg                              Caps
┌──────────────────┬──────────────────┬──────────────┬──────────────────────┐
│ CURSOR:  <-- -->  │          UP DOWN │   DELETE     │ Insert Mode:    Ins  │
│ Char:     ← →     │ Line:     ↑  ↓   │ Char:   Del  │ Insert line:    ^N   │
│ Word:   Home End  │ Page: PgUp PgDn  │ Word:   ^T   │ Save: ^W  Abort:Esc  │
│ Line:    ^← ^→    │ Find:    ^KF     │ Line:   ^Y   │ Read file:      ^KR  │
│ Reformat: ^KB     │ Refind:  ^KL     │              │ Write file:     ^KW  │
└──────────────────┴──────────────────┴──────────────┴──────────────────────┘
```

Fig. 9.21. *dBASE III Plus word processor.*

The dBASE III Plus word processor operates in much the same manner as it does for entering memo field data. When writing programs, however, remember to end each command with a Return. The return character is indicated on the screen by a less-than sign (<) in the rightmost column.

Step 2: Enter comment lines to identify the program's name and overall purpose. On subsequent lines type

```
* MX_PERF.PRG
* Calculates performance statistics for salespersons
```

Your screen should look like figure 9.22.

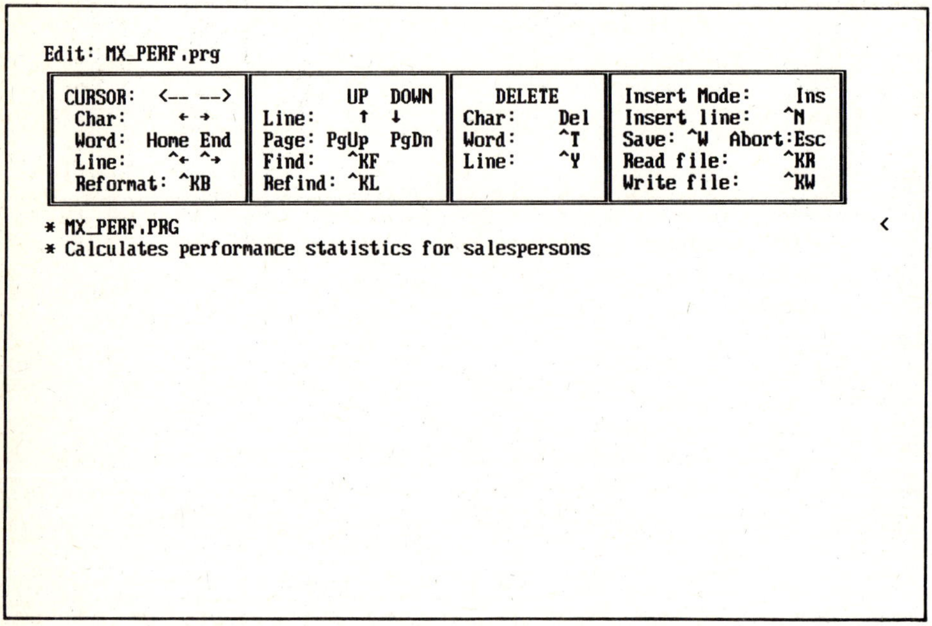

```
Edit: MX_PERF.prg
┌───────────────────────┬───────────────────────┬───────────────────────┬───────────────────────┐
│ CURSOR:   <-- -->     │           UP   DOWN   │     DELETE            │ Insert Mode:     Ins  │
│ Char:       ← →       │ Line:      ↑    ↓     │ Char:       Del       │ Insert line:     ^N   │
│ Word:    Home End     │ Page: PgUp   PgDn     │ Word:       ^T        │ Save: ^W  Abort:Esc   │
│ Line:     ^← ^→       │ Find:     ^KF         │ Line:       ^Y        │ Read file:       ^KR  │
│ Reformat: ^KB         │ Refind: ^KL           │                       │ Write file:      ^KW  │
└───────────────────────┴───────────────────────┴───────────────────────┴───────────────────────┘
* MX_PERF.PRG                                                                                   <
* Calculates performance statistics for salespersons
```

Fig. 9.22. *Comment lines for MX_PERF.*

Step 3: Enter the commands to process statistics for Doug Kornfeld. Add the following lines to the program:

```
COUNT FOR ESP = 'DWK' TO mcount
SUM PAMT FOR ESP = 'DWK' TO mtotal
AVERAGE FOR ESP = 'DWK' TO maver
? 'Initials of Salesperson: DWK'
? 'Number of Sales:', mcount
? 'Total of Sales:', mtotal
? 'Average Sales:', maver
RETURN
```

The completed program looks like figure 9.23.

```
Edit: B:mx_perf.prg                      Ins

 CURSOR: <-- -->               UP  DOWN   DELETE        Insert Mode:    Ins
 Char:     ← →       Line:    ↑   ↓       Char:   Del   Insert line:    ^N
 Word:  Home End     Page: PgUp PgDn      Word:   ^T    Save: ^W Abort:Esc
 Line:    ^← ^→      Find:      ^KF       Line:   ^Y    Read file:      ^KR
 Reformat: ^KB       Refind:    ^KL                     Write file:     ^KW

* MX_PERF.PRG                                                             <
* Calculates performance statistics for salespersons                     <
COUNT FOR ESP = 'DWK' TO mcount                                          <
SUM PAMT FOR ESP = 'DWK' TO mtotal                                      <
AVERAGE PAMT FOR ESP = 'DWK' TO maver                                   <
? 'Initials of Salesperson: DWK'                                        <
? 'Number of Sales: ', mcount                                          <
? 'Total of Sales: ', mtotal                                           <
? 'Average Sales: ', maver                                             <
RETURN
```

Fig. 9.23. *Commands to report DWK's performance.*

Step 4: Save and run the program. Press Ctrl-End to save the program. At the dot prompt, make sure that the MX_SALES database is in use. Type *DO MX_PERF* to run the program. Compare your screen with figure 9.24.

The "chit-chat" on the screen preceding the results of the program is called *talk*. It includes comments from dBASE concerning what it did in carrying out the program, and the results of any storage or retrieval operations requested. After all the "bugs" have been eliminated from the program, you can use the SET TALK OFF command so that the talk does not interfere with the information as you want it presented.

```
. do mx_perf
      4 records
      4 records summed
      PAMT
15772.69
      4 records averaged
   PAMT
3943.17
Initials of Salesperson: DWK
Number of Sales:         4
Total of Sales:      15772.69
Average Sales:       3943.17
.
Command Line    ‖<B:>‖MX_SALES          ‖Rec: EOF/10    ‖Ins ‖‖

         Enter a dBASE III PLUS command.
```

Fig. 9.24. *Running program MX_PERF.*

Interacting with the Program

One problem with the program is that the initials of Doug Kornfeld are *hard-coded* into the program. In other words, this program only gives Kornfeld's performance data. Having the program request which Saltwater Sally's salesperson you need performance statistics for is preferable. This kind of capability would mean that the program is *interacting* with the user, pausing to ask for information it needs to continue operation.

Before the interactive version of the program can run correctly, a memory variable, here referred to as *minit*, must be created. The GET command does not create a memory variable; it expects one to have been created already. In Lesson 5 you learned how to create memory variables with the statistics commands. A more general way of creating a memory variable is to use the STORE command. Rather than calculating a value to store, as the statistics commands do, STORE names a specific value for the variable. For example, the command

    STORE SPACE(3) TO minit

uses the SPACE function to store three blanks to the variable named minit.

The dBASE III Plus command language allows you several ways to build user interaction into programs. This workbook shows you how to make programs interactive through use of the commands @ . . . SAY . . . GET . . . and READ. These commands do three things:

- They put a prompt at a specific location on the screen asking the operator for certain information

- They pause the program

- They take the information the operator types and store it into a memory variable or a database field

The dots in the general form of the @ . . . SAY . . . GET . . . command indicate places where you specify the three requirements of the command. The first dots, after the at sign (@), indicate the screen location where the prompt is to appear. The location is specified using coordinates representing the row number and the column number where the prompt is to start. Row numbers range from 0 to 24, and column numbers range from 0 to 79. The row position comes first, followed by a comma, and then followed by the column number: for example @ 4,15 SAY . . . GET . . . .

The second set of dots indicates the prompt. The prompt is enclosed in quotation marks: for example, @ 4,15 SAY 'Enter initials for salesperson' GET . . . The third set of dots indicates the name of the memory variable to save the operator's response to: for example,

    @ 4,15 SAY 'Enter initials for salesperson' GET minit

NOTES

The READ command follows @ . . . SAY . . . GET . . . and is responsible for pausing the screen and "reading the GET" at the location where the operator will enter the salesperson's initials.

Step 1: Make the MX_PERF program interactive. Type *MODIFY COMMAND MX_PERF* to edit the program.

Step 2: Insert blank lines for the new commands. Move the cursor so that it lies under the C of the COUNT command, and press Ctrl-N to insert a new line above the COUNT command. Press the Ins key to put the word processor into INSERT mode.

Step 3: Enter the new program lines. Starting at the new line, type the following commands:

```
STORE SPACE(3) TO minit
@ 4,15 SAY 'Enter initials for salesperson' GET minit
READ
```

Compare your program to figure 9.25.

```
Edit: B:mx_perf.prg                    Ins

CURSOR: <-- -->              UP   DOWN    DELETE        Insert Mode:     Ins
Char:      ←  →     Line:    ↑    ↓       Char:    Del  Insert line:    ^N
Word:   Home End    Page: PgUp  PgDn      Word:    ^T   Save: ^W Abort:Esc
Line:      ^←  ^→   Find:    ^KF          Line:    ^Y   Read file:      ^KR
Reformat: ^KB       Refind:  ^KL                        Write file:     ^KW

* MX_PERF.PRG                                                            <
* Calculates performance statistics for salespersons                    <
STORE SPACE(3) TO minit                                                  <
@ 4,15 SAY 'Enter initials for salesperson' GET minit                   <
READ                                                                     <
COUNT FOR ESP = 'DWK' TO mcount                                          <
SUM PAMT FOR ESP = 'DWK' TO mtotal                                       <
AVERAGE PAMT FOR ESP = 'DWK' TO maver                                    <
? 'Initials of Salesperson: DWK'                                        <
? 'Number of Sales: ', mcount                                           <
? 'Total of Sales: ', mtotal                                            <
? 'Average Sales: ', maver                                             <
RETURN
```

Fig. 9.25. *Interactive lines added to MX_PERF.*

NOTES

Step 4: Edit the processing lines of the program. Edit each line that makes a direct reference to DWK. Change each mention of DWK to *minit*, the memory variable that stores the initials of the salesperson. Pay particular attention to the line that prints the initials of the salesperson. The changed lines should now read as follows:

```
COUNT FOR ESP = minit TO mcount
SUM PAMT FOR ESP = minit TO mtotal
AVERAGE PAMT FOR ESP = minit TO maver
? 'Initials of Salesperson:', minit
```

The edited program should now look as it does in figure 9.26.

```
Edit: B:mx_perf.prg                     Ins

 CURSOR:  <-- -->        UP  DOWN    DELETE        Insert Mode:    Ins
 Char:      + +     Line:   t  +     Char:   Del   Insert line:    ^N
 Word:  Home End    Page: PgUp PgDn  Word:   ^T    Save: ^W  Abort:Esc
 Line:    ^+ ^+     Find:    ^KF     Line:   ^Y    Read file:      ^KR
 Reformat: ^KB      Refind:  ^KL                   Write file:     ^KW

* MX_PERF.PRG                                                        <
* Calculates performance statistics for salespersons                <
STORE SPACE(3) TO minit                                              <
@ 4,15 SAY 'Enter initials for salesperson' GET minit               <
READ                                                                 <
COUNT FOR ESP = minit TO mcount                                      <
SUM PAMT FOR ESP = minit TO mtotal                                   <
AVERAGE PAMT FOR ESP = minit TO maver                               <
? 'Initials of Salesperson:', minit                                 <
? 'Number of Sales: ', mcount                                        <
? 'Total of Sales: ', mtotal                                         <
? 'Average Sales: ', maver                                           <
RETURN
```

Fig. 9.26. *Edited program with interactive lines.*

Step 5: Save and run the program. Press Ctrl-End and type *DO MX_PERF*. When the program prompts for the salesperson's initials, type *LEM*. Compare figure 9.27 with the completed run.

Looping the Program

The program now works well at reporting the performance statistics for a single salesperson, but then the program ends. To run statistics for another salesperson, you must repeat the DO MX_PERF command. Having the program recycle itself would be better, prompting for another set of initials until you indicated that you were finished.

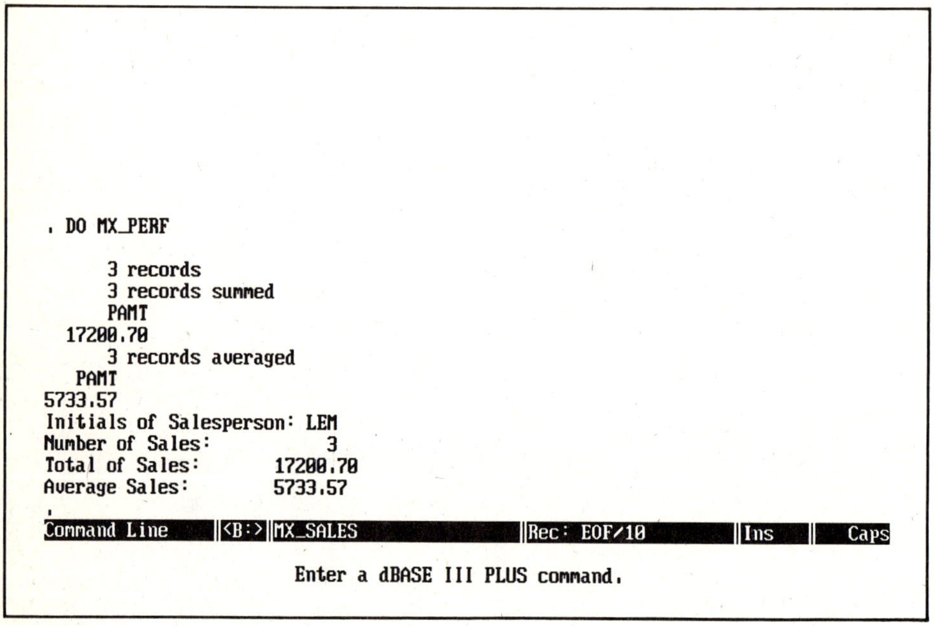

```
. DO MX_PERF

       3 records
       3 records summed
       PAMT
  17200.70
       3 records averaged
    PAMT
 5733.57
 Initials of Salesperson: LEM
 Number of Sales:         3
 Total of Sales:       17200.70
 Average Sales:         5733.57
 .
```

Command Line	<B:> MX_SALES	Rec: EOF/10	Ins	Caps

Enter a dBASE III PLUS command.

Fig. 9.27. *Running edited MX_PERF.*

Repeating a set of commands is done in dBASE III Plus with a program control mechanism called a *loop*. Loops have a beginning and an end, and they have some way of indicating how many times they should run. The start of a loop is indicated with the command DO WHILE and the end with the command ENDDO. Between DO WHILE and the ENDDO come all the commands that are to be repeated.

The loop control can be set in a number of ways. For Saltwater Sally's, which has three salespeople, you can set a control to have the loop operate just three times. This is done by setting up a memory variable to keep track of how many times the loop has already run. When this *counter* goes past three, the loop ends. The loop control is written as part of the DO WHILE command:

DO WHILE counter < 4

A loop requires two additional commands: one to create the memory variable counter (STORE 1 TO counter), and one to advance the counter when the loop has processed a salesperson (STORE 1 + counter TO counter).

Step 1: Add a program loop to MX_PERF. Type *MODIFY COMMAND MX_PERF* to edit the program. Add the lines indicated in the program listing below.

```
* MX_PERF.PRG
* Calculates performance statistics for salespersons

STORE 1 TO counter                                        <== Add
DO WHILE counter < 4                                      <== Add

STORE SPACE(3) TO minit
@ 4,15 SAY 'Enter initials for salesperson' GET minit
READ

COUNT FOR ESP = minit TO mcount
SUM PAMT FOR ESP = minit TO mtotal
AVERAGE PAMT FOR ESP = minit TO maver

? 'Initials of Salesperson:', minit
? 'Number of Sales: ', mcount
? 'Total of Sales: ', mtotal
? 'Average Sales: ', maver

STORE 1 + counter TO counter                             <== Add

ENDDO                                                     <== Add

RETURN
```

NOTES

Notice that the counter variable is set to the value 1 outside the loop, because this command should be carried out only once. However, the counter is incremented within the loop, once for every time the loop runs. When the counter advances to 4, the loop condition is no longer true; the program then drops out of the loop and continues at the command following ENDDO.

Step 2: Save and run the program. Press Ctrl-End. At the dot prompt, type *DO MX_PERF*. At the first prompt type *LEM*, at the second type *DWK*, and at the third type *FSM*.

Running a Loop Indefinitely

A disadvantage in running a loop a set number of times is that you might type some initials inaccurately, getting no useful information but still having that run counted. A more practical way of controlling the loop is to let the user decide how many times the loop should run. For instance, when the program prompts for initials, the operator might type END, which would act as the signal to terminate the loop.

Making a loop run indefinitely involves a different type of loop control than the counter approach. It involves using a logical variable set initially to true (.T.) and running the loop while the variable stays true. For instance, if the variable is called *continue*, the loop control would be DO WHILE continue. More simply, the command DO WHILE .T. also will set up a perpetual loop, and it does not require creating a memory variable ahead of time.

The means for exiting the loop is tied to a program *branch control*, which specifies one thing to do if a condition is true and another thing if it is not true. The most common type of branch control in dBASE III Plus is an IF statement.

An IF statement is written with at least three parts. First is an IF command that sets up the test condition: IF minit = 'END'. Recall that minit is the memory variable that stores the operator's response to the prompt Enter initials for salesperson. Following the IF command is an instruction for what to do if the test condition is true. In this case the action to take would be to EXIT. The EXIT command causes the program to drop out of the loop and continue with the command following ENDDO. Finally, an ENDIF command indicates that the IF statement has completed.

Step 1: Edit the MX_PERF program to set an indefinite loop control. Type *MODIFY COMMAND MX_PERF*.

Step 2: Change the loop control. In place of DO WHILE counter < 4, type *DO WHILE .T.* to set up an indefinite loop.

Step 3: Delete the two lines that mention the counter variable: STORE 1 TO counter, and STORE 1 + counter TO counter. Move to those lines and press Ctrl-Y.

NOTES

Step 4: Add the test condition. After the @ ... SAY ... GET ... command, add this conditional statement:

```
IF minit = 'END'
    EXIT
ENDIF
```

The completed program should look like figure 9.28.

```
* MX_PERF.PRG
* Calculates performance statistics for salespersons

DO WHILE .T.

    STORE SPACE(3) TO minit
    @4,33 SAY 'Enter initials for salesperson' GET minit
    READ

    IF minit = 'END'
        EXIT
    ENDIF

    COUNT FOR ESP = minit TO mcount
    SUM PAMT FOR ESP = minit TO mtotal
    AVERAGE PAMT FOR ESP = minit TO maver

    ? 'Initials of Salesperson:', minit
    ? 'Number of Sales: ', mcount
    ? 'Total of Sales: ', mtotal
    ? 'Average Sales: ', maver

ENDDO

RETURN
```

Fig. 9.28. *Adding an indefinite loop.*

Step 5: Save and test the program. Press Ctrl-End and type *DO MX_PERF*. Enter the initials *LEM* at the first pass. At the second pass, type *END* to make sure the loop is exited properly.

Cleaning Up the Program

You probably have noticed that, after you enter the initials of a salesperson, the program does not pause to allow you to edit the line. If you make a mistake at the last initial, it can't be corrected. The solution to this problem is to make the program pause after GET until a Return is pressed. This is done most easily with the command SET CONFIRM ON, given at the beginning of the program.

NOTES

At this point it also would be useful to set any other system controls—for instance, to turn the bell off, to set talk off, and to open the MX_SALES database specifically. It also would be helpful to have the screen clear after running one salesperson.

Step 1: Set the system controls in the program. Type *MODIFY COMMAND MX_PERF.* After the initial comment lines, add the following lines:

```
SET TALK OFF
SET BELL OFF
SET CONFIRM ON

USE MX_SALES
```

Step 2: Change the system controls back to their defaults. Immediately before the RETURN command at the end of the program, add these lines:

```
SET TALK ON
SET BELL ON
SET CONFIRM OFF
```

Step 3: Enter a command to clear the screen. Immediately after the DO WHILE .T. command, type the command *CLEAR.*

Because the screen clears immediately after reporting the program results, you have no time to read the results.

Step 4: Pause the screen after reporting a salesperson's performance statistics. Immediately before ENDDO, type the command *WAIT.*

The program with all its cleanup commands should look similar to figure 9.29.

Step 5: Test the program. Press Ctrl-End to save your changes, and type *DO MX_PERF* to run the program. Test the program by typing the initials *FSM* on one pass, and end it on another pass by typing *END.*

```
* MX_PERF.PRG
* Calculates performance statistics for salespersons

SET TALK OFF
SET BELL OFF
SET CONFIRM ON

USE MX_SALES

DO WHILE .T.

    CLEAR
    STORE SPACE(3) TO minit
    @4,33 SAY 'Enter initials for salesperson' GET minit
    READ

    IF minit = 'END'
        EXIT
    ENDIF

    COUNT FOR ESP = minit TO mcount
    SUM PAMT FOR ESP = minit TO mtotal
    AVERAGE PAMT FOR ESP = minit TO maver

    ? 'Initials of Salesperson:', minit
    ? 'Number of Sales: ', mcount
    ? 'Total of Sales: ', mtotal
    ? 'Average Sales: ', maver

    WAIT
ENDDO

SET TALK ON
SET BELL ON
SET CONFIRM OFF

RETURN
```

Fig. 9.29. *Completed MX_PERF program.*

SUMMARY OF CONCEPTS
PRESENTED IN LESSON 9

1. You can enter commands into program or command files. dBASE III Plus reads and executes each command.

2. An operator can enter further instructions to alter program execution. One way to do this is with an @ . . . SAY . . . GET . . . command.

3. Use MODIFY COMMAND to enter programs. The dBASE III Plus word processor appears. The text is entered in the same way as text is entered into a memo field.

4. Always document a program with comments about the program's name and purpose. An asterisk is the comment character.

5. The WAIT command halts a program until any character is typed at the keyboard.

6. CLEAR erases the screen.

7. Start a program by issuing DO and the name of the program. A RETURN ends the processing of a program file.

8. When an IF expression is true, dBASE III Plus processes all commands between an IF and its corresponding ENDIF.

9. All commands between a DO WHILE and its corresponding ENDDO are repeated if the DO WHILE condition is true. An EXIT unconditionally leaves the program, and execution continues with the first command below the loop.

10. Like SUM TO, the STORE command can create memory variables.

11. SAY statements place prompts or values at any coordinates on the screen. GET statements do the same, but they also allow entry of new values of existing fields or variables if a READ command is issued.

NOTES

Design a program called BILLS, which counts the number of bills a vendor has sent to Saltwater Sally's and totals their amount. The operator will supply the name of the vendor whose bills should be reported. MX_PERF can serve as a model for this program.

Step 1: Activate the dBASE III Plus word processor to write the program. Type *MODIFY COMMAND BILLS.*

Step 2: Enter the following code. Save your work by pressing Ctrl-End.

```
* BILLS.PRG
* Produces totals of all bills for single vendor.
* Uses SSBILLS data file.

SET TALK OFF
SET BELL OFF
SET CONFIRM ON

USE SSBILLS
DO WHILE .T.
  CLEAR
  STORE SPACE(20) TO mvend
  @ 4,15 SAY 'Enter name of vendor ' GET mvend
  @ 6,15 SAY 'Type END to leave the program'
  READ

  IF mvend = 'END'
    EXIT
  ENDIF

  COUNT FOR VNAME = mvend TO mcount
  SUM VAMT FOR VNAME = mvend to msum

  ? 'Name of vendor: ', mvend
  ? 'Number of bills: ', mcount
  ? 'Amount of bills: ', msum

  WAIT
ENDDO

SET TALK ON
SET BELL ON
SET CONFIRM OFF
RETURN
```

NOTES

Step 3: Test your work by typing *DO BILLS.* At the prompt, type the complete vendor name exactly as it is stored in the database. If the program does not work properly, type *END* to return to the dot prompt, and then type *MODIFY COMMAND BILLS* to check your program code for errors.

NOTES

10

The Ties That Bind: Writing Menus

Related sections in *dBASE III Plus Handbook*, 2nd Edition: Chapters 9 and 11.

In Lesson 9 you learned some basic programming techniques to automate reporting salespeople's performance. In this lesson and the next, those same techniques are used and extended in order to integrate an *application*, a coordinated set of functions that contribute to doing some larger job. In dBASE III Plus, each function is written as a separate program, and all the programs are tied together and accessed through a menu. The menu itself is written as another program. In this lesson you will learn how to do the following:

- Construct a simple menu
- Avoid using @ . . . SAY commands
- Branch by using a DO CASE command
- Deal with errors users may make

Jogging Your Memory with a Menu

In Lesson 8, you wrote specifications for three reports to present various information from the MX_SALES database. Each of these reports (SALES, SALEFIN, and CUST-NOTE) was saved and stored as a report form file. Using any of the three requires you to remember the name of the form file. You will be surprised at how often you forget the names of these and other files you have created.

NOTES

To ease your overtaxed memory, you can program a menu to "remember" the names for you. A menu has two main parts: a set of options and a set of actions. The options are laid out so that each option is identified by a letter or number. To call up a particular program action, the user types the letter or number for that selection.

Using a menu in dBASE is like ordering by the numbers from a menu in a Chinese restaurant. If you tell the waiter that you want number 6, the waiter gives the order to the cook, who prepares the dish you want. Number 6, along with a description of the dish, corresponds to a menu option. Giving your order to the waiter corresponds to selecting a menu option. And the cook preparing your meal corresponds to the program action for your menu choice.

A dBASE menu, like a restaurant menu, includes a list of available options. These options can be anything dBASE is capable of doing: adding and editing records, searching a database, running a report, and so on. In previous lessons, you wrote the program "recipes" for each of these actions. In the menu, you link each option with the program that carries it out.

To best get your order, a dBASE menu consists of three parts: the list of options, the user's choice, and the list of actions. Also, to allow users to make more than one choice during a menu session, the menu is enclosed in a program loop. Figure 10.1 illustrates the main elements and the order they occur in.

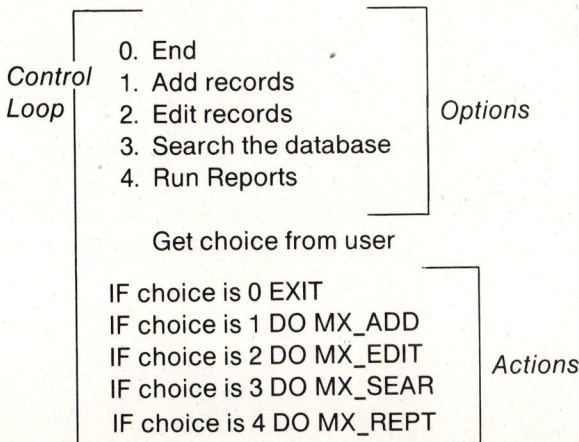

```
                    ┌──────────────────────┐
                    │  0. End              │
        Control     │  1. Add records      │
        Loop        │  2. Edit records     │      Options
                    │  3. Search the database │
                    │  4. Run Reports      │
                    └──────────────────────┘

                      Get choice from user

                    ┌──────────────────────┐
                    │ IF choice is 0 EXIT  │
                    │ IF choice is 1 DO MX_ADD │
                    │ IF choice is 2 DO MX_EDIT │   Actions
                    │ IF choice is 3 DO MX_SEAR │
                    │ IF choice is 4 DO MX_REPT │
                    └──────────────────────┘
```

Fig. 10.1. *Main elements of a dBASE menu.*

NOTES

The first step in writing a menu that calls up the sales reports (MX_REPT.PRG) is planning where the options are to appear on the screen and then writing a series of @ . . . SAY statements to lock in the starting location of each line. If the menu is to appear to the user as it does in figure 10.2, it needs to start close to the top of the screen and be indented somewhat from the left margin.

```
SALTWATER SALLY'S SALES REPORTS


   1 - Summary Report

   2 - Detailed Report

   3 - Customer Notes

Choose One  ███████ 0
```

Fig. 10.2. *Plan for Sales Reports menu.*

Step 1: Type *DO QPREP*. Select Lesson 10

Step 2: Write a menu program called MX_REPT. Type *MODIFY COMMAND MX_REPT*. In the word processor, type the following comment lines:

```
* MX_REPT.PRG
* Menu program to access sales system reports
```

Step 3: Write the set of options. Type the following statements after the comments:

```
CLEAR
STORE 0 TO mchoice

@ 5,10 SAY "SALTWATER SALLY'S SALES REPORTS"
@ 9,15 SAY '1 - Summary Report'
@ 11,15 SAY '2 - Detailed Report'
@ 13,15 SAY '3 - Customer Notes'
@ 16,15 SAY 'Choose One' GET mchoice
READ
```

Note the menu title. Because it includes a single quotation mark in the word SALLY'S, you must enclose the string in double quotation marks.

NOTES

Step 4: Review the appearance of the menu. Press Ctrl-End and type *DO MX_REPT.* Your screen should resemble the plan you originally laid out (refer to fig. 10.2).

Step 5: Specify the set of actions for the menu options. Type *MODIFY COMMAND MX_REPT* to reenter the word processor. Move the cursor past the last program line, and add the following statements:

```
IF mchoice = 1
   REPORT FORM sales
ENDIF

IF mchoice = 2
   REPORT FORM salefin
ENDIF

IF mchoice = 3
   REPORT FORM custnote
ENDIF
```

The program now should resemble figure 10.3.

```
* MX_REPT.PRG
* Menu program to access sales system reports

   CLEAR
   STORE 0 TO mchoice

   @ 5,10 SAY "SALTWATER SALLY'S SALES REPORTS"
   @9,15 SAY '1 - Summary Report'
   @11,15 SAY '2 - Detailed Report'
   @ 13,15 SAY '3 - Customer Notes'
   @ 16,15 SAY 'Choose One ' GET mchoice
   READ

   IF mchoice = 1
       REPORT FORM sales
   ENDIF

   IF mchoice = 2
       REPORT FORM salefin
   ENDIF

   IF mchoice = 3
       REPORT FORM custnote
   ENDIF
```

Fig. 10.3. *Program core of Sales Reports menu.*

NOTES

Step 6: Test the menu program again. Press Ctrl-End. At the dot prompt, press the up-arrow key twice and then press Return.

dBASE III Plus stores a record of the last twenty commands typed at the dot prompt in a *history buffer*. You can recall any of those twenty commands by using the up-arrow and down-arrow keys to bring the commands back to the dot prompt. Once a command is back at the dot prompt, you can execute it as usual by pressing Return.

When you write programs, you will enter and leave the word processor often, to write and then test your program. Instead of typing MODIFY COMMAND and DO repeatedly, use the history buffer to give yourself a typing break.

You also can use the history buffer to correct or modify command lines. Bring the command to the dot prompt, and use the editing keys to make the changes.

Step 7: Build the program loop for the menu. Press the up-arrow key twice to bring the MODIFY COMMAND MX_REPT line to the dot prompt, and press Return. Insert the following line immediately after the comment lines:

```
DO WHILE .T.
```

After the last program line, close the loop with the command *ENDDO*. Figure 10.4 shows how your program should look.

Step 8: Add an option and an action to exit the user from the loop. After the line beginning @ 5,10 SAY, insert the command @ 7,15 SAY '0 - Exit'. Before the command IF mchoice = 1, add the following lines:

```
IF mchoice = 0
    EXIT
ENDIF
```

Step 9: Clean up the display of the menu, and pause the screen after a report is displayed. Immediately before the ENDDO command, insert a *WAIT* command. Immediately after the comments, enter the command *SET TALK OFF*. Your program now should look similar to figure 10.5.

Step 10: Save and test the program. Press Ctrl-End. At the dot prompt, use the up-arrow key to bring the DO MX_REPT line back to the dot prompt. Press Return and select a report to run. When the report is displayed, type *0* to end the program.

The program should now work correctly, with one exception. The SALEFIN report (option 2) needs to be run on an indexed database for the reasons discussed in Lesson 8. You must add program commands to correct this situation.

```
* MX_REPT.PRG
* Menu program to access sales system reports

DO WHILE .T.

    CLEAR
    STORE 0 TO mchoice

    @  5,10 SAY "SALTWATER SALLY'S SALES REPORTS"
    @  9,15 SAY '1 - Summary Report'
    @ 11,15 SAY '2 - Detailed Report'
    @ 13,15 SAY '3 - Customer Notes'
    @ 16,15 SAY 'Choose One ' GET mchoice
    READ

    IF mchoice = 1
        REPORT FORM sales
    ENDIF

    IF mchoice = 2
        REPORT FORM salefin
    ENDIF

    IF mchoice = 3
        REPORT FORM custnote
    ENDIF

ENDDO
```

Fig. 10.4. *Sales Reports menu program with loop added.*

```
* MX_REPT.PRG
* Menu program to access sales system reports

SET TALK OFF
DO WHILE .T.

    CLEAR
    STORE 0 TO mchoice

    @  5,10 SAY "SALTWATER SALLY'S SALES REPORTS"
    @  7,15 SAY '0 - Exit'
    @  9,15 SAY '1 - Summary Report'
    @ 11,15 SAY '2 - Detailed Report'
    @ 13,15 SAY '3 - Customer Notes'
    @ 16,15 SAY 'Choose One ' GET mchoice
    READ

    IF mchoice = 0
        EXIT
    ENDIF

    IF mchoice = 1
        REPORT FORM sales
    ENDIF

    IF mchoice = 2
        REPORT FORM salefin
    ENDIF

    IF mchoice = 3
        REPORT FORM custnote
    ENDIF

    WAIT
ENDDO
```

Fig. 10.5. *Sales Reports menu program with pause and cleanup added.*

NOTES

Step 11: Open the database within the program. Enter *MODIFY COMMAND MX_REPT,* and immediately below the SET TALK OFF command, type *USE MX_SALES.*

Step 12: Index MX_SALES on the ESP field for option 2. Move the cursor to the line below IF mchoice = 2. Insert a blank line, and type *INDEX ON esp TO temp.* On another blank line below the REPORT FORM salefin line, type *CLOSE INDEX.*

Step 13: Delete the TEMP index file, and reset all defaults. After the ENDDO command, type the following lines:

```
ERASE TEMP.NDX
SET TALK ON
RETURN
```

Compare your program with the listing in figure 10.6.

Building the Main Menu

An integrated application consists of more functions than just those that report on the database. The application also should have automated programs to handle at least the most common housekeeping chores:

- Appending new records

- Locating a particular record

- Editing a record

Lesson 11 covers building programs to handle these housekeeping tasks. In this lesson, you will anticipate these programs and build a menu for users to access them.

Step 1: Call up the word processor. Type *MODIFY COMMAND MX_MENU.* MX_MENU is the name of the Main Menu program file.

Step 2: Enter comments and set up commands. Type the following lines to get the program started:

```
* MX_MENU.PRG
* Main menu for sales system
* Manages MX_SALES database

USE MX_SALES
```

In the next step, you will write the program lines for the list of options. In writing the report program, MX_REPT, you used a series of @ . . . SAY statements to write the list. In this exercise you will use the TEXT . . . ENDTEXT commands to avoid having to calculate the screen locations.

```
* MX_REPT.PRG
* Menu program to access sales system reports

SET TALK OFF
USE MX_SALES
DO WHILE .T.

    CLEAR
    STORE 0 TO mchoice

    @  5,10 SAY "SALTWATER SALLY'S SALES REPORTS"
    @  7,15 SAY '0 - Exit'
    @  9,15 SAY '1 - Summary Report'
    @ 11,15 SAY '2 - Detailed Report'
    @ 13,15 SAY '3 - Customer Notes'
    @ 16,15 SAY 'Choose One ' GET mchoice
    READ

    IF mchoice = 0
        EXIT
    ENDIF

    IF mchoice = 1
        REPORT FORM sales
    ENDIF

    IF mchoice = 2
        INDEX ON esp TO temp
        REPORT FORM salefin
        CLOSE INDEX
    ENDIF

    IF mchoice = 3
        REPORT FORM custnote
    ENDIF

    WAIT
ENDDO

ERASE TEMP.NDX
SET TALK ON
RETURN
```

Fig. 10.6. *Completed Sales Reports menu program.*

The TEXT command is useful because any lines following TEXT are displayed on the screen in exactly the column and row locations they occupy in the program. For instance, suppose you want your menu to appear as it does in figure 10.7, approximately centered toward the top of the screen. To achieve this arrangement, simply design the menu in the word processor as you want it to appear, and enclose the menu options between the TEXT and ENDTEXT commands.

```
SALTWATER SALLY'S SALES SYSTEM
      === MAIN MENU ===

   0 - Exit to dBASE

   1 - Add Sales

   2 - Edit Sales

   3 - Locate a Sale

   4 - Report Sales
```

Fig. 10.7. *Plan for Main Menu.*

Step 3: Enter the list of options. Type the command *TEXT*. Starting on the next line, enter the menu design shown in figure 10.7. End the options list by typing *ENDTEXT*. Compare your program to the one in figure 10.8.

Because you have not calculated a position for the last menu line, you do not know at what position to GET the user's menu selection. To solve this problem, you can use the INPUT command in place of the @ . . . SAY . . . GET you used in MX_REPT. INPUT provides a prompt following the command name and stores the number the user chooses to a numeric memory variable.

Step 4: Record the user's menu selection. On the line following ENDTEXT, type *INPUT 'Please Choose an Option ' TO mselect*.

Step 5: Save the program and test it at this stage of completion. Press Ctrl-End; then type *DO MX_MENU*. Enter an option. Because no actions have been specified yet, all options exit the program (see fig. 10.9).

```
* MX_MENU.PRG
* Main menu for sales system
* Manages MX_SALES database

USE MX_SALES

TEXT
                    SALTWATER SALLY'S SALES SYSTEM
                        === MAIN MENU ===

                    0 - Exit to dBASE

                    1 - Add Sales

                    2 - Edit Sales

                    3 - Locate a Sale

                    4 - Report Sales

ENDTEXT
```

Fig. 10.8. *Main Menu program with TEXT command.*

```
. DO MX_MENU
                    SALTWATER SALLY'S SALES SYSTEM
                        === MAIN MENU ===

                    0 - Exit to dBASE

                    1 - Add Sales

                    2 - Edit Sales

                    3 - Locate a Sale

                    4 - Report Sales

Please Choose an Option 4

Command Line     <B:> MX_SALES            Rec: 1/10            Caps
                    Enter a dBASE III PLUS command.
```

Fig. 10.9. *Running the Main Menu options list.*

In the next step, you will record the set of actions for the menu items. To reduce the amount of typing and to make processing more efficient, you will use a DO CASE . . . ENDCASE structure.

The DO CASE statement can do essentially the same job as the series of IF statements used in writing the actions in MX_REPT, but with less programming on your part and less processing time on dBASE's part. In place of an IF . . . ENDIF pair, substitute a CASE command followed on the same line by a test condition. On the lines following the CASE command, type the action to take if the condition holds true. Write one CASE command and one action for each menu choice.

Step 6: Write the set of actions. Following the INPUT command, type the following commands:

```
DO CASE
   CASE mselect = Ø
      EXIT
   CASE mselect = 1
      DO MX_ADD
   CASE mselect = 2
      DO MX_EDIT
   CASE mselect = 3
      DO MX_SEAR
   CASE mselect = 4
      DO MX_REPT
ENDCASE
```

Step 7: Build a menu control loop. Immediately after the USE MX_SALES command, type the following commands:

```
DO WHILE .T.
   CLEAR
```

On the line following the ENDCASE command, type *ENDDO*.

Step 8: Complete the program. After the comments at the beginning of the program, type *SET TALK OFF*. After ENDDO at the end of the program, type these commands:

```
SET TALK ON
RETURN
```

Your completed program now should look similar to the one shown in figure 10.10.

```
* MX_MENU.PRG
* Main menu for sales system
* Manages MX_SALES database

SET TALK OFF
USE MX_SALES

DO WHILE .T.

    CLEAR
    TEXT
                    SALTWATER SALLY'S SALES SYSTEM
                        === MAIN MENU ===

                    0 - Exit to dBASE

                    1 - Add Sales

                    2 - Edit Sales

                    3 - Locate a Sale

                    4 - Report Sales

    ENDTEXT

    INPUT 'Please Choose an Option ' TO mselect

    DO CASE
        CASE mselect = 0
            EXIT
        CASE mselect = 1
            DO MX_ADD
        CASE mselect = 2
            DO MX_EDIT
        CASE mselect = 3
            DO MX_SEAR
        CASE mselect =4
            DO MX_REPT
    ENDCASE

ENDDO

SET TALK ON
RETURN
```

Fig. 10.10. *Completed Main Menu program.*

Step 9: Run the completed program. Press Ctrl_End, and then type *DO MX_MENU*. Test option *4*, to report sales. You should see the Saltwater Sally's Sales Reports menu (MX_REPT.PRG). Select option *0* from the report menu to return to the Main Menu.

Because the menu is a program, you can nest menus—that is, an option on one menu can call up another menu.

Step 10: Try a different menu option. Select option *2* from the Main Menu. The message that results, File does not exist, indicates that the MX_EDIT program the menu called for is not available (see fig. 10.11). Type *C* to cancel the program.

```
                SALTWATER SALLY'S SALES SYSTEM
                    === MAIN MENU ===

                    0 - Exit to dBASE

                    1 - Add Sales

                    2 - Edit Sales

                    3 - Locate a Sale

                    4 - Report Sales

Please Choose an Option 2
File does not exist.
                    ?
            DO MX_EDIT
Called from - B:MX_MENU.prg




Command        |<B:>|MX_SALES              |Rec: 1/10    |Ins  |  Caps
            Cancel, Ignore, or Suspend? (C, I, or S)
                Enter a dBASE III PLUS command.
```

Fig. 10.11. Calling a non-existent program from the Main Menu.

If you choose an option that dBASE cannot carry out for some reason, a message appears on the message line asking you to choose one of three options:

Cancel, Ignore, or Suspend? (C, I, or S)

- Canceling a program simply returns system control to the dot prompt. At that point you can use MODIFY COMMAND to correct the error.

NOTES

- Ignoring the error forces the program past the offending line. The results can be unpredictable, because an early error can affect later statements in the program. These statements may be written correctly, but they may not work correctly because of the error.

- Suspending the program sends control temporarily back to the dot prompt, where you can give commands to check or verify the situation. For instance, if the message reports that a file does not exist, you can suspend the program and give a DIR command to check the spelling of the file. You cannot correct the error while the program is suspended, but if the error is not fatal, you can resume the program and check for other errors. After suspending a program, continue the program by using the RESUME command at the dot prompt.

Que Tip: To print the MX_MENU program file within dBASE III Plus, type *TYPE MX_MENU.PRG TO PRINT.*

Trapping User Errors

Anyone sitting at a keyboard interacting with a program is likely to make an error at one time or another. If the program does not spot these errors and point them out to the user, the error may either "crash" the program or corrupt the database. Therefore, a program should be written to anticipate the most common user errors. It is considered a "courtesy" for the program to help the user by pointing out that an error was made and what the user should do to correct it.

dBASE III Plus has several means for coping with errors. One way is to send an error message and ask whether and how the program should continue. This kind of message is helpful for people who develop the programs but disconcerting for those who use them. Therefore, the program should not include any errors that lead to a dBASE error message. Eliminating errors of this kind is part of the normal "debugging" process of writing, then testing, then rewriting the program code.

Most programs operate on the assumption that users will confine their choices to legitimate program options. Programmers, however, would be naive to think that users will always choose correctly. Therefore, you should think ahead to the kinds of mistakes users will—not might—make, and add "traps" to catch these errors. An *error trap* is a section of program code that identifies for the user when an error has occurred, suggests how to correct it, and allows the user to make amends without "crashing" the program.

NOTES

The dBASE III Plus programming language has built-in devices that make error traps easy to write. Two of these devices are included as alternative actions to the IF . . . ENDIF and DO CASE . . . ENDCASE commands. You can insert an ELSE statement into an IF . . . ENDIF command to give the program some direction about what to do if the test condition is not true. The DO CASE . . . ENDCASE command has a similar OTHERWISE statement.

For the Main Menu program, you will use the OTHERWISE statement to trap user responses that are not legitimate options.

Step 1: Reenter the word processor. Type *MODIFY COMMAND MX_MENU,* or use the up-arrow key to bring this command back to the command line.

Step 2: Insert an error trap for invalid option selections. Use the PgDn and down-arrow keys to move the cursor to the ENDCASE statement. Press Ctrl-N to insert a blank line, and type the following lines:

```
OTHERWISE
  ? 'Not a valid option.'
  ? 'Please choose a number from 1 to 4.'
  WAIT
```

The program should now look as it does in figure 10.12.

Step 3: Test the error trap. Press Ctrl-End, and type *DO MX_MENU.* At the select option, type *6* and compare your screen with figure 10.13.

```
* MX_MENU.PRG
* Main menu for sales system
* Manages MX_SALES database

SET TALK OFF
USE MX_SALES

DO WHILE .T.

    CLEAR
    TEXT
                    SALTWATER SALLY'S SALES SYSTEM
                          === MAIN MENU ===

                        0 - Exit to dBASE

                        1 - Add Sales

                        2 - Edit Sales

                        3 - Locate a Sale

                        4 - Report Sales

    ENDTEXT

    INPUT 'Please Choose an Option ' TO mselect

    DO CASE
        CASE mselect = 0
             EXIT
        CASE mselect = 1
             DO MX_ADD
        CASE mselect = 2
             DO MX_EDIT
        CASE mselect = 3
             DO MX_SEAR
        CASE mselect =4
             DO MX_REPT
        OTHERWISE
             ? 'Not a valid option.'
             ? 'Please choose a number from 1 to 4.'
             WAIT
    ENDCASE

ENDDO

SET TALK ON
RETURN
```

Fig. 10.12. *Programming an error trap in the Main Menu.*

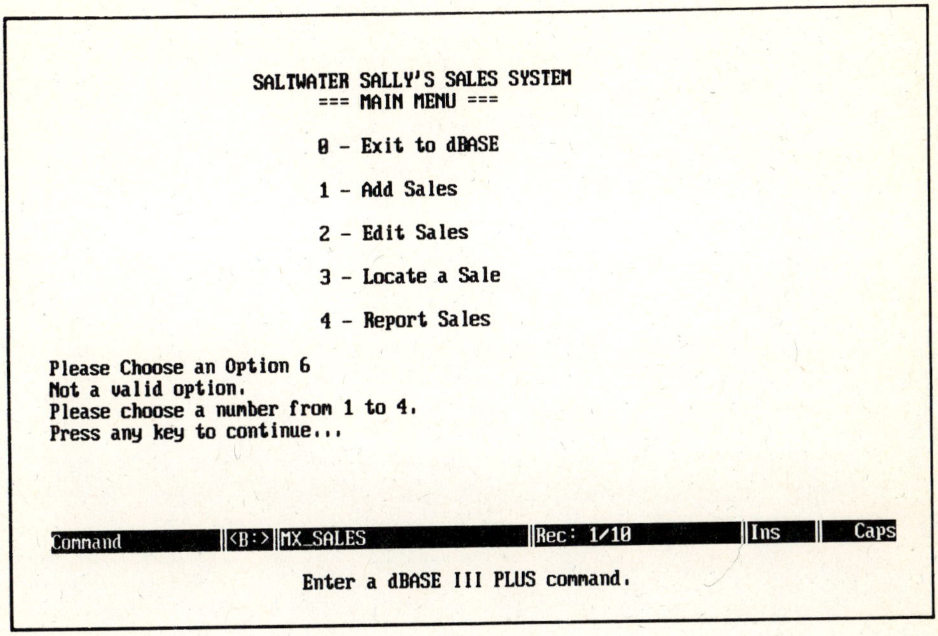

```
                  SALTWATER SALLY'S SALES SYSTEM
                      === MAIN MENU ===

                       0 - Exit to dBASE

                       1 - Add Sales

                       2 - Edit Sales

                       3 - Locate a Sale

                       4 - Report Sales

Please Choose an Option 6
Not a valid option.
Please choose a number from 1 to 4.
Press any key to continue...




Command         ||<B:>||MX_SALES            ||Rec: 1/10      ||Ins  ||   Caps
                  Enter a dBASE III PLUS command.
```

Fig. 10.13. *Testing the Main Menu error trap.*

SUMMARY OF CONCEPTS PRESENTED IN LESSON 10

1. An application can consist of many program files. The Main Menu coordinates the program files.

2. Menus display a list of options, obtain a menu selection, and branch to the action corresponding to the selection.

3. DO CASE . . . ENDCASE, like IF . . . ENDIF, tests for a condition and executes actions if the condition is met.

4. TEXT . . . ENDTEXT organizes the display screen and avoids the use of @ . . . SAY statements.

5. The dBASE III Plus history buffer stores the last twenty commands typed at the dot prompt. Stored commands can be recalled to the dot prompt by using the up-arrow and down-arrow keys, and then executed.

6. Menus can be nested within one another; an option on one menu can call up another menu.

7. A menu is embedded within an infinite loop to allow users to make more than one selection during a session. An infinite loop must provide an option for leaving the loop.

8. dBASE III Plus identifies program errors as they occur and allows the programmer to cancel the program, ignore the error, or suspend the program. You restart a suspended program by using the RESUME command.

9. Error traps can catch user errors. An error trap can be an ELSE statement within an IF . . . ENDIF command, or an OTHERWISE statement within a DO CASE . . . ENDCASE command.

Design menus for the billing system. First, design a menu to generate GENBILLS. Unlike MX_REPT, which offers a choice of reports, SS_REPT produces only one report but offers a choice of destinations: either to the screen only or to both the screen and the printer.

Step 1: Activate the dBASE III Plus word processor to enter the SS_REPT program file. Type *MODIFY COMMAND SS_REPT*.

Step 2: Enter the code that follows. Save your work by pressing Ctrl-End.

```
* SS_REPT.PRG
* Produces choice of printer or screen for GENBILLS report.
* Uses SSBILLS data file.
USE SSBILLS
DO WHILE .T.
   STORE 0 TO sschoice
   CLEAR
   @ 5,10 SAY "--- GENERAL BILLS REPORT --- "
   @ 7,10 SAY "0 - EXIT"
   @ 8,10 SAY "1 - Report to the Printer"
   @ 9,10 SAY "2 - Screen Only "
   @ 10,10 SAY "Choose One " GET sschoice
   READ
   IF sschoice = 0
      EXIT
   ENDIF

   IF sschoice = 1
      ? "Prepare Printer "
      WAIT
      REPORT FORM GENBILLS TO PRINT
      ENDIF

   IF sschoice = 2
         REPORT FORM GENBILLS
         WAIT
   ENDIF

ENDDO
RETURN
```

NOTES

Step 3: Test your work. Type *DO SS_REPT*. Select the option to report to the screen. If a printer is available, send the report to the printer. If the program is not working properly, type *MODIFY COMMAND* to verify that the code has been entered properly.

Now design the Main Menu for the billing system. The procedures are virtually identical to those used for the sales system. Call the billing Main Menu SS_MENU.

Step 4: Activate the dBASE III Plus word processor to enter the Main Menu. Type *MODIFY COMMAND SS_MENU*.

Step 5: Enter the code that follows. Save by pressing Ctrl-End.

```
* SS_MENU.PRG
* Main Menu for Bills
* Applications Purpose:
* Track the Bills Owed by Sally's
SET TALK OFF
SET SAFETY OFF
USE SSBILLS
DO WHILE .T.
   CLEAR
   STORE 0 TO SSCHOICE
   @ 3,25 SAY "SALTWATER SALLY'S BILLING SYSTEM"
   @ 5,25 SAY "====== MAIN MENU ======"
   @ 7,25 SAY "0 - EXIT TO dBASE"
   @ 8,25 SAY "1 - ADD BILLS"
   @ 9,25 SAY "2 - EDIT BILLS"
   @ 10,25 SAY "3 - LOCATE A BILL"
   @ 11,25 SAY "4 - REPORT BILLS BY MONTH"
   @ 14,30 SAY "PLEASE CHOOSE AN OPTION" GET SSCHOICE
      READ

      * Execute according to option selected.
   DO CASE

   CASE SSCHOICE = 0
         * Prepare for exit.
         EXIT

   CASE SSCHOICE = 1
         * Add a record to Bills
         DO SS_ADD
```

NOTES

```
            CASE SSCHOICE = 2
                  * Edit records
                  DO SS_EDIT

            CASE SSCHOICE = 3
                  * Locate records
                  DO SS_SEAR

            CASE SSCHOICE = 4
                  * REPORT OPTIONS
                  DO SS_REPT

            OTHERWISE
              @ 20,0 SAY "NOT A VALID OPTION"
              WAIT
            ENDCASE
      ENDDO

      CLOSE DATABASES

      RETURN
```

Step 6: Test your work. Type *DO SS_MENU.* Select the report option, and generate the report on the screen.

NOTES

11

Screen Formatting: The Add, Edit, and Search Programs

Related sections in *dBASE III Plus Handbook*, 2nd Edition: Chapters 7 and 10.

Many of the dBASE III Plus operations that update a database make use of a screen showing the field names along with a highlight bar representing the length of the field (see fig. 11.1). This screen allows you to get and change values for any of the fields.

The screen works as it should, but it can be improved. The screen can be organized more logically, and the labels can be more informative than the field names. Also, the screen can help the user by inserting default characters that either do not change or change infrequently from one record to the next. Formatting a new screen to substitute for the default screen can add these improvements as well as some additional benefits.

In this lesson you will learn how to operate the dBASE III Plus screen generator to format screens for database updating operations. Then you will construct programs to do the following:

- Add records to the database
- Edit the database
- Search the database

Each of these programs will make use of the screen you design.

```
┌─────────────────────────────────────────────────────────────────────────┐
│                                                                           │
│   ┌──────────────────┬──────────────────┬────────────────┬────────────┐  │
│   │ CURSOR   <-- -->  │         UP   DOWN │   DELETE       │Insert Mode: Ins│
│   │ Char:    ←   →    │ Field:   ↑    ↓   │ Char:    Del   │Exit/Save:  ^End│
│   │ Word:  Home End   │ Page:  PgUp  PgDn │ Field:   ^Y    │Abort:      Esc │
│   │                   │ Help:    F1       │ Record:  ^U    │Memo:     ^Home │
│   └──────────────────┴──────────────────┴────────────────┴────────────┘  │
│    CFNAME                                                                  │
│    CLNAME                                                                  │
│    CSTREET                                                                 │
│    CCITY                                                                   │
│    CST                                                                     │
│    CZIP                                                                    │
│    CPHONE                                                                  │
│    CNOTE        memo                                                       │
│    PDATE         / /                                                       │
│    PINDATE       / /                                                       │
│    PCODE                                                                   │
│                                                                           │
│   ─────────────────────────────────────────────────────────────────────  │
│   APPEND          <B:> MX_SALES              Rec: EOF/10                   │
└─────────────────────────────────────────────────────────────────────────┘
```

Fig. 11.1. *Default data entry screen.*

Creating Screens and Format Files

Making a new screen for database updating operations is a two-stage process. The first step is for you to create a "blueprint" detailing what you want to appear on the screen and where. The resulting screen file (.SCR) holds the specifications for the screen. The second step is for dBASE to automatically generate a format file (.FMT) from the screen file. The format file is a list of @ . . . SAY and @ . . . GET statements that pinpoint the starting locations of each screen label or field.

A new screen is built by using the CREATE SCREEN command and giving the screen file a name. The format file generated from the screen file will have the same root name but a different extension.

The screen creator in dBASE III Plus acts like other Assistant menu systems, such as the report creator and the label creator. The screen creator adds another component, called the *blackboard*, to the menu system. The blackboard is a computer slate on which you design the screen form. You move the blackboard cursor to where you want a label or field, and either type the label or load the field. For the Sales System application, you will use the blackboard to design a screen similar to figure 11.2.

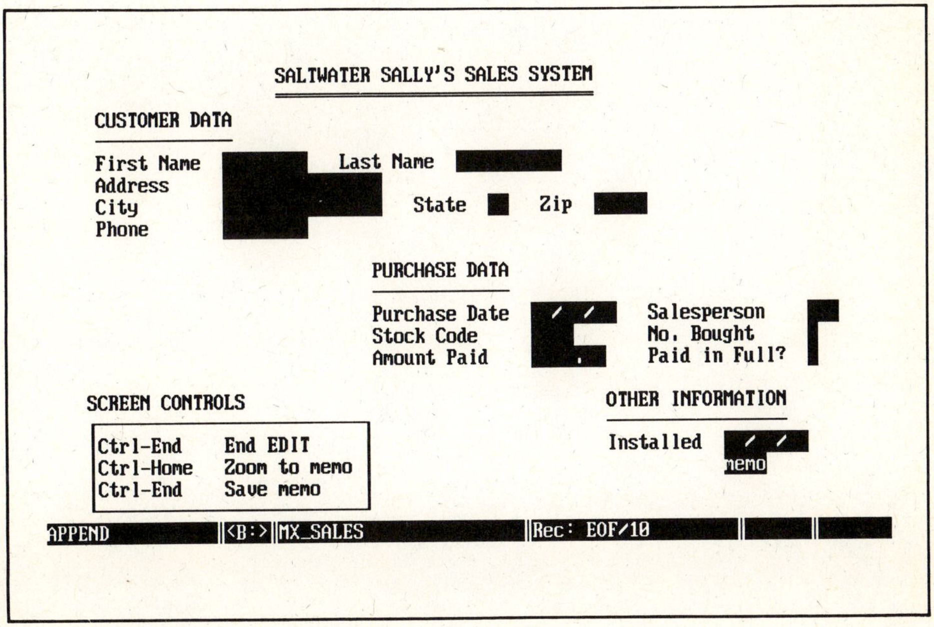

Fig. 11.2. *Plan for revised data entry screen.*

NOTES

The CREATE SCREEN menu includes four options (see fig. 11.3). These options allow you to **Set Up** databases and fields to appear on the screen, **Modify** the settings for fields, choose **Options** for drawing boxes and lines on the screen, and **Exit** the screen creator. The blackboard is used to arrange fields and labels into the desired pattern. Either the menu or the blackboard is active at any time. You switch between the two by pressing the F10 key.

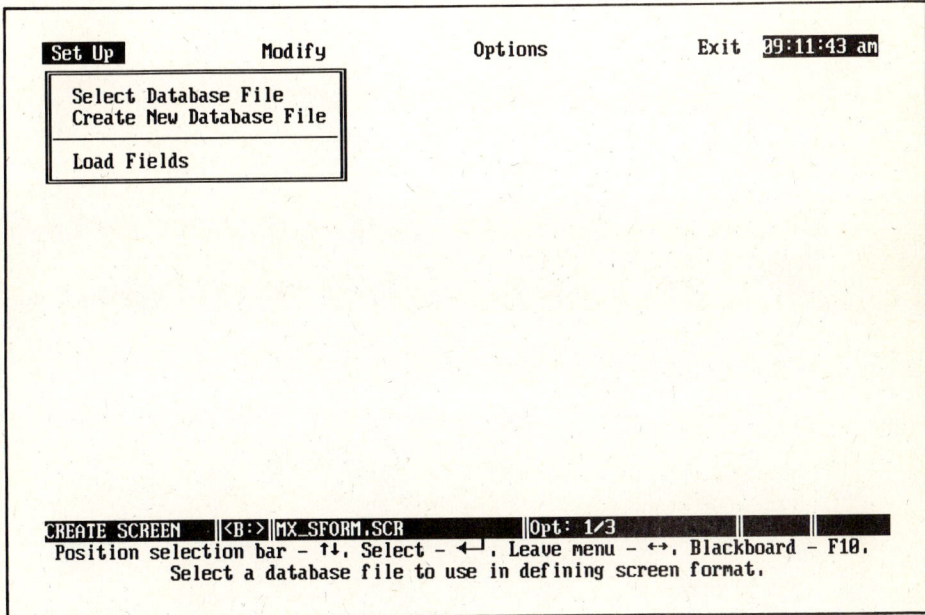

```
 Set Up              Modify            Options           Exit  09:11:43 am
 ┌──────────────────────────┐
 │ Select Database File     │
 │ Create New Database File │
 ├──────────────────────────┤
 │ Load Fields              │
 └──────────────────────────┘




















 CREATE SCREEN   │<B:>│MX_SFORM.SCR         │Opt: 1/3
   Position selection bar - ↑↓, Select - ←┘, Leave menu - ↔, Blackboard - F10.
         Select a database file to use in defining screen format.
```

Fig. 11.3. *Main menu of screen creator.*

Step 1: Type *DO QPREP*. Select Lesson 11.

Step 2: Load the screen creator. Type *CREATE SCREEN MX_SFORM*.

Step 3: Set up the database. From the CREATE SCREEN menu, highlight the **Set Up** submenu and then the **Select Database File** option. Select the database **MX_SALES.DBF** (see fig. 11.4).

Step 4: Enter the screen title. Press F10 to enter the blackboard. Note that the position of the blackboard cursor is indicated in the fourth panel of the status bar. Move the cursor to row 01, column 22 and type *SALTWATER SALLY'S SALES SYSTEM*.

```
 Set Up              Modify          Options            Exit  09:12:15 am
 ┌─────────────────────────────┐ ┌───────────────┐
 │ Select Database File         │ │QX1SALES.DBF   │
 │ Create New Database File     │ │QX4SALES.DBF   │
 │                              │ │MX_SALES.DBF   │
 │ Load Fields                  │ └───────────────┘
 └─────────────────────────────┘




 CREATE SCREEN    <B:> MX_SFORM.SCR           Opt: 3/3
 Position selection bar - ↑↓, Select - ←┘, Leave menu - ↔, Blackboard - F10.
         Select a database file to use in defining screen format.
```

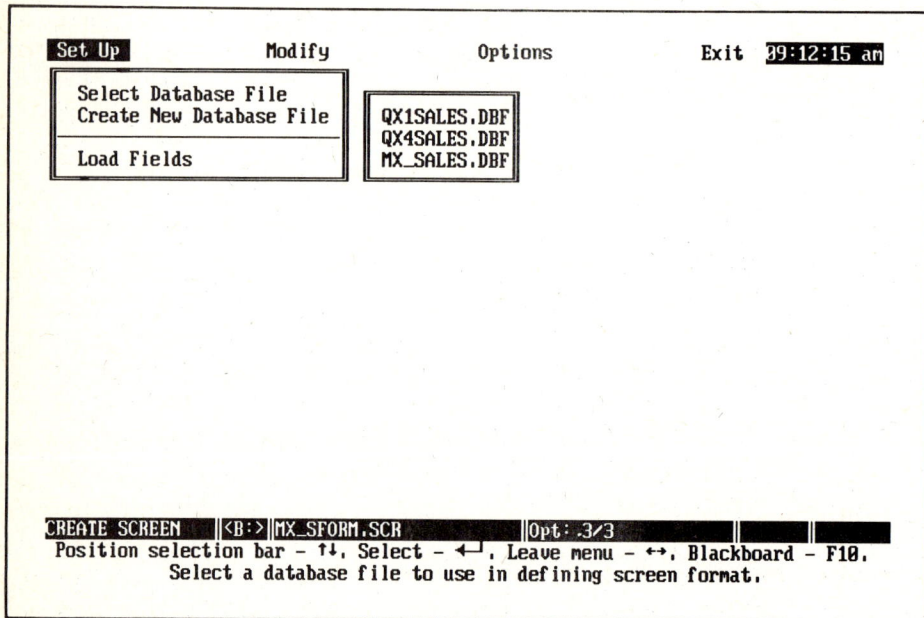

Fig. 11.4. *Setting up a database in the screen creator.*

Step 5: Underline the screen title. Press F10, move to the **Options** submenu, and select **Double bar**. Pressing Return puts you back in the blackboard automatically. Move the cursor to row 02, column 22 and press Return. Now move the cursor to row 02, column 51 and press Return again.

Drawing lines and boxes is done with **Options**. Lines can be either **Single bar** or **Double bar**. In the blackboard, move the cursor to the leftmost position of the line (where the line is to begin), and lock in the position by pressing Return. Then move the cursor to the rightmost position of the line and press Return again. For a box, the upper left corner and lower right corner are located and locked.

If a box or line has been drawn incorrectly, you can eliminate it by moving the cursor onto the box or line and pressing Ctrl-U. You can move a box or line from one location to another by putting the cursor on it, pressing Return, moving the cursor to the new location, and pressing Return again to complete the move. This procedure is called *dragging*. A box or line can be resized using a similar technique.

Step 6: Enter the title for the customer data. Move the cursor to row 03, column 05 and type *CUSTOMER DATA*.

Step 7: Underline the title on row 04 with a single line. Press F10, select **Options**, select the **Single bar** option, and press Return. Locate the cursor under the letter C and press Return. Move the cursor under the second A and press Return again. Compare your screen with figure 11.5.

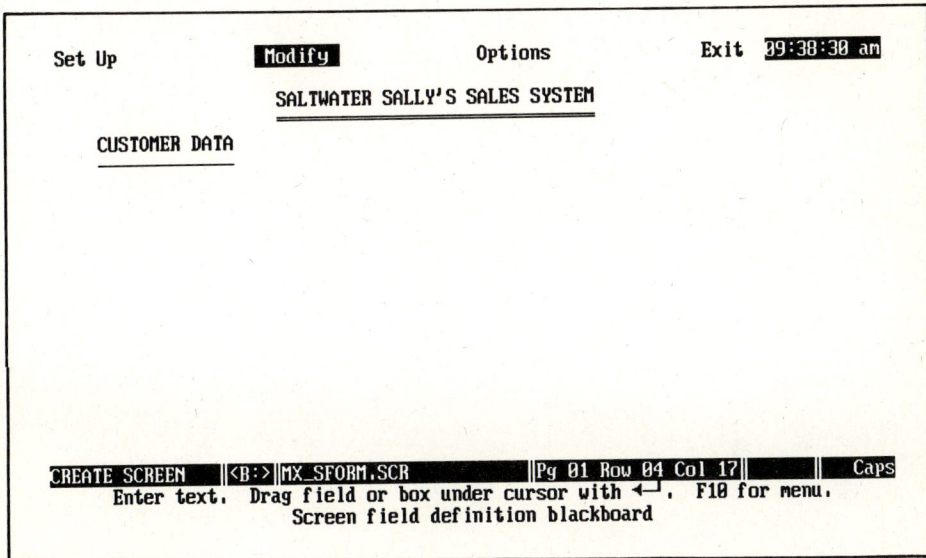

```
 Set Up              Modify            Options         Exit  09:38:30 am
                    SALTWATER SALLY'S SALES SYSTEM
                    ─────────────────────────────
         CUSTOMER DATA
         ─────────────





 

 
 CREATE SCREEN    <B:> MX_SFORM.SCR          Pg 01 Row 04 Col 17      Caps
     Enter text.  Drag field or box under cursor with ↵.  F10 for menu.
                   Screen field definition blackboard
```

Fig. 11.5. *Entering screen and customer data titles on the blackboard.*

NOTES

Step 8: Load the customer name fields. Move the cursor to row 05, column 05 and press F10 to move to the **Set Up** submenu. Select **Load Fields**. From the field list submenu, select the fields **CFNAME** and **CLNAME** by highlighting each and pressing Return. Both fields are marked with an arrow. Compare your screen with figure 11.6.

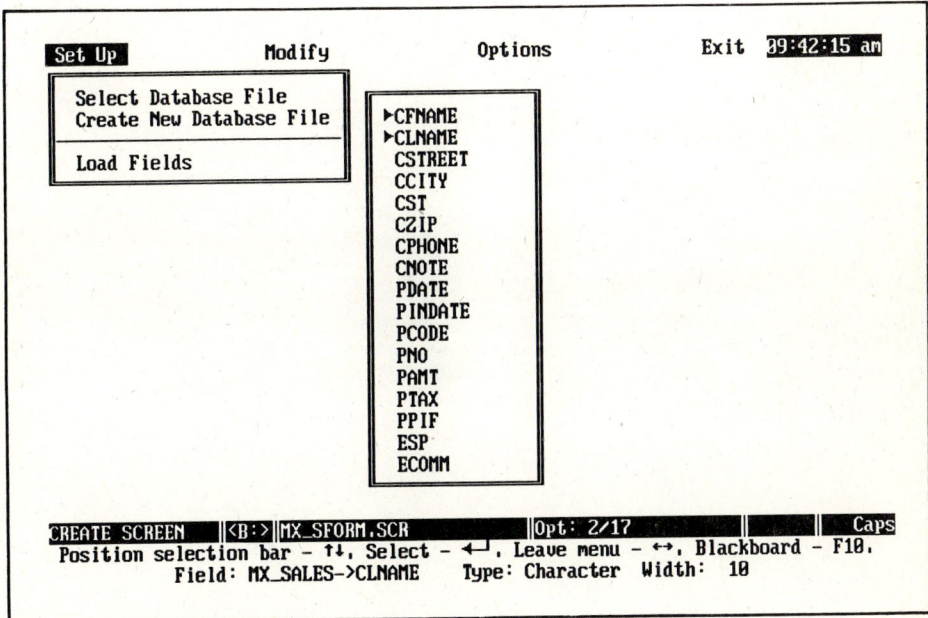

```
 Set Up          Modify            Options           Exit  09:42:15 am
┌─────────────────────────────┐ ┌──────────────┐
│ Select Database File        │ │ ►CFNAME      │
│ Create New Database File    │ │ ►CLNAME      │
│                             │ │  CSTREET     │
│ Load Fields                 │ │  CCITY       │
└─────────────────────────────┘ │  CST         │
                                 │  CZIP        │
                                 │  CPHONE      │
                                 │  CNOTE       │
                                 │  PDATE       │
                                 │  PINDATE     │
                                 │  PCODE       │
                                 │  PNO         │
                                 │  PAMT        │
                                 │  PTAX        │
                                 │  PPIF        │
                                 │  ESP         │
                                 │  ECOMM       │
                                 └──────────────┘

 CREATE SCREEN   <B:>MX_SFORM.SCR        Opt: 2/17              Caps
    Position selection bar - ↑↓, Select - ◄─┘, Leave menu - ↔, Blackboard - F10.
           Field: MX_SALES->CLNAME    Type: Character   Width:  10
```

Fig. 11.6. *Loading customer name fields.*

After selecting the second field, press F10 to return to the blackboard.

Step 9: Enter new field labels. The field labels now correspond to the names of the fields in the database. Change the name of CFNAME to *First Name*. If necessary, adjust the starting position of the *field bar* (the highlighted string of X's) to column 17. Move the cursor to row 05, column 28 and type *Last Name.*

Step 10: Rearrange the fields. Move the cursor into the CLNAME field bar, press Return, move the cursor back to row 05, column 39, and press Return again. Doing this drags the field from one location to another.

Step 11: Eliminate the old label, CLNAME. Do this by moving to line 06 and pressing Ctrl-Y. Compare your screen with figure 11.7.

```
 Set Up              Modify              Options              Exit  09:52:31 am

                     SALTWATER SALLY'S SALES SYSTEM
                     ─────────────────────────────
   CUSTOMER DATA
   ─────────────
   First Name  XXXXXXX    Last Name  XXXXXXXXX




 CREATE SCREEN    <B:> MX_SFORM.SCR          Pg 01 Row 06 Col 39
      Enter text.  Drag field or box under cursor with ←┘.  F10 for menu.
                     Screen field definition blackboard
```

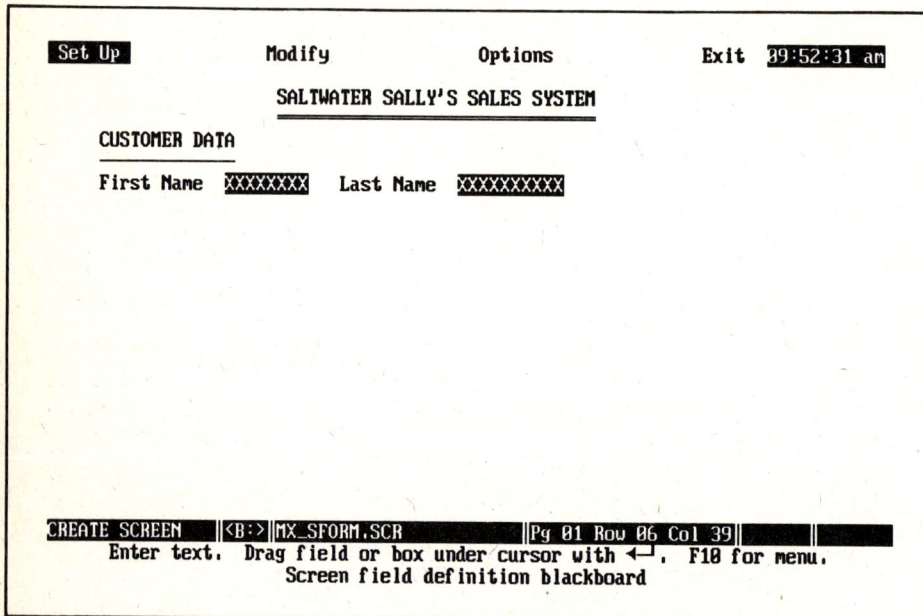

Fig. 11.7. *Customer name fields arranged on blackboard.*

Step 12: Enter the customer address information. Move to row 06, column 05. Using the same method used with CFNAME and CLNAME, load the following fields:

> **CSTREET**
> **CCITY**
> **CST**
> **CZIP**
> **CPHONE**

Step 13: Relabel all the fields and drag the CST and CZIP fields to row 07. The new field labels and their positions are as follows:

Street		
City	State	Zip
Phone		

Use the same methods used with CFNAME and CLNAME to drag the fields and eliminate unnecessary lines. Compare your screen with figure 11.8.

```
 Set Up            Modify           Options          Exit  10:06:09 am

                   SALTWATER SALLY'S SALES SYSTEM
                   ══════════════════════════════

   CUSTOMER DATA
   ─────────────
   First Name  XXXXXXX   Last Name  XXXXXXXXXX
   Street      XXXXXXXXXXXXXX
   City        XXXXXXXXXXXXXX   State  XX   Zip  XXXXX
   Phone       XXXXXXX




CREATE SCREEN   ‖<B:>‖MX_SFORM.SCR        ‖Pg 01 Row 08 Col 11‖‖      ‖
      Enter text.  Drag field or box under cursor with ↵.  F10 for menu.
                   Screen field definition blackboard
```

Fig. 11.8. *Customer address and phone fields arranged on blackboard.*

NOTES

Step 14: Enter the title for the purchase information. Position the cursor at row 10, column 31 and type *PURCHASE DATA*. Underline the title with a single bar.

Step 15: Load the purchase information fields. Move to row 12, column 31 and press F10. Move to the **Set Up** submenu, and select **Load Fields**. Mark the following fields:

PDATE
PCODE
PNO
PAMT
PPIF
ESP

Press the F10 key to enter the blackboard.

Step 16: Enter new field labels. In place of the field names type the following labels in the positions indicated:

Purch Date	Salesperson
Stock Code	No. Bought
Amount Paid	Paid in Full?

Drag the fields to their new locations, and eliminate the field names (see fig. 11.9).

Step 17: Load other data fields. Position the cursor at row 16, column 53, type *OTHER INFORMATION*, and underline it with a single bar. Reposition the cursor at row 18, column 53, and press F10. Go to the **Set Up** submenu, and select the **Load Fields** option. Select **CNOTE** and **PINDATE**.

Step 18: Relabel and rearrange the fields. Reverse the position of the two fields; the memo field should follow the PINDATE field. Erase the word CNOTE by pressing Ctrl-T. In place of the word PINDATE, type *Installed*. Compare your screen with the one illustrated in figure 11.10.

Step 19: Provide some information to users to control entry and exit from memo and EDIT. Move to row 16, column 04 and type *SCREEN CONTROLS*. Type the following lines at the positions indicated:

Row	Col	Text
18	05	Ctrl-End - Exit EDIT
19	05	Ctrl-Home - Zoom to Memo
20	05	Ctrl-End - Exit Memo

```
 Set Up            Modify          Options          Exit  10:19:28 am
                    SALTWATER SALLY'S SALES SYSTEM

   CUSTOMER DATA

   First Name  XXXXXXX    Last Name  XXXXXXXXX
   Street      XXXXXXXXXXXXXX
   City        XXXXXXXXXXXXXX    State  XX   Zip  XXXX
   Phone       XXXXXXX

                         PURCHASE DATA

                         Purch Date  99/99/99     Salesperson   XXX
                         Stock Code  XXXX         No. Bought    9
                         Amount Paid 9999.99      Paid in Full? L


 CREATE SCREEN   <B:> MX_SFORM.SCR            Pg 01 Row 15 Col 43
        Enter text.  Drag field or box under cursor with ←┘.  F10 for menu.
                     Screen field definition blackboard
```

Fig. 11.9. *Purchase data fields arranged on blackboard.*

```
 Set Up            Modify          Options          Exit  10:26:50 am
                    SALTWATER SALLY'S SALES SYSTEM

   CUSTOMER DATA

   First Name  XXXXXXX    Last Name  XXXXXXXXX
   Street      XXXXXXXXXXXXXX
   City        XXXXXXXXXXXXXX    State  XX   Zip  XXXX
   Phone       XXXXXXX

                         PURCHASE DATA

                         Purch Date  99/99/99     Salesperson   XXX
                         Stock Code  XXXX         No. Bought    9
                         Amount Paid 9999.99      Paid in Full? L

                                      OTHER INFORMATION

                                      Installed  99/99/99
                                                 MEMO
 CREATE SCREEN   <B:> MX_SFORM.SCR            Pg 01 Row 19 Col 62
        Enter text.  Drag field or box under cursor with ←┘.  F10 for menu.
                     Screen field definition blackboard
```

Fig. 11.10. *Other information fields arranged on blackboard.*

Step 20: Draw a box around the screen controls. Move the cursor to row 17, column 04, press F10, move to **Options**, and select **Single bar**. Back in the blackboard, press Return to lock the upper left corner of the box. Move the cursor to row 21, column 30 and press Return again.

The completed screen now should resemble figure 11.11.

```
Set Up              Modify          Options            Exit  10:39:02 am
                    SALTWATER SALLY'S SALES SYSTEM

    CUSTOMER DATA

    First Name  XXXXXXX    Last Name  XXXXXXXXX
    Street      XXXXXXXXXXXXXX
    City        XXXXXXXXXXXXXX    State  XX   Zip  XXXX
    Phone       XXXXXXX

                            PURCHASE DATA

                            Purch Date  99/99/99    Salesperson  XXX
                            Stock Code  XXXX        No. Bought   9
                            Amount Paid 9999.99     Paid in Full? L

    SCREEN CONTROLS                     OTHER INFORMATION

    Ctrl-End  - Exit EDIT               Installed  99/99/99
    Ctrl-Home - Zoom to Memo                       MEMO
    Ctrl-End  - Exit Memo

 CREATE SCREEN   <B:> MX_SFORM.SCR         Pg 01 Row 21 Col 30 Ins
       Enter text.  Drag field or box under cursor with ◄┘.  F10 for menu.
                    Screen field definition blackboard
```

Fig. 11.11. *Screen control instructions added to blackboard.*

Step 21: Exit and save the screen and format file. Press F10 and move to the **Exit** submenu. With **Save** selected, press Return.

Step 22: Test the screen. At the dot prompt, type *APPEND*. Figure 11.2 shows the result. Press Esc to leave APPEND.

When a format file is created, it is set to the active database. In later sessions, the command SET FORMAT TO MX_SFORM activates the file. A format also can be set within a view file.

To check the status of the format file, use the command DISPLAY STATUS. Any set format file will be identified with the open database. To close a format file, use CLOSE FORMAT. A format file also is closed if the database it is linked to is closed.

NOTES

Using Pictures and Ranges To Prevent Errors

A format file's primary purpose is putting data onto the display in a form that makes entering and editing the database easier for users. As part of this process, a format file also can include error traps that catch certain kinds of data entry errors. A format file does this through pictures and ranges.

Pictures

A *picture* is a model of how data is supposed to look when it is entered into a particular field. A picture can be specified on a character-by-character basis for each position in the field, or it can be specified for all positions in the field. The first possibility is called a *picture template*, the second a *picture function*.

By default, each field in the format file is defined with a picture template according to the type of field it is. The template is represented in the blackboard by the symbols within the highlighted field bar. The default picture templates and what they represent are listed in table 11.1.

Table 11.1
Default Picture Templates

Field Type	Default Template	Characters Allowed in the Field
Character	X	Any printable character
Numeric	9	Any numeral or number sign
Date	99/99/99	Numerals separated by slashes
Logical	L	The letters T, F, Y, or N
Memo	memo	Any character when activated

In addition, character and numeric fields have other picture symbols that can mix with or replace the default symbols. Table 11.2 lists these special picture symbols.

Any other symbols included in a picture template take on their own values and over-write anything else that might be typed in that location. The slash (/) in the date field template is an example of a *literal symbol*; nothing else can be typed in place of the slash.

In the following steps, you will add special picture templates to the State, Stock Code, and Salesperson fields. The State field and Salesperson field should accept only up-percase letters. The Stock Code field should be represented with an uppercase letter, a hyphen (-), and two numerals: for example, H-89. Adding these templates can cut down on the number of data entry errors, because dBASE III Plus will not accept any values that violate the picture template.

Table 11.2
Special Picture Symbols

For Character Fields

Symbol	Action
!	Converts typed character to uppercase
A	Accepts only alphabetic characters (no numerals)
N	Accepts only alphabetic characters and numerals
9	Accepts only numerals or number signs
#	Accepts numerals, number signs, spaces, and periods

For Numeric Fields

Symbol	Action
#	Accepts numerals, spaces, and signs
,	Displays a comma within the number
.	Specifies a decimal point location

Step 1: Modify the MX_SFORM screen. Type *MODIFY SCREEN MX_SFORM* and press F10 to enter the blackboard.

Step 2: Specify a picture template for the State field. Move the cursor into the field bar for the State field, and press F10. In the **Modify** submenu, move the selection bar to **Picture Template:** and press Return. For the **Picture value**, type two exclamation points, *!!* (see fig. 11.12). Press Return to complete the template.

```
 Set Up          Modify        Options           Exit  12:09:45 pm

                 Screen Field Definition
                  Action : Edit/GET
                  Source:  MX_SALES
                  Content: CST                 Character Input Symbols
                  Type   : Character
                  Width:     2                 A     Any alpha character
                  Decimal:                     L     Allow T, F, Y, or N
                                               N     Alpha and digits
                  Picture Function:            X     Any character
                  Picture Template:            Y     Allow Y, or N
                  Range:                       #     Allow digits, spaces,
                                                     signs, and periods
                                               9     Allow digits and signs
                                               !     Convert to uppercase
                                               other Overwrite data unless
                                                     @R function is used

     Picture value!!

 MODIFY SCREEN    <B:> MX_SFORM.SCR          Opt: 6/6        Ins
        Enter a picture template without using quotes. Finish with ←┘.
        Enter a picture template for editing or displaying this field.
```

Fig. 11.12. *Adding a picture value to CST field.*

A picture function is much the same as a picture template, except that the function applies to all positions in the field. The available functions will be listed when you activate the option from the menu.

Step 3: Specify a picture function for the Salesperson field. Press F10 to return to the blackboard, and move the cursor into the Salesperson field bar. Press F10 again to return to the **Modify** submenu. Move the selection bar down to **Picture Function:**, press Return, and type a single exclamation point, *!* (see fig. 11.13). Press Return again.

```
   Set Up            Modify              Options              Exit  12:27:35 pm

                    ┌─────────────────────────────────┐
                    │ Screen Field Definition         │
                    │  Action : Edit/GET              │
                    │  Source:  MX_SALES              │
                    │  Content: ESP                   │
                    │  Type   : Character             │
                    │  Width:      3                  │
                    │  Decimal:                       │
                    │                              █  │
                    │  Picture Function:              │      ┌────────────────────────────────┐
                    │  Picture Template:              │      │ Character Input Functions      │
                    │  Range:                         │      │                                │
                    └─────────────────────────────────┘      │  !   convert to uppercase      │
                                                             │  A   display only alpha chars  │
                                                             │  D   American mm/dd/yy date    │
                                                             │  E   European dd/mm/yy date    │
                                                             │  S   horizontal scrolling      │
                                                             │  R   insert <other> char       │
                                                             │      don't overwrite it        │
                                                             └────────────────────────────────┘

     ┌─────────────────────────────────────────┐
     │ Function value▶!                         │
     └─────────────────────────────────────────┘
   MODIFY SCREEN  ║<B:>║MX_SFORM.SCR            ║Pg 01 Row 12 Col 72║      ║
     Enter one or more function symbols without using quotes. Finish with ◄─┘.
        Enter a picture function for editing or displaying this field.
```

Fig. 11.13. *Adding a function value to ESP field.*

Step 4: Specify a picture template for the Stock Code field. Press F10 to reenter the blackboard, and move the cursor into the Stock Code field bar. Press F10 and move the **Modify** selection bar to **Picture Template:**. Press Return and type *!-99* as the **Picture value** (see fig. 11.14).

```
   Set Up          Modify          Options          Exit  12:31:18 pm

                  Screen Field Definition
                   Action : Edit/GET
                   Source : MX_SALES
                   Content: PCODE
                   Type   : Character          Character Input Symbols
                   Width :      4
                   Decimal:                    A     Any alpha character
                                               L     Allow T, F, Y, or N
                                               N     Alpha and digits
                   Picture Function:           X     Any character
                   Picture Template:           Y     Allow Y, or N
                   Range:                      #     Allow digits, spaces,
                                                     signs, and periods
                                               9     Allow digits and signs
                                               !     Convert to uppercase
                                               other Overwrite data unless
                                                     @R function is used

         Picture value !-99

  MODIFY SCREEN    <B:> MX_SFORM.SCR          Pg 01 Row 13 Col 43
         Enter a picture template without using quotes. Finish with ↵.
         Enter a picture template for editing or displaying this field.
```

Fig. 11.14. *Adding a picture value to PCODE field.*

Press Return and then F10. Compare the new appearance of the screen with figure 11.15. Notice that the State field and Stock Code field are now specified with the new picture templates.

Ranges

A range offers a way to prevent values from being entered into the database that are either less than a lower limit or greater than an upper limit. Ranges apply to numeric and date fields only.

```
  Set Up              Modify              Options            Exit  12:32:33 pm
                      SALTWATER SALLY'S SALES SYSTEM
      CUSTOMER DATA
      ─────────────
      First Name  XXXXXXX    Last Name  XXXXXXXXX
      Street      XXXXXXXXXXXXX
      City        XXXXXXXXXXXXXX     State  !!   Zip  XXXXX
      Phone       XXXXXXX

                           PURCHASE DATA
                           ─────────────
                           Purch Date  99/99/99    Salesperson  XXX
                           Stock Code  !-99        No. Bought   9
                           Amount Paid 9999.99     Paid in Full? L

      SCREEN CONTROLS                      OTHER INFORMATION
      ───────────────                      ─────────────────
      ┌──────────────────────────────┐
      │ Ctrl-End  - Exit EDIT         │     Installed  99/99/99
      │ Ctrl-Home - Zoom to Memo      │                MEMO
      │ Ctrl-End  - Exit Memo         │
      └──────────────────────────────┘
  MODIFY SCREEN    <B:> MX_SFORM.SCR            Pg 01 Row 21 Col 43
      Enter text.  Drag field or box under cursor with ←┘.  F10 for menu.
                    Screen field definition blackboard
```

Fig. 11.15. *Screen with modified pictures.*

Step 1: Enter a lower limit for the purchase date. Saltwater Sally's was incorporated on January 1, 1985, so no sales were recorded before that date. Move into the Purch Date field bar and press F10. Move the selection bar to **Range:** in the **Modify** submenu, and press Return. In the **Range:** submenu, activate the **Lower Limit:** option and type *01/01/85.* The slashes are already provided (see fig. 11.16).

Press the right-arrow key to leave the menu and then F10 to return to the blackboard.

```
 Set Up          Modify          Options          Exit  12:44:38 pm

                   Screen Field Definition
                   Action : Edit/GET
                   Source:  MX_SALES
                   Content: PDATE
                   Type   : Date
                   Width:      8
                   Decimal:

                   Picture Function:
                   Picture Template:
                   Range:                  █   Input Range
                                               Lower Limit:01/01/85
                                               Upper Limit:



 MODIFY SCREEN    <B:> MX_SFORM.SCR          Pg 01 Row 12 Col 43
                   Enter new value. Finish with ←.
              Enter the maximum and minimum values allowed for this field.
```

Fig. 11.16. *Specifying a range for PDATE field.*

Step 2: Enter a lower limit for the installed date. Move the cursor into the Installed field bar, and repeat Step 1.

Step 3: Test the completed format file again. **Exit** and **Save** the screen and format files. At the dot prompt, type *APPEND* to enter APPEND mode. Enter your first name into the First Name field bar.

Step 4: Test the State field. Press Return until the cursor reaches the State field bar. With Caps Lock off, type *md.* Note that the format screen records the lowercase entry as MD.

NOTES

Step 5: Test the Salesperson field. Move to the Salesperson field bar and type *esp* in lowercase. Again the format file converts the entry to uppercase: ESP.

Step 6: Test the Stock Code field. In the Stock Code field bar, try typing the entry *7-at*. Note that dBASE beeps and does not allow you to continue. Backspace to the beginning of the field bar, and type *h-65*. Again, the format file converts to uppercase and permits the entry.

Step 7: Test the Installed field. Move to the Installed field bar and attempt to enter the date *12/15/84*. Notice the error message that appears at the bottom of the screen:

> RANGE is 01/01/85 to None (press SPACE)

Press the space bar and reenter the date as *12/15/85*.

Step 8: Check access to the memo field. Notice that the memo field is the last field on the screen. Follow the instructions in the SCREEN CONTROLS box to zoom to the memo field by pressing Ctrl-Home. Exit the memo field by pressing Ctrl-End.

Step 9: Exit the APPEND mode without saving the trial record. Press Esc.

Writing the Screen-Oriented Programs

The rest of the programs used in Saltwater Sally's Sales Information System—the add, edit, and search programs—use the MX_SFORM format file. The first, MX_ADD, adds new records to the database. This program contains features designed to save data entry time for the user.

One way MX_ADD saves time is that it sets up two fields—PDATE and PNO—with default values of today's date and the number 1. These fields will have to be changed only if the values differ from the defaults.

Another time-saver is a short programming routine that calculates the data for the fields PTAX and ECOMM. MX_ADD calculates the sales tax at 5% of the sale. The program calculates the commission at 35% if the sale is $4000 or above, and 27% if the sale is below $4000. The program includes two REPLACE commands to handle the calculations.

Step 1: Enter the MX_ADD program file. Type *MODIFY COMMAND MX_ADD* and enter the following code:

```
* MX_ADD.PRG
* Allows one record to be added

* First prepare empty record
APPEND BLANK
```

NOTES

Sales occur one at a time, rarely in groups. MX_ADD allows only one sale to be added before returning to the Main Menu. APPEND BLANK differs from APPEND in that only one record can be added to the database.

Step 2: Add the default values for PDATE and PNO. Add the following lines to the program:

```
* Add in default data to appear on screen
REPLACE pdate WITH DATE()
REPLACE pno WITH 1
```

Step 3: Specify the format file to read in new values. Add the following lines:

```
* Get data values from keyboard operator
SET FORMAT TO MX_SFORM
READ
CLOSE FORMAT
```

Step 4: Calculate taxes and commissions. Continue the program with these lines:

```
* Calculate tax and commission fields
REPLACE ptax WITH pamt * .05
IF pamt >= 4000
   REPLACE ecomm WITH pamt * .35
ELSE
   REPLACE ecomm WITH pamt * .27
ENDIF

RETURN
```

The completed program should look as it does in figure 11.17.

Step 5: Test the program. Press Ctrl-End to save the program, and type *DO MX_ADD*. The format screen with the default values should appear (see fig. 11.18). Fill in the name fields with your own name, move the cursor down to the Amount Paid field, and enter *2000*. Press Ctrl-End, or press Return until you pass the memo field.

Step 6: Examine the test record. Type *CLEAR*. Then press Return and type *DISPLAY PAMT,PTAX,ECOMM* to verify that the tax and commission have been calculated and entered (see fig. 11.19).

Step 7: Delete the test record. Type *DELETE*. dBASE returns the message `1 record deleted`.

The program to edit records, MX_EDIT, has fewer features than MX_ADD. MX_EDIT simply sets up the format file and calls the EDIT command.

```
* MX_ADD.PRG
* Allows one record to be added

* First prepare empty record
APPEND BLANK

* Add in default data to appear on screen
REPLACE pdate WITH DATE()
REPLACE pno WITH 1

* Get data values from keyboard operator
SET FORMAT TO MX_SFORM
READ
CLOSE FORMAT

* Calculate tax and commission fields
REPLACE ptax WITH pamt * .05
IF pamt >= 4000
     REPLACE ecomm WITH pamt * .35
ELSE
     REPLACE ecomm WITH pamt * .27
ENDIF

RETURN
```

Fig. 11.17. *Completed data entry program.*

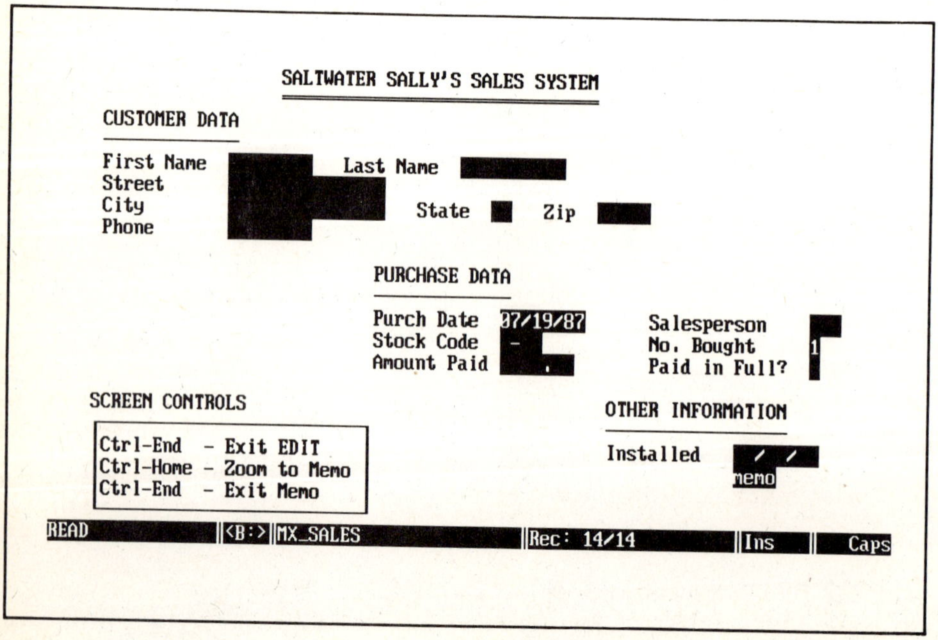

SALTWATER SALLY'S SALES SYSTEM

CUSTOMER DATA

First Name
Street
City   Last Name
Phone   State   Zip

PURCHASE DATA

Purch Date 07/19/87   Salesperson
Stock Code -   No. Bought   1
Amount Paid .   Paid in Full?

SCREEN CONTROLS   OTHER INFORMATION

Ctrl-End - Exit EDIT   Installed   / /
Ctrl-Home - Zoom to Memo   memo
Ctrl-End - Exit Memo

READ   <B:> MX_SALES   Rec: 14/14   Ins   Caps

Fig. 11.18. *Running the data entry program.*

```
, DISPLAY PAMT,PTAX,ECOMM
Record#    PAMT    PTAX    ECOMM
    11   2000.00 100.00  540.00

Command Line    ||<B:>||MX_SALES           ||Rec: 11/11        ||Ins  ||   Caps
              Enter a dBASE III PLUS command.
```

Fig. 11.19. *Display of fields calculated in the data entry program.*

Step 8: Enter the MX_EDIT program. Type *MODIFY COMMAND MX_EDIT* and type the following program lines:

```
* MX_EDIT.PRG
* Edits records

SET FORMAT TO MX_SFORM
EDIT
CLOSE FORMAT

RETURN
```

Figure 11.20 shows how your program should look.

Step 9: Test the program. Press Ctrl-End to save the file, type *GO TOP*, and then type *DO MX_EDIT* (see fig. 11.21). To exit EDIT mode, press Ctrl-End.

The search program, MX_SEAR, uses the LOCATE command to test each record in the data file until LOCATE finds the first record that meets the search condition. The main purpose of searching is to locate a particular record so that the installation date of the hot tub or pool can be entered. LOCATE finds the correct record and brings it to the screen for editing.

```
* MX_EDIT.PRG
* Edits records

SET FORMAT TO MX_SFORM
EDIT
CLOSE FORMAT

RETURN
```

Fig. 11.20. *Completed edit program.*

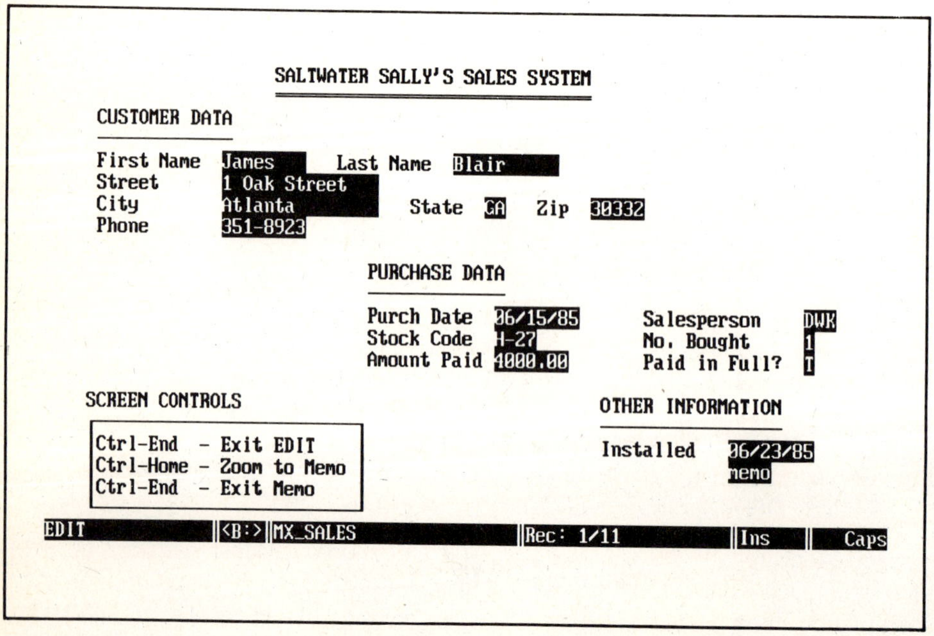

```
                    SALTWATER SALLY'S SALES SYSTEM

   CUSTOMER DATA

   First Name   James        Last Name   Blair
   Street       1 Oak Street
   City         Atlanta          State   CA   Zip   30332
   Phone        351-8923

                         PURCHASE DATA

                    Purch Date   06/15/85    Salesperson     DWK
                    Stock Code   H-27        No. Bought      1
                    Amount Paid  4000.00     Paid in Full?   T

   SCREEN CONTROLS                         OTHER INFORMATION

   ┌─────────────────────────────┐        Installed     06/23/85
   │ Ctrl-End  - Exit EDIT       │                      memo
   │ Ctrl-Home - Zoom to Memo    │
   │ Ctrl-End  - Exit Memo       │
   └─────────────────────────────┘

  EDIT          ║<B:>║MX_SALES          ║Rec: 1/11    ║Ins  ║  Caps
```

Fig. 11.21. *Running the edit program.*

Step 10: Get a customer name to search for from the operator. Type *MODIFY COMMAND MX_SEAR* and enter the following lines:

```
* MX_SEAR.PRG
* Searches for purchase record using customer name
* If found record is brought to screen for editing

CLEAR
@ 10,0
ACCEPT "Enter Customer's First Name " TO mcfname
?
ACCEPT "Enter Customer's Last Name " TO mclname
```

The ACCEPT command operates similarly to the INPUT command introduced in Lesson 10. The difference is that ACCEPT can create only a character memory variable. This limitation is useful because the user does not have to type surrounding quotation marks to enter a character value into the memory variable when the program is run.

The purpose of the @ command without a SAY statement is to position the cursor at the specified screen coordinates so that the ACCEPT prompts are at the correct location. Also, note that the quotation marks surrounding the prompts in the program must be double, because the prompts contain an apostrophe in the word *Customer's.*

Step 11: Search the database for the target record. Continue the program by typing this command on a single line:

```
LOCATE FOR UPPER(TRIM(clname)+cfname) = UPPER(mclname+mcfname)
```

The UPPER function converts the CLNAME+CFNAME and MCLNAME+MCFNAME to uppercase so that a lowercase memory variable can be compared correctly with an uppercase database field. The function sets a common denominator for the search comparison so that even if the user types the customer's last name as JONES, the function still will match the Jones stored in the database.

The TRIM function trims off any trailing blanks in the CLNAME field before that field is "added to" the CFNAME field. The field variable CLNAME stores ten characters, whether or not a particular last name requires all ten. Without trimming the blanks, the comparison to the memory variables would not work correctly. For instance, if Molly Brown's record is being searched, accepting the last and first names and then adding them would give this string for UPPER(mclname+mcfname):

```
BROWNMOLLY
```

Without the TRIM, the field variables would yield a different string:

```
BROWN     MOLLY
```

This string would not match the memory variable.

NOTES

Step 12: Bring a found record to the screen for editing. Type the following program lines:

```
IF .NOT. EOF()
    SET FORMAT TO MX_SFORM
    READ
    CLOSE FORMAT
ELSE
    @ 20,0 SAY "Name Not Found. Returning to Menu."
    WAIT
ENDIF

RETURN
```

The completed program should look as it does in figure 11.22.

```
* MX_SEAR.PRG
* Searches for purchase record using customer name
* If found record is brought to screen for editing

CLEAR
@ 10,0
ACCEPT "Enter Customer's First Name " TO mcfname
?
ACCEPT "Enter Customer's Last Name  " TO mclname

LOCATE FOR UPPER(TRIM(clname)+cfname) = UPPER(mclname+mcfname)

IF .NOT. EOF()
    SET FORMAT TO MX_SFORM
    READ
    CLOSE FORMAT
ELSE
    @ 20,0 SAY "Name Not Found. Returning to Menu."
    WAIT
ENDIF

RETURN
```

Fig. 11.22. *Completed search program.*

Step 13: Test the program. Press Ctrl-End and then type *DO MX_SEAR*. When the prompts appear, type *MOLLY* for the first name and *BROWN* for the last name. The record should appear on the screen (see fig. 11.23). Press Ctrl-End to leave the format screen.

```
                    SALTWATER SALLY'S SALES SYSTEM

      CUSTOMER DATA

      First Name  Molly      Last Name  Brown
      Street      92 Aqua Vita
      City        Riverdale        State  CA    Zip  30274
      Phone       876-1252

                         PURCHASE DATA

                    Purch Date  06/22/85      Salesperson    LEM
                    Stock Code  H-22          No. Bought     1
                    Amount Paid 6600.35       Paid in Full?  F

      SCREEN CONTROLS                    OTHER INFORMATION

      Ctrl-End  - Exit EDIT              Installed      06/27/85
      Ctrl-Home - Zoom to Memo                          memo
      Ctrl-End  - Exit Memo

    READ              <B:> MX_SALES              Rec: 6/11          Ins      Caps
```

Fig. 11.23. *Running the search program.*

Step 14: Retest the program with an incorrect name. Type *DO MX_SEAR* and cue
for *JAMES BROWN*. Entering an incorrect name causes the program to
branch to the error trap and return this message:

Name Not Found. Returning to Menu.

Step 15: Test the programs from the Main Menu. Type *DO MX_MENU* and access
each of the three screen-based programs to assure that they are called
correctly from the Main Menu.

SUMMARY OF CONCEPTS
PRESENTED IN LESSON 11

1. A format file configures the screen for entry and display of data.

2. A format file is created through the CREATE SCREEN command and modified through MODIFY SCREEN. Format files have the extension .FMT. The screen file that generates the format has the extension .SCR.

3. CREATE SCREEN allows fields and labels to be repositioned on the display screen.

4. Picture templates, picture functions, and ranges can be set in a format file to reduce the burden of data entry and to build in error trapping.

5. If the format file has been activated with SET FORMAT TO and the format file name, then when a READ statement is issued, the fields and variables are displayed under the influence of the format file.

6. APPEND, EDIT, and CHANGE can function through an active format file.

7. Inactivate a format file with CLOSE FORMAT.

8. APPEND BLANK prepares one (and only one) new record for entry. REPLACE can be used to enter default data before the entire record is viewed.

9. You can use the UPPER( ) function with LOCATE to find a search phrase of mixed uppercase and lowercase letters.

10. The TRIM( ) function removes trailing blanks from a field value.

LESSON 11
EXERCISE

Design the same routines for the billing file. Enter them as outlined and save them by pressing Ctrl-End. Then run and test each routine.

Step 1: Open the billing file by typing *USE GENBILLS.*

Step 2: Enter the screen form. Type *MODIFY FILE SSSFORM.FMT* and enter the following statements:

```
* SSSFORM.FMT
* Obtain Vendor data
@ 3,20 SAY "SALTWATER SALLY'S BILLING SYSTEM"
@ 4,20 SAY "================================"
@ 6, 1 SAY "VENDOR DATA"
@ 7, 1 SAY "------------"
@ 9, 1 SAY "COMPANY NAME :"
@ 9,15 GET VNAME
@ 11, 1 SAY "DIRECT TO :"
@ 11,15 GET VATTN
@ 13, 1 SAY "PHONE NUMBER :"
@ 13,15 GET VPHONE

* Display Cursor Commands
@ 19, 1 SAY "MAJOR COMMANDS"
@ 20, 1 SAY "------------"
@ 22, 1 SAY "PgDn Key - Next Record"
@ 23, 1 SAY "Control-End - Saves and Exits"

* Obtain Billing data
@ 6,45 SAY "PAYABLES DATA"
@ 7,45 SAY "------------"
@ 9,45 SAY "DATE RECEIVED:"
@ 9,60 GET DATEIN
@ 11,45 SAY "DATE DUE :"
@ 11,60 GET DATEDUE
@ 13,45 SAY "BILL NUMBER :"
@ 13,60 GET VBILLNO
@ 15,45 SAY "BILL AMOUNT :"
@ 15,60 GET VAMT
@ 17,45 SAY "PAID IN FULL?:"
@ 17,60 GET VPIF
* End of screen form file.
```

NOTES

Step 3: Enter the addition routine. Type *MODIFY COMMAND SS_ADD* and enter the following lines:

```
* SS_ADD.PRG

APPEND BLANK
* Add in default information to appear on screen.
* Assume that the date of entry is the DOS date.
* Assume that the due date is thirty days from today.
REPLACE datein WITH DATE()
REPLACE datedue WITH DATE() + 30

* Acquire input of billing data.
SET FORMAT TO SSSFORM
READ
CLOSE FORMAT

RETURN
```

Step 4: Enter the following editing routine. Type *MODIFY COMMAND SS_EDIT* and enter the lines that follow:

```
* SS_EDIT.PRG
* Edits billing records
SET FORMAT TO SSSFORM
EDIT
CLOSE FORMAT
RETURN
```

Step 5: Enter the following search routine. Type *MODIFY COMMAND SS_SEAR* and enter these lines:

```
* SS_SEAR.PRG
* Searches for bill.
* Allows Date Paid and Paid in Full fields to be entered.
* Search phrase is the Vendor company name, VNAME.
CLEAR
STORE SPACE(20) TO mvname
@ 10,10 SAY Enter the Company Name GET mvname
READ
```

NOTES

```
LOCATE FOR UPPER(vname) = UPPER(mvname)

IF .NOT. EOF()
   SET FORMAT TO SSSFORM
   READ
   CLOSE FORMAT
ELSE
   @ 20,0 SAY "Name Not Found. Returning to Menu. "
   WAIT
ENDIF
RETURN
```

NOTES

12

The Professional Touch: Relating Databases

Related sections in *dBASE III Plus Handbook*, 2nd Edition: Chapters 1 and 6.

Doug's efforts so far have worked out nicely. The sales information system manages the data on all sales transactions and summarizes the data into useful findings. Doug was justifiably pleased when he showed Henry Hacker the automated version. Henry was pleased, too; but then Henry dropped the other shoe.

"I'm impressed, Doug. You've brought this system a long way in a short time. But have you thought about how to handle sales where the customer buys more than one item?"

"Sure," said Doug. "I just write each item as a separate record."

"That does work," Henry replied, "But then you have to repeat the same customer data for each item in the sale. If a customer buys ten different items, that's ten times you'll be typing the same name and address."

Doug's paternal instincts surfaced. He defended his baby. "Okay, but with a little extra programming I could tell the system to fill in those repeated fields automatically."

"Yes, you could," Henry acknowledged, "But the point is that you still would be storing the data ten times. That's a waste of disk space."

Doug's curiosity overcame his defensiveness. "I have a feeling that if we continue this conversation, I'll have some more work to do. But I guess I'm game. What's your plan?"

Henry outlined a strategy that involves setting up two different databases: one to hold data on customers and one to hold data on the items sold. The two databases would

NOTES

be "related" to one another by adding a common field, such as an invoice number, to each. Then, to pull together a report such as the general sales report, the customer's name and phone number would be drawn from one database, and the details of the sale from the other database. The invoice number would act as the point on which to match records, to make sure the correct name got reported with the correct sale.

"Your idea sounds good, but won't it involve a lot of complicated programming?" Doug asked.

"Not nearly as much as you would expect," Henry said reassuringly.

Henry went on to explain that dBASE III Plus is a *relational database management system*, meaning that it has capabilities to manage several databases simultaneously. These capabilities include commands that

- Put the record pointers in the databases into lockstep with each other

- Shift dBASE's attention from one database to the other as needs require

- Specify the source database for a reported field

In this lesson, you will see how, with Henry's assistance, Doug reworked the sales information system by splitting the customer information into a second database and building relational links between it and the purchase information database. You also will see how he reworked the data entry program to accommodate the revised system.

Splitting the MX_SALES Database

The first step in making the sales information system relational is to split the current database, MX_SALES, into a customer database (MX_CUST) and a purchase database (MX_PURCH). As preparation for the split, the database needs an invoice number field.

Step 1: Type *DO QPREP*. Select Lesson 12.

Step 2: Type *USE MX_SALES*.

Step 3: Modify the structure of MX_SALES by adding a field named INVOICE. At the dot prompt, type *MODIFY STRUCTURE*. With the selection bar on the first field, press Ctrl-N to insert a blank line. Type *INVOICE* as the field name, select character as the type, and enter *6* as the width (see fig. 12.1).

Press Ctrl-End and then Return to save the modification.

You must now add values for the new INVOICE field to the current records. Each invoice number is made up of the last two digits of the year, a hyphen (-), and a three-digit sequence number. For example, the first invoice of 1985 would be coded 85-001. Figure 12.2 shows the invoice numbers to apply to the current set of records.

```
                                            Bytes remaining:   3876

  ┌────────────────┬────────────────┬────────────────┬──────────────────────┐
  │ CURSOR  <-- -->│    INSERT      │    DELETE      │ Up a field:       ↑  │
  │ Char:    ← →   │ Char:    Ins   │ Char:    Del   │ Down a field:     ↓  │
  │ Word: Home End │ Field:   ^N    │ Word:    ^Y    │ Exit/Save:      ^End │
  │ Pan:    ^← ^→  │ Help:    F1    │ Field:   ^U    │ Abort:           Esc │
  └────────────────┴────────────────┴────────────────┴──────────────────────┘

       Field Name  Type      Width Dec        Field Name  Type      Width Dec
  ─────────────────────────────────────   ────────────────────────────────────
   1  INVOICE     Character    6        9  CNOTE       Memo       10
   2  CFNAME      Character    8       10  PDATE       Date        8
   3  CLNAME      Character   10       11  PINDATE     Date        8
   4  CSTREET     Character   15       12  PCODE       Character   4
   5  CCITY       Character   15       13  PNO         Numeric     1    0
   6  CST         Character    2       14  PAMT        Numeric     7    2
   7  CZIP        Character    5       15  PTAX        Numeric     6    2
   8  CPHONE      Character    8       16  PPIF        Logical     1
  ──────────────────────────────────────────────────────────────────────────
  MODIFY STRUCTURE  <B:>  MX_SALES              Field: 2/18            Caps
                        Enter the field name.
  Field names begin with a letter and may contain letters, digits and underscores
```

Fig. 12.1. *Adding an invoice number field to the MX_SALES database.*

```
  CLNAME----  CFNAME--  INVOICE
  Blair       James     85-001
  Connors     Francis   85-002
  Jones       Thomas    85-003
  Aster       Sam       85-004
  Stevens     Harold    85-005
  Drown       Molly     85-006
  Clark       John      85-007
  Jones       Susan     85-008
  Abbott      William   85-009
  Hoffsmith   Barbara   85-010
```

Fig. 12.2. *Invoice numbers for current records.*

Step 4: Add values for the INVOICE field. At the dot prompt, type these commands:

> GO TOP
> BROWSE FIELDS CLNAME,CFNAME,INVOICE

Press Ctrl-Home to bring up the BROWSE menu, and move the cursor to the **Freeze** option. Press Return and type *INVOICE* as the field to freeze (see fig. 12.3). Freezing a field makes edits possible only in that field. Press Return once more.

```
 Bottom          Top          Lock        Record No,      ▐Freeze▌ 08:51:26 pm
 ┌─────────────────────────────┬──────────────────────────────────────────────┐
 │ CURSOR    <-- -->       UP  │Enter field name to freeze: ▐INVOICE▌          │
 │ Char:      ← →     Record: ↑│                                               │
 │ Field: Home End   Page: PgUp PgDn │ Field: ^Y    │ Abort:        Esc        │
 │ Pan:      ^← ^→   Help:  F1 │ Record: ^U   │ Set Options: ^Home            │
 └─────────────────────────────┴──────────────────────────────────────────────┘
 CFNAME-- CLNAME---- INVOICE
 James    Blair     ▐     ▌
 Francis  Connors
 Thomas   Jones
 Sam      Aster
 Harold   Stevens
 Molly    Brown
 John     Clark
 Susan    Jones
 William  Abbott
 Barbara  Hoffsmith



 BROWSE        <C:> MX_SALES          Rec: 1/10              Caps
                Enter new value,  Finish with ◄┘.
                Enter a single field name to edit,
```

Fig. 12.3. *Freezing a field in BROWSE.*

Starting with the first record, type the invoice numbers listed in figure 12.2. As you complete one invoice number, you will automatically be positioned to enter the next number.

At the prompt ==> Add new records? (Y/N), press N for No and then Ctrl-End to save the changes.

Splitting the database amounts to putting some fields in one database and some fields in a second database. To do this, you will use the dBASE III Plus COPY TO command. Among other actions, COPY TO specifies a list of fields in the current database to include in a new database given after the TO keyword. The structure of the new database is created automatically from the field definitions of the current database.

NOTES

Step 5: Copy the invoice number field and the customer data fields to a new database called MX_CUST. Type the following command (all on one line):

PY TO MX_CUST FIELDS INVOICE,CLNAME,CFNAME,CSTREET,CCITY,CST,CZIP,CPHONE,CNOTE

Step 6: Copy the invoice number field and the purchase data fields to a new database called MX_PURCH. Type this command (all on one line):

PY TO MX_PURCH FIELDS INVOICE,PDATE,PINDATE,PCODE,PNO,PAMT,PTAX,PPIF,ESP,ECOMM

Setting a Relation

With two databases created, the next step is to set a *relation* between them—a link between the databases that moves the record pointers in both databases to records that
share the same value on a key field. The *key field* is a field that both databases share
and that has the same name, type, and length in both databases. Doug's key field is the
invoice number. A relation between the databases on the invoice number means that
at any one time the record pointers in both databases are pointing to records with the
same invoice number.

To set the relation between the databases, both database files must be open at the
same time. Ordinarily, this is impossible, because opening a new database closes an
open database automatically. However, dBASE III Plus can internally partition the computer's memory into ten distinct work areas. Each work area is independent of the others, although they can communicate with one another through dBASE's relational
commands. Each work area can keep one database and its index and format files open.

Each work area is identified by a number (from 1 to 10), a letter (from A to J), or an alias.
The alias is generally the same as the name of the database in use in that area. If you
take no special action, the USE command opens a database in the first work area,
which is identified as work area 1, work area A, or by the name of the database it
houses.

If two or more databases need to be open simultaneously, the subsequent database(s)
must each be put into a different work area than the first. To do this, you first would
choose any of the other nine work areas, identify it by letter or number using the SE-
LECT command, and open the database in it. For instance, to open a database called
SURVEY in work area 3, type SELECT 3 (or SELECT C) and then USE SURVEY. Later,
you can select this work area by its alias—that is, by using the command SELECT
SURVEY.

Step 1: Open the MX_CUST database in work area 1. Type *USE MX_CUST.*

NOTES

Step 2: Open the MX_PURCH database in work area 2. Type these commands on successive lines:

> SELECT 2
> USE MX_PURCH

Step 3: Check the status of the system. Type *DISPLAY STATUS* to verify that the databases were assigned correctly. Your screen should resemble figure 12.4.

```
. DISPLAY STATUS

Select area: 1, Database in Use: B:MX_CUST.dbf    Alias: MX_CUST
            Memo file:   B:MX_CUST.dbt

Currently Selected Database:
Select area: 2, Database in Use: B:MX_PURCH.dbf    Alias: MX_PURCH

File search path:
Default disk drive: B:
Print destination: PRN:
Margin =      0
Current work area =    2

Press any key to continue...
Command Line    |<B:>|MX_PURCH             |Rec: 1/10      ||       | Caps
            Enter a dBASE III PLUS command.
```

Fig. 12.4. *System status after splitting MX_SALES.*

Step 4: Index the MX_PURCH database on the key field. While in work area 2, type *INDEX ON INVOICE TO PRCH_INV.*

Step 5: Index the MX_CUST database on the key field. Move back to work area 1 by typing *SELECT 1.* Then type *INDEX ON INVOICE TO CUST_INV.*

Both databases currently act independently. When you move the record pointer in one database with LOCATE, FIND, GO, LIST, BROWSE, or another command, doing so has no effect on the record pointer in the other database. That pointer stays in the same position.

NOTES

To relate the two databases, you must SELECT one of the databases to be the active database. This is the database in which you will typically initiate a search operation, such as FIND, SEEK, or LOCATE. Then you need to use the SET RELATION TO command to set the link into the passive database.

The SET RELATION TO command will automatically move the record pointer in the passive database to a record with the same value on the key field, whenever the pointer moves in the active database. The passive database must be indexed on the key field beforehand, and the index file must be open. The SET RELATION TO command requires that you give the key field after the keyword TO and that you give the work area of the passive database after a keyword INTO. For instance, if you are relating the active database into the database SURVEY in work area 3 on the common field SSN, you would type either

SET RELATION TO SSN INTO SURVEY

or

SET RELATION TO SSN INTO C

Step 6: Relate the purchase database into the customer database. Type *SELECT B.* With MX_PURCH as the active database, type *SET RELATION TO INVOICE INTO MX_CUST.*

Step 7: Check the status again. Type *DISPLAY STATUS* and verify that the relation was set correctly (see fig. 12.5).

Step 8: Test the relation. Type the following commands. Note that the record pointer in the customer database moves automatically to the record with the same invoice number in the purchase database.

    FIND 85-004
    DISPLAY
    SELECT 1
    DISPLAY

The relation works in one direction only. Moving the record pointer in work area 1 has no effect on the pointer in work area 2.

When databases are related, you can access fields in the related database from the active database work area. You do this by preceding the field name with the work area letter or alias and joining the two with an "arrow." The arrow is constructed using a hyphen (-) and a greater-than ($>$) sign—for example, A -$>$ CLNAME or MX_CUST -$>$ CLNAME.

```
Select area:  1, Database in Use: B:MX_CUST.DBF   Alias: MX_CUST
     Master index file:  B:CUST_INV.NDX  Key: INVOICE
             Memo file:    B:MX_CUST.dbt

Currently Selected Database:
Select area:  2, Database in Use: B:MX_PURCH.DBF   Alias: MX_PURCH
     Master index file:  B:PRCH_INV.NDX  Key: INVOICE
     Related into: MX_CUST
     Relation: INVOICE

File search path:
Default disk drive: B:
Print destination:  PRN:
Margin =      0
Current work area =    2

Press any key to continue...
Command Line    ||<B:>||MX_PURCH              ||Rec: EOF/10    ||Ins  ||  Caps

             Enter a dBASE III PLUS command.
```

Fig. 12.5. *System status with a relation set.*

Step 9: Display data from related databases. Move back to work area 2 by typing *SELECT B*. Type the command *DISPLAY ALL INVOICE,A -> CLNAME,A -> CFNAME,PDATE,PCODE,PAMT* (see fig. 12.6).

```
. DISPLAY ALL INVOICE,A -> CLNAME,A -> CFNAME,PDATE,PCODE,PAMT
Record#   INVOICE A -> CLNAME A -> CFNAME PDATE     PCODE    PAMT
      1   85-001  Blair     James       06/15/85  H-27   4000.00
      2   85-002  Connors   Francis     06/16/85  H-22   6600.35
      3   85-003  Jones     Thomas      06/17/85  H-19   3523.17
      4   85-004  Aster     Sam         06/18/85  P-11   9042.00
      5   85-005  Stevens   Harold      06/19/85  H-19   3523.17
      6   85-006  Brown     Molly       06/22/85  H-22   6600.35
      7   85-007  Clark     John        06/25/85  P-14   8097.00
      8   85-008  Jones     Susan       06/27/85  H-27   4000.00
      9   85-009  Abbott    William     07/01/85  P-11   9042.00
     10   85-010  Hoffsmith Barbara     07/02/85  P-10    152.52
.
```

Command Line	\<B:>|MX_PURCH	Rec: EOF/10	Ins	Caps

Enter a dBASE III PLUS command.

Fig. 12.6. *Displaying data from two databases.*

Using a Relation To Write a Report

In this exercise you will write a report that collects data from the two related databases. The report (named MX_OWED) will generate a list of customers who still owe money on their account. It will include the following columns of data:

CUSTOMER NAME	PHONE	INVOICE	PURCHASE DATE	PURCHASE AMOUNT

Once constructed, the report will display data for only those customers recorded as not having paid in full (.NOT. PPIF).

Step 1: Create the report form. Type *SELECT B* to make MX_PURCH the active database. Type *CREATE REPORT MX_OWED* to enter the report generator.

Step 2: Title the report. Activate the **Page title** line and type *ACCOUNTS OUTSTANDING* (see fig. 12.7). Press Ctrl-End.

```
┌─────────────────────────────────────────────────────────────────┐
│ Options          Groups        Columns        Locate      Exit  09:13:31 pm │
│ ┌─────────────────────────────┐                                  │
│ │ Page title              ⊇   │                                  │
│ │ Page width (positions)  80  │   ┌───────────────────────────┐  │
│ │ Left margin              8  │   │ACCOUNTS OUTSTANDING       │  │
│ │ Right margin             0  │   │                           │  │
│ │ Lines per page          58  │   │                           │  │
│ │ Double space report     No  │   │                           │  │
│ │ Page eject before printing Yes │ └───────────────────────────┘  │
│ │ Page eject after printing  No │                                 │
│ │ Plain page              No  │                                  │
│ └─────────────────────────────┘                                  │
│                                                                   │
│                                                                   │
│ ┌──────────────────┬──────────────────┬─────────────────┬──────────────┐ │
│ │ CURSOR  <-- -->  │ Delete char:  Del │ Insert column: ^N │ Insert:  Ins │ │
│ │ Char:    ← →     │ Delete word:   ^T │ Report format: F1 │ Zoom in:  ^PgDn │ │
│ │ Word:  Home End  │ Delete column: ^U │ Abandon:      Esc │ Zoom out: ^PgUp │ │
│ └──────────────────┴──────────────────┴─────────────────┴──────────────┘ │
│ CREATE REPORT   |<C:>|MX_OWED.FRM              |Opt: 1/9      |        | Caps │
│              Enter report title.  Exit - Ctrl-End.                │
│    Enter up to four lines of text to be displayed at the top of each report page. │
└─────────────────────────────────────────────────────────────────┘
```

Fig. 12.7. *Entering a title for MX_OWED report form.*

Step 3: Define the first column of the report. Move to the **Columns** option and enter the **Contents** line. Type *TRIM(MX_CUST -> CFNAME)+' '+MX_CUST -> CLNAME*. Lock in the contents by pressing Return. Enter the **Heading** line and type *CUSTOMER NAME*. Lock in the heading by pressing Ctrl-End (see fig. 12.8).

dBASE uses the default width and decimal settings for each field unless you override the settings.

```
Options          Groups        Columns         Locate      Exit  09:18:45 pm

                     Contents            TRIM(MX_CUST -> CFNAME)+' '+MX_CUST
                     Heading             CUSTOMER NAME
                     Width               19
                     Decimal places
                     Total this column



   ┌─Report Format────────────────────────────────────────────────────────
   >>>>>>>>CUSTOMER NAME         ─────────────────────────────────────────



          XXXXXXXXXXXXXXXXXXX

CREATE REPORT   <C:> MX_OWED.FRM              Column: 1                  Caps
     Position selection bar - ↑↓.  Select - ←┘.  Prev/Next column - PgUp/PgDn.
     Enter up to four lines of text to display above the indicated column.
```

Fig. 12.8. *Completing the first column of MX_OWED report form.*

Step 4: Define the second column. Press the PgDn key to move to column 2, and enter the following:

    Contents   *MX_CUST -> CPHONE*
    Heading   *PHONE*

Step 5: Define the third column. Press PgDn to move to column 3, and enter the following:

    Contents   *INVOICE*
    Heading   *INVOICE*

NOTES

Step 6: Define the fourth column. PgDn to column 4 and enter the following:

Contents	*PDATE*
Heading	*PURCHASE;DATE*

The semicolon indicates that you want a two-line heading. You also can type *PURCHASE* on the first **Heading** line and *DATE* on the second line.

Step 7: Define the fifth column. PgDn to column 5 and enter the following:

Contents	*PAMT*
Heading	*PURCHASE;AMOUNT*
Width	*8*

The completed report format should look as it does in figure 12.9.

```
 Options        Groups      Columns         Locate      Exit  09:38:37 pm
                    Contents          PAMT
                    Heading           PURCHASE:AMOUNT
                    Width                 8
                    Decimal places        2
                    Total this column   Yes




   ┌Report Format─────────────────────────────────────────────────
   │ER NAME        PHONE     INVOICE PURCHASE    PURCHASE ────────────
   │                                 DATE        AMOUNT
   │
   │
   │
   │ XXXXXXXXXXXXX XXXXXXXX XXXXXX   mm/dd/yy        ####.##

 CREATE REPORT    <C:> MX_OWED.FRM              Column: 5              Caps
     Position selection bar - ↑↓.   Select - ←┘.   Prev/Next column - PgUp/PgDn.
     Enter a field or expression to display in the indicated report column.
```

Fig. 12.9. *Format for report drawing data from two databases.*

Step 8: Run the completed report. Move to the **Exit** option and **Save** the report. At the dot prompt, type *REPORT FORM MX_OWED FOR .NOT. PPIF.* Your report should resemble figure 12.10.

```
, REPORT FORM MX_OWED FOR .NOT. PPIF
        Page No,    1
        07/28/87
                                ACCOUNTS OUTSTANDING

        CUSTOMER NAME       PHONE      INVOICE PURCHASE PURCHASE
                                               DATE     AMOUNT


        Aster Sam           371-2341 85-004   06/18/85  9042.00
        Stevens Harold      543-9850 85-005   06/19/85  3523.17
        Brown Molly         876-1252 85-006   06/22/85  6600.35
        Clark John          351-1118 85-007   06/25/85  8097.00
        *** Total ***
                                                       27262.52


Command Line    ||<B:>||MX_PURCH         ||Rec: EOF/10    ||Ins  ||  Caps

            Enter a dBASE III PLUS command,
```

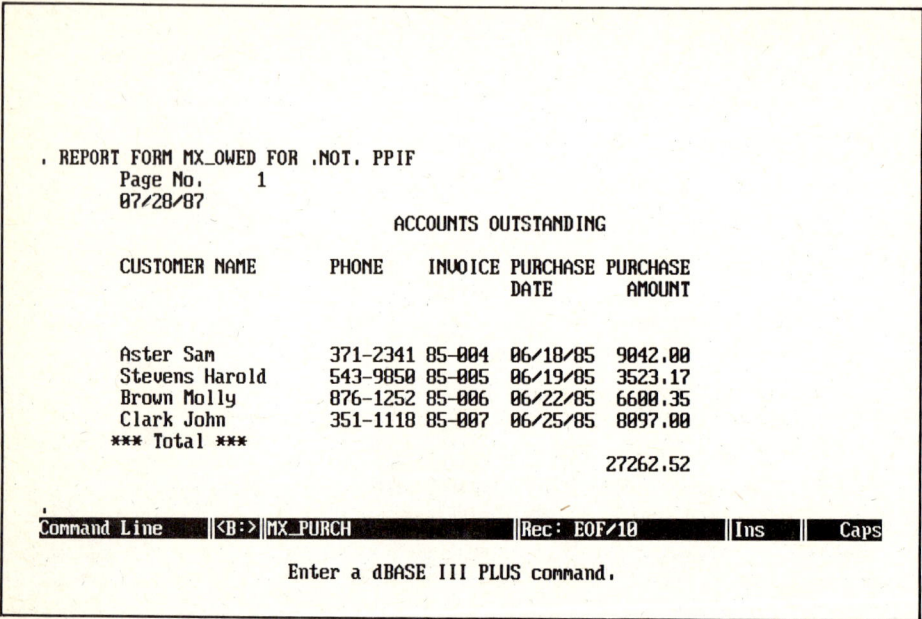

Fig. 12.10. *Report consolidated from two databases.*

Building a Data Entry Program for Two Related Databases

The process of recording and storing data for a new invoice is more complicated when two databases must be fed. Moreover, the MX_PURCH database can have more than one entry for a single invoice. To accommodate these conditions, a new data entry procedure must be programmed—one that allows the operator to enter the customer information and then enter one or more stock code items.

The Format Files

Before you build the data entry program, you will design two format files: one to enter data into the MX_CUST database, and one to enter data into the MX_PURCH database.

Step 1: Generate a format file named CUSTOMER for the MX_CUST database. At the dot prompt, type *SELECT A.* Then type *CREATE SCREEN CUSTOMER.* Select the database file **MX_CUST** and load all the fields. Press F10 to enter the blackboard.

Step 2: Relabel and rearrange the fields into a data entry screen. Use the techniques learned in Lesson 11 to redesign the blackboard. Use figure 12.11 as a model of how the completed screen should look.

```
 Set Up              Modify              Options          Exit  01:05:59 am
CUSTOMER INFORMATION

   Invoice Number: XXXXX

   Customer Last Name: XXXXXXXXX  First Name: XXXXXXX

   Street: XXXXXXXXXXXXXX

   City: XXXXXXXXXXXXXX   State: XX   Zip Code: XXXXX

   Phone Number: XXXXXXX      Comments: MEMO



 CREATE SCREEN    <B:> CUSTOMER.SCR            Pg 01 Row 02 Col 00 Ins
      Enter text. Drag field or box under cursor with ↵, F10 for menu.
                    Screen field definition blackboard
```

Fig. 12.11. *Screen for MX_CUST database.*

NOTES

Step 3: Test the completed screen. **Exit** and **Save** the completed screen. At the dot prompt type *EDIT*, and check that the format file performs correctly. Your screen should resemble figure 12.12. Press Esc to exit EDIT mode.

```
CUSTOMER INFORMATION
─────────────────────

   Invoice Number:  85-001

   Customer Last Name: Blair      First Name: James

   Street: 1 Oak Street

   City: Atlanta        State: CA   Zip Code: 30332

   Phone Number: 351-8923    Comments: memo




 EDIT          <B:> MX_CUST              Rec: 1/14              Caps
```

Fig. 12.12. *CUSTOMER screen in EDIT mode.*

Step 4: Generate a format file named PURCHASE for the MX_PURCH database. At the dot prompt, type *SELECT B* to make MX_PURCH the active database. Then type *CREATE SCREEN PURCHASE*, select the database **MX_PURCH**, and load all the fields except PTAX and ECOMM. Press F10 to enter the blackboard.

Step 5: Relabel and rearrange the fields. Use figure 12.13 as a guide to filling in the screen.

In the next step you will change the action of the INVOICE field to make it a display-only field. This allows the current contents of the field to be displayed without possibly being changed. You do this so that the invoice number needs to be entered only once.

Step 6: Make the INVOICE field a display-only field. Move the blackboard cursor into the INVOICE field, and press F10. In the **Modify** submenu, change the **Action:** to **Display/SAY** by pressing Return (see fig. 12.14).

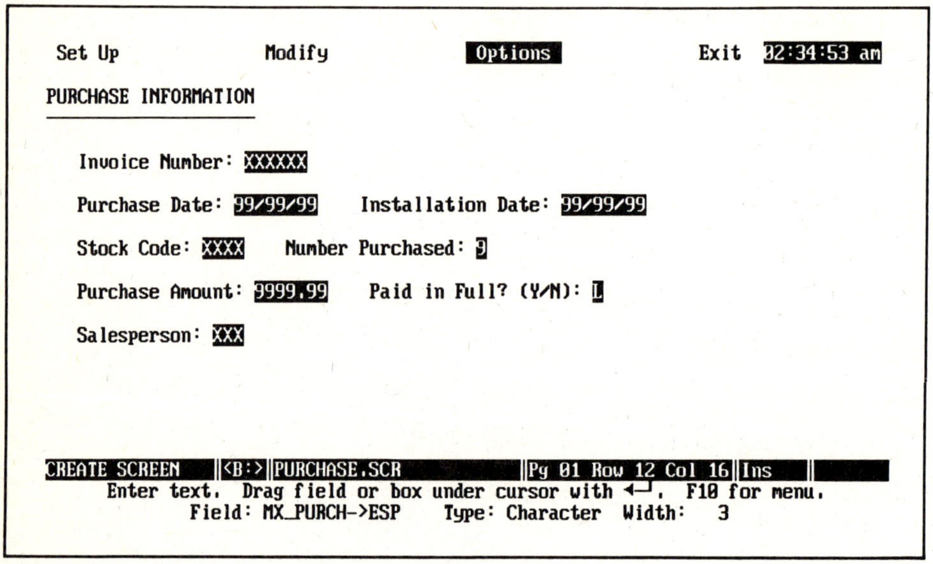

```
  Set Up            Modify            Options            Exit   02:34:53 am
  PURCHASE INFORMATION


     Invoice Number: XXXXX

     Purchase Date: 99/99/99     Installation Date: 99/99/99

     Stock Code: XXXX    Number Purchased: 9

     Purchase Amount: 9999.99     Paid in Full? (Y/N): L

     Salesperson: XXX



 CREATE SCREEN   |<B:>|PURCHASE.SCR        |Pg 01 Row 12 Col 16||Ins
       Enter text. Drag field or box under cursor with ←┘. F10 for menu.
            Field: MX_PURCH->ESP   Type: Character  Width:   3
```

Fig. 12.13. *Screen for MX_PURCH database.*

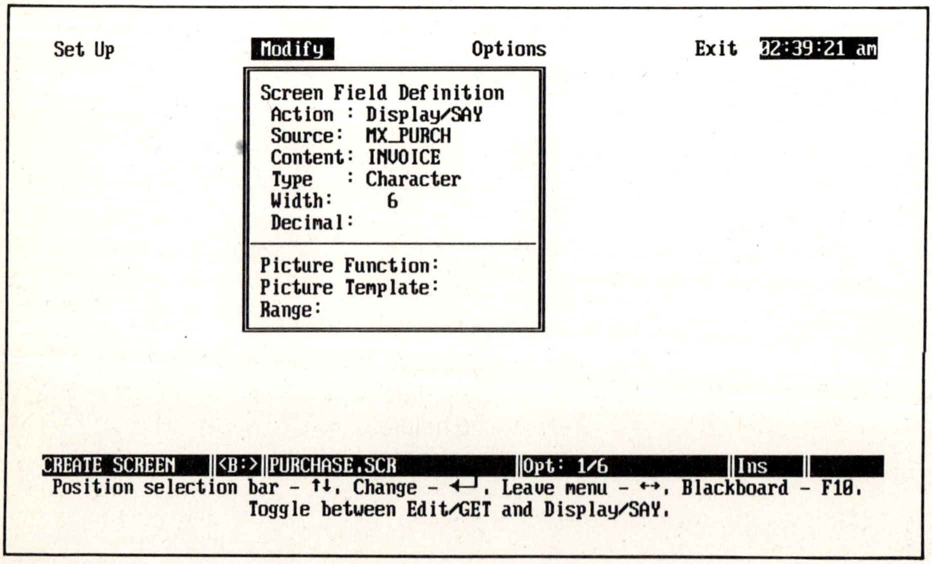

```
  Set Up            Modify            Options            Exit   02:39:21 am

                    ┌─────────────────────────────┐
                    │ Screen Field Definition     │
                    │ Action : Display/SAY        │
                    │ Source:  MX_PURCH           │
                    │ Content: INVOICE            │
                    │ Type   : Character          │
                    │ Width:      6               │
                    │ Decimal:                    │
                    │─────────────────────────────│
                    │ Picture Function:           │
                    │ Picture Template:           │
                    │ Range:                      │
                    └─────────────────────────────┘



 CREATE SCREEN   |<B:>|PURCHASE.SCR        |Opt: 1/6      ||Ins  ||
       Position selection bar - ↑↓. Change - ←┘. Leave menu - ↔. Blackboard - F10.
                Toggle between Edit/GET and Display/SAY.
```

Fig. 12.14. *Changing the action of the INVOICE field.*

Step 7: Test the completed screen. **Exit** and **Save** the screen. At the dot prompt, type *EDIT* to check the format file. Your screen should resemble figure 12.15. Press Esc to exit EDIT mode. Note that you cannot change the invoice number in this screen.

```
PURCHASE INFORMATION

    Invoice Number: 85-001

    Purchase Date: 06/15/85     Installation Date: 06/23/85

    Stock Code: 1-27   Number Purchased: 1

    Purchase Amount: 1000.00   Paid in Full? (Y/N): T

    Salesperson: DWK




EDIT            <B:>  MX_PURCH              Rec: 1/15            Ins
```

Fig. 12.15. *PURCHASE screen used in EDIT mode.*

The Data Entry Program

In the next steps you will build the format files into a data entry program that can be used to enter multiple purchases under a single invoice number.

The current system status, revealed by typing DISPLAY STATUS, includes the two selected databases, their indexes, their respective format files, and the relation from MX_CUST into MX_PURCH. Because the new data entry program must set up this same status, including it in a view file would be helpful. The correct status is already in operation, so you can create the view file most simply by specifying that you want it created from the environment. The *environment* is the collection of files currently open—in other words, those that determine the system status. The only command required is

CREATE VIEW <name of view file> FROM ENVIRONMENT

NOTES

Step 1: Create a view file named INVOICE from the environment. Type *CREATE VIEW INVOICE FROM ENVIRONMENT.*

Step 2: Begin a program called ADD_INV, which will add data from invoices to the two databases. Type *MODIFY COMMAND ADD_INV.* In the word processor, type the following comment and setup lines:

```
* ADD_INV.PRG
* Data entry program to add invoice records
* Adds a single customer record to MX_CUST and one to several
* purchase records to MX_PURCH

SET TALK OFF
SET CONFIRM ON
SET BELL OFF
SET VIEW TO INVOICE
```

Step 3: Program the addition of customer information to MX_CUST. Type the following lines:

```
DO WHILE .T.

  SELECT MX_CUST
  APPEND BLANK
  READ
  STORE invoice TO minvoice
```

A loop is set up to allow for adding data from more than one invoice. The INVOICE value is stored to a memory variable, MINVOICE, so that it can be automatically entered into the purchase database.

Step 4: Program the addition of purchase information to MX_PURCH. Type the following lines:

```
  SELECT B
  DO WHILE .T.
   CLEAR
   APPEND BLANK
   REPLACE invoice WITH minvoice
   READ
```

A second loop is set up within the first loop to allow the operator to enter more than one purchase from the invoice. The REPLACE command is used to display the value of IN-VOICE, which the user will have already entered into the MX_CUST database. To assure that data will not be corrupted, the user cannot change the value of the invoice number.

NOTES

Step 5: Program a way out of the second loop, and end it. Type the following lines:

```
ACCEPT 'Enter another purchase for this invoice? (Y/N) ' TO ask
IF UPPER(ask) = 'Y'
   LOOP
ELSE
   EXIT
ENDIF

ENDDO
```

Step 6: Program a way out of the first loop, and end it. Type

```
ACCEPT 'Add another invoice? (Y/N) ' TO doagain
IF UPPER(doagain) = 'Y'
   LOOP
ELSE
   EXIT
ENDIF

ENDDO
```

Step 7: Reset the defaults and close the program. Type these lines:

```
SET TALK ON
SET CONFIRM OFF
SET BELL ON

RETURN
```

The completed program should look as it does in figure 12.16.

Step 8: Test the completed program. Type *DO ADD_INV*. When prompted, add the following data:

> CUSTOMER INFORMATION
>   Invoice Number: *85-011*
>   Customer Last Name: *Wiggins*
>   First Name: *Angela*
>   Street: *1215 W. Wilson*
>   City: *Marietta*
>   State: *GA*
>   Zip Code: *31575*
>   Phone Number: *234-9843*
>   Comments: *None*

Compare your completed screen with figure 12.17.

```
* ADD_INV.PRG
* Data entry program to add invoice records.
* Adds a single customer record to MX_CUST and one to several
* purchase records to MX_PURCH

SET TALK OFF
SET CONFIRM ON
SET BELL OFF
SET VIEW TO INVOICE

DO WHILE .T.

  SELECT MX_CUST
  APPEND BLANK
  READ
  STORE invoice TO minvoice

  SELECT B
  DO WHILE .T.
   CLEAR
   APPEND BLANK
   REPLACE invoice WITH minvoice
   READ
   ACCEPT 'Enter another purchase for this invoice? (Y/N) ' TO ask
   IF UPPER(ask) = 'Y'
     LOOP
   ELSE
     EXIT
   ENDIF

  ENDDO

  ACCEPT 'Add another invoice? (Y/N) ' TO doagain
  IF UPPER(doagain) = 'Y'
     LOOP
  ELSE
     EXIT
  ENDIF

ENDDO

SET TALK ON
SET CONFIRM OFF
SET BELL ON

RETURN
```

Fig. 12.16. *Listing of ADD_INV program.*

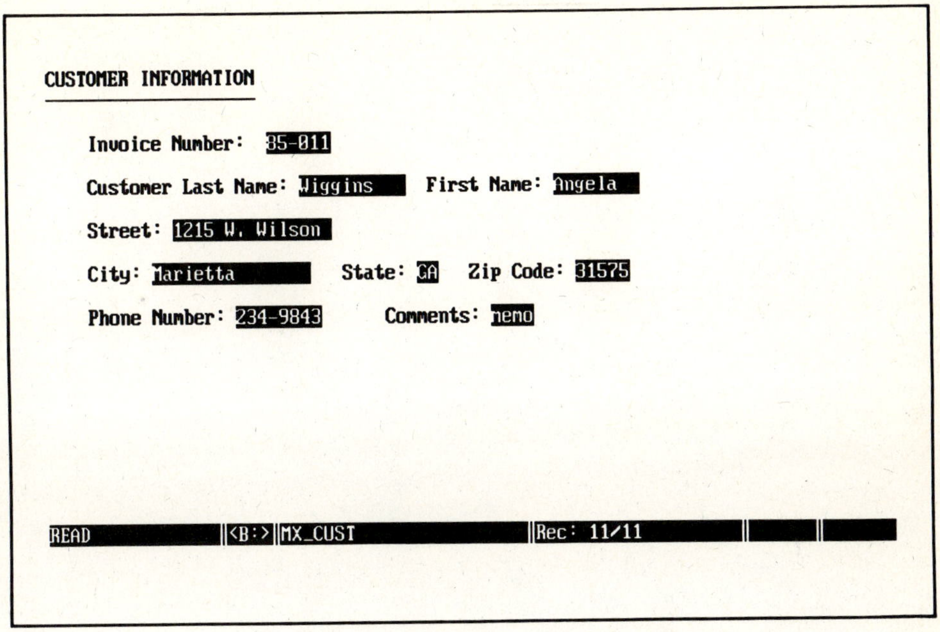

```
CUSTOMER INFORMATION

    Invoice Number:  85-011

    Customer Last Name: Wiggins      First Name: Angela

    Street: 1215 W. Wilson

    City: Marietta          State: GA   Zip Code: 31575

    Phone Number: 234-9843       Comments: memo




READ              <B:> MX_CUST                Rec: 11/11
```

Fig. 12.17. *Using CUSTOMER screen from within the ADD_INV program.*

Step 9: Add the following data when prompted:

> PURCHASE INFORMATION (Item 1)
> Purchase Date: *07/05/85*
> Installation Date: *07/15/85*
> Stock Code: *H-24*
> Number Purchased: *1*
> Purchase Amount: *3520*
> Paid in Full? (Y/N): *N*
> Salesperson: *DWK*

Compare your completed screen with figure 12.18.

When you press the Return key after completing the Salesperson field, you will be asked if you want to add another purchase item to this invoice. Respond Yes.

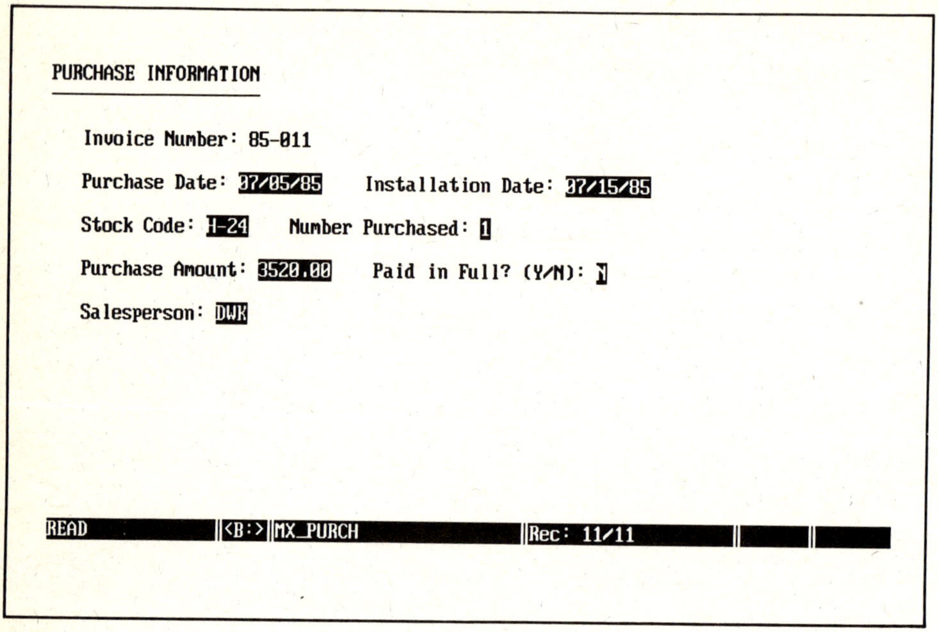

```
 PURCHASE INFORMATION
 ───────────────────

    Invoice Number: 85-011

    Purchase Date: 07/05/85    Installation Date: 07/15/85

    Stock Code: 1-24   Number Purchased: 1

    Purchase Amount: 3520.00    Paid in Full? (Y/N): Y

    Salesperson: DWK




 READ            <B:> MX_PURCH              Rec: 11/11
```

Fig. 12.18. *Using PURCHASE screen from within the ADD_INV program.*

Step 10: Add the following record:

> PURCHASE INFORMATION (Item 2)
> > Purchase Date: *07/06/85*
> > Installation Date:
> > Stock Code: *I-15*
> > Number Purchased: *2*
> > Purchase Amount: *25.65*
> > Paid in Full? (Y/N): *N*
> > Salesperson: *DWK*

No additional items are on this invoice, so respond No to the first prompt. When asked if you want to add another invoice, respond No again (see fig. 12.19).

```
PURCHASE INFORMATION
─────────────────────

   Invoice Number: 85-011

   Purchase Date: 07/06/85    Installation Date:   /  /

   Stock Code: I-15    Number Purchased: 2

   Purchase Amount:    25.65    Paid in Full? (Y/N): N

   Salesperson: DWK
 Enter another purchase for this invoice? (Y/N) N
 Add another invoice? (Y/N) N




 Command        <B:> MX_PURCH           Rec: 12/12      Ins      Caps
```

Fig. 12.19. *Testing the branch options in the ADD_INV program.*

Step 11: Rerun the report MX_OWED. Type *REPORT FORM MX_OWED FOR .NOT. PPIF*. Note that Wiggins appears twice in the listing for the same invoice number (see fig. 12.20).

```
, REPORT FORM MX_OWED FOR .NOT. PPIF
        Page No.     1
        07/28/87
                              ACCOUNTS OUTSTANDING

        CUSTOMER NAME        PHONE      INVOICE PURCHASE PURCHASE
                                                DATE     AMOUNT


        Aster Sam            371-2341 85-004  06/18/85  9042.00
        Stevens Harold       543-9050 85-005  06/19/85  3523.17
        Brown Molly          876-1252 85-006  06/22/85  6600.35
        Clark John           351-1118 85-007  06/25/85  8097.00
        Wiggins Angela       234-9843 85-011  07/05/85  3520.00
        Wiggins Angela       234-9843 85-011  07/06/85    25.65
        *** Total ***

                                                        30808.17
```

```
Command Line    ||<B:>||MX_PURCH              ||Rec: EOF/12    ||Ins  || Caps

              Enter a dBASE III PLUS command.
```

Fig. 12.20. *Final report from MX_OWED.*

Going through the New Menu

Despite the extra work involved, Doug was impressed with the power of dBASE III Plus to handle almost any kind of information management problem. Over the next few weeks, with some assistance from Henry, he perfected the application, using dBASE's relational properties to advantage. Perfecting the application meant redoing all the other programs in the application, but the system he ended up with had much greater capability to handle Saltwater Sally's growth. Doug felt it was worth the work. He re-named the new menu SALESYS, for **SALE**s **SYS**tem.

Step 1: Type *DO SALESYS* and go through all the options in the menu to see how they work.

Step 2: See the underlying programs and how they control the different functions of the system. Enter *TYPE SALESYS.PRG* if you don't have a printer. If you have a printer, enter *TYPE SALESYS.PRG TO PRINT*. Look at the options specified in the CASE statement to see the names of the other programs called from the menu. Repeat this step for each of these programs in turn.

The End of the Beginning

Doug's efforts and Henry's assistance paid off. Admiral Hornblower turned from fence-sitter to fan. He began to see other possibilities of extending the system and integrating it with other business functions. He and Doug considered the future of dBASE III Plus at Saltwater Sally's.

"I think this experiment proves the real usefulness of managing the sales system with dBASE," the Admiral admitted. "What do you see dBASE doing for us in managing our sales prospects?"

"Funny, I've just been thinking about the prospects," Doug said. "We salespeople find ourselves missing sales opportunities because we lose track of who our walk-ins are, who we send mailings to, when we last contacted old customers, what reactions people have to the product line, and so on. I think we could develop a prospect tracking system with dBASE that would solve a lot of these problems. I bet we even could tie it in with the customer database we already have."

"Good idea," agreed the Admiral. "What else?"

NOTES

Doug let his creative energies run. "Well, how about a staff payroll system feeding off the sales commission data we have? And a tie-in to an inventory system is possible. We're keeping track of what we sell. It shouldn't be that difficult to subtract what we sell from inventory and learn what we have left to sell. That would be a little bit of work, but we're up to it. Even without that much trouble, we could have dBASE pump out our customer invoices and age our receivables. We probably even could have dBASE run our whole accounting system."

Admiral Hornblower summed up the outlook nicely. "It sounds to me like Sally's found herself a real friend in dBASE and that you are becoming quite a manager."

SUMMARY OF CONCEPTS
PRESENTED IN LESSON 12

1. dBASE III Plus allows up to ten databases to be open, each in a separate work area. Different work areas are chosen using the SELECT command.

2. Databases can be related to one another if they share a common field and if a SET RELATION TO command has been defined.

3. Data in different databases can be pulled together into a single listing, report, or display if the databases are related.

4. Selected fields or records can be copied into another database using the COPY TO command. COPY TO automatically creates the structure of the new database.

5. A view file can select one or more databases, and assign indexes and format files to each. It also can set a relation between databases.

6. A single data entry program can be used to append records into different databases.

■ LESSON 12
    EXERCISE

The Saltwater Sally's billing system could benefit from the same relational treatment you gave to the sales system. The billing system currently must repeat information on a vendor's name, phone number, and contact. As bills to the same vendor accumulate, the billing database (SSBILLS) becomes redundant on these fields. Splitting this database would be better, keeping the vendor's name, phone, and contact person in one database (SSACCTS) and the billing data itself in a second database (SSBILLS1).

To create the new databases, you can follow roughly the same steps you used to set up the revised sales system. The critical first step is to set up a field that both databases will share and that can be the basis for relational searches. We will call this common field VACCT for **V**endor **ACC**oun**T**.

Step 1: Open the SSBILLS database and modify it. Type *USE SSBILLS* and then *MODIFY STRUCTURE.*

Step 2: Add the VACCT field. With the cursor on the first field, press Ctrl-N to insert a blank field line. Type the name of the field as *VACCT*, leave the field type as character, and make the length 3. Press Ctrl-End to save your changes, and then press Return to verify your modifications.

Step 3: Add the vendor account numbers to the SSBILLS database. Type *BROWSE FIELDS VACCT,VNAME* and enter the account numbers shown.

VACCT	VNAME
101	Aquarius Pool Supp.
102	Tidewater Tillie's
103	Acme Chlorine
104	Southern Bell
105	Trust Realty Co.

Save your work by pressing Ctrl-End.

Step 4: Create the SSACCTS database by copying selected fields from SSBILLS to it. Type *COPY FIELDS VACCT,VNAME,VATTN,VPHONE TO SSACCTS.*

Step 5: Create the SSBILLS1 database by copying the remaining fields from SSBILLS to it. Type *COPY FIELDS VACCT,DATEIN,VBILLNO,VAMT,VPIF TO SSBILLS1.*

Step 6: Close the SSBILLS database. Type *CLOSE DATABASES.*

In the next series of steps you will set up the relational work environment for the two new databases. Doing so allows you access to the fields in either database while one database is active.

NOTES

Because the two new databases are relatable on the common VACCT field, setting a relation between the two to make searches easier is helpful. The best direction for the relation is from the SSACCTS database into the SSBILLS1 database, to let you find a vendor in the SSACCTS file and then pull up all the billing information on that vendor from the SSBILLS file. As you might remember, to permit this type of searching you must first index both databases on the common field.

Step 7: Set up a work area for the SSACCTS database, and create an index in this area. Type the following commands:

    SELECT A
    USE SSACCTS
    INDEX ON VACCT TO SSACCTS

Step 8: Set up a work area for the SSBILLS1 database, and create an index for it in this area. Type the following commands:

    SELECT B
    USE SSBILLS1
    INDEX ON VACCT TO SSBILLS1

You will next set up the relation between SSACCTS and SSBILLS1. Because SSACCTS will be the active search database, you will move back to its work area and set the relation from it to SSBILLS1.

Step 9: Move to work area A by typing *SELECT A*.

Remember that after you assign a database to a work area, you can refer to the work area by the database alias. In other words, you could have typed SELECT SSACCTS, rather than SELECT A, to move to this work area.

Step 10: Set the relation. Type *SET RELATION TO VACCT INTO SSBILLS1*.

In the next set of steps you will test the relation to assure that it works as expected. To test the relation, you will FIND a record by account number in the SSACCTS database and then switch to the SSBILLS1 database to display all the records that match this account number. Remember that, because of the relation between the databases, the record pointer in the SSBILLS1 database is already pointing at the first record with the same account number as the found record in the SSACCTS database.

Step 11: Find account number 103. Type *FIND 103*. Notice that the status line updates the record number indicator.

Step 12: Move into the SSBILLS1 work area. Type *SELECT SSBILLS1*.

NOTES

Step 13: Display all the billing amounts for records with the current account number. Display also the name of the vendor. Type

DISPLAY ALL SSACCTS->VNAME,VAMT WHILE VACCT=VACCT.

The DISPLAY command asks to display the VNAME field from the SSACCTS database (SSACCTS->VNAME), and the VAMT from the current work area for records whose account number equals that of the current record in SSBILLS.

After you have set up and related the new databases, you can build relational reports and relational data entry procedures similar to those for the sales system.

More Computer Knowledge from Que

LOTUS SOFTWARE TITLES

1-2-3 QueCards	21.95
1-2-3 for Business, 2nd Edition	19.95
1-2-3 Business Formula Handbook	19.95
1-2-3 Command Language	21.95
1-2-3 Macro Library, 2nd Edition	21.95
1-2-3 Tips, Tricks, and Traps, 2nd Edition	19.95
Using 1-2-3, Special Edition	24.95
Using 1-2-3 Workbook and Disk, 2nd Edition	29.95
Using Lotus HAL	19.95
Using Symphony, 2nd Edition	24.95

DATABASE TITLES

dBASE III Plus Applications Library	21.95
dBASE III Plus Handbook, 2nd Edition	21.95
dBASE III Plus Advanced Programming, 2nd Edition	22.95
dBASE III Plus Tips, Tricks, and Traps	19.95
R:BASE Solutions: Applications and Resources	19.95
R:BASE System V Techniques and Applications	21.95
R:BASE System V User's Guide, 2nd Edition	19.95
Using Reflex	19.95
Using Paradox, 2nd Edition	22.95
Using Q & A	19.95

MACINTOSH AND APPLE II TITLES

HyperCard QuickStart: A Graphics Approach	21.95
Using AppleWorks, 2nd Edition	19.95
Using dBASE Mac	19.95
Using Dollars and Sense	18.95
Using Excel	19.95
Using HyperCard: From Home to HyperTalk	24.95
Using Microsoft Word: Macintosh Version	19.95
Using Microsoft Works	18.95
Using WordPerfect: Macintosh Version	19.95

APPLICATIONS SOFTWARE TITLES

Smart Tips, Tricks, and Traps	23.95
Using Dollars and Sense on the IBM	18.95
Using Enable, 2nd Edition	22.95
Using Excel: IBM Version	19.95
Using Managing Your Money	18.95
Using Quattro	21.95
Using Smart	22.95
Using SuperCalc4	19.95

WORD-PROCESSING AND DESKTOP PUBLISHING TITLES

Microsoft Word Tips, Tricks, and Traps	
Using DisplayWrite 4	
Using Microsoft Word, 2nd Edition	
Using MultiMate Advantage, 2nd Edition	
Using PageMaker on the IBM	
Using Ventura Publisher	
Using WordPerfect, 3rd Edition	
Using WordPerfect 5	
Using WordPerfect Workbook and Disk	
Using WordStar	
WordPerfect QueCards	
WordPerfect Tips, Tricks, and Traps	
WordPerfect Advanced Techniques	

HARDWARE AND SYSTEMS TITLES

DOS Programmer's Reference	
DOS QueCards	
DOS Workbook and Disk	
IBM PS/2 Handbook	
Managing Your Hard Disk	
MS-DOS User's Guide, 3rd Edition	
Networking IBM PCs, 2nd Edition	
Programming with Windows	
Understanding UNIX: A Conceptual Guide, 2nd Edition	
Using Microsoft Windows	
Using PC DOS, 2nd Edition	

PROGRAMMING AND TECHNICAL TITLES

Advanced C: Techniques and Applications	
C Programmer's Library	
C Programming Guide, 2nd Edition	
C Self-Study Guide	
C Standard Library	
Debugging C	
Turbo Pascal for BASIC Programmers	
Turbo Pascal Program Library	
Turbo Pascal Tips, Tricks, and Traps	
Using Assembly Language	
Using QuickBASIC 4	
Using Turbo Prolog	

QUE®

Que Order Line: **1-800-428-5331**

All prices subject to change without notice. Prices and charges are for domestic orders only.
Non-U.S. prices might be higher.

ORDER FROM QUE TODAY

m	Title	Price	Quantity	Extension
8	dBASE III Plus Handbook, 2nd Edition	$21.95		
7	Using PC DOS, 2nd Edition	22.95		
5	dBASE III Plus Tips, Tricks, and Traps	19.95		
2	dBASE III Plus Applications Library	19.95		

Book Subtotal

Shipping & Handling ($2.50 per item)

Indiana Residents Add 5% Sales Tax

GRAND TOTAL

d of Payment:

☐ eck   ☐ VISA   ☐ MasterCard   ☐ American Express

Number _____ Exp. Date _____

holder's Name _____

o _____

ess _____

_____ State _____ ZIP _____

If you can't wait, call **1-800-428-5331**, ext. 888 and order TODAY.

All prices subject to change without notice.

FOLD HERE

Place
Stamp
Here

Que Corporation
P.O. Box 90
Carmel, IN 46032

REGISTRATION CARD

gister your copy of *dBASE III Plus Workbook and Disk* and receive information about Que's newest prod-
s. Complete this registration card and return it to Que Corporation, P.O. Box 90, Carmel, IN 46032.

me _____Phone _____

mpany _____Title _____

dress _____

y _____ST _____ZIP _____

ase check the appropriate answers:

ere did you buy *dBASE III Plus Workbook and
k?*
- ☐ Bookstore (name: _____)
- ☐ Computer store (name: _____)
- ☐ Catalog (name: _____)
- ☐ Direct from Que
- ☐ Other: _____

w many computer books do you buy a year?
- ☐ 1 or less   ☐ 6-10
- ☐ 2-5   ☐ More than 10

w many Que books do you own?
- ☐ 1   ☐ 6-10
- ☐ 2-5   ☐ More than 10

w long have you been using dBASE software?
- ☐ Less than 6 months   ☐ 1 to 3 years
- ☐ 6 months to 1 year   ☐ Over 3 years

nat influenced your purchase of *dBASE III Plus
orkbook and Disk?*
- ☐ Personal recommendation
- ☐ Advertisement
- ☐ In-store display
- ☐ Price
- ☐ Que catalog
- ☐ Que postcard
- ☐ Que's reputation
- ☐ Other:_____

ow would you rate the overall content of *dBASE
Plus Workbook and Disk?*
- ☐ Very good
- ☐ Good
- ☐ Not useful
- ☐ Poor

How would you rate the *lessons disk?*
- ☐ Very good
- ☐ Good
- ☐ Not useful
- ☐ Poor

How would you rate the *individual lessons?*
- ☐ Very good
- ☐ Good
- ☐ Not useful
- ☐ Poor

What do you like *best* about *dBASE III Plus Workbook and Disk?*

What do you like *least* about *dBASE III Plus Workbook and Disk?*

How do you use *dBASE III Plus Workbook and
Disk?*

What other Que products do you own?

What other software do you own?

Please feel free to list any other comments you may
have about *dBASE III Plus Workbook and Disk.*

_____

_____

_____

_____

_____

_____

_____

FOLD HERE

_____

_____

_____

_____

Que Corporation
P.O. Box 90
Carmel, IN 46032

MORE COMPUTER KNOWLEDGE FROM QUE

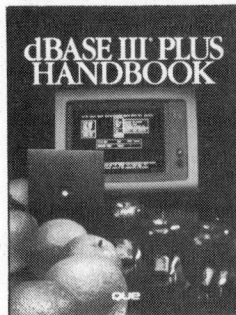

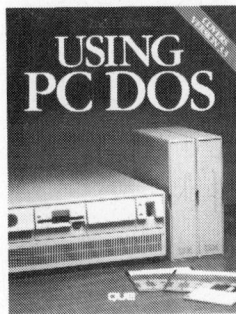

If your computer uses 3 1/2-inch disks . . .

While most personal computers use 5 1/4-inch disks to store information, some newer computers are switching to 3 1/2-inch disks for information storage. If your computer uses 3 1/2-inch disks, you can return this form to Que to obtain a 3 1/2-inch disk to use with this workbook. Simply fill out the remainder of this form, and mail to:

dBASE III Plus
Workbook Disk Exchange
Que Corporation
11711 N. College Ave.
Carmel, IN 46032

We will then send you, free of charge, the 3 1/2-inch version of the workbook software.

Name _____ Phone _____

Company _____ Title _____

Address _____

City _____ St ____ ZIP ____

FOLD HERE

_____

_____

_____

_____

Que Corporation
P.O. Box 90
Carmel, IN 46032